Fighting to Preserve
a Nation's Soul

Fighting to Preserve a Nation's Soul

America's Ecumenical War on Poverty

ROBERT BAUMAN

The University of Georgia Press
ATHENS

© 2019 by the University of Georgia Press
Athens, Georgia 30602
www.ugapress.org
All rights reserved
Set in 9.5/13 Miller Text Roman
by Graphic Composition, Inc.

Most University of Georgia Press titles are
available from popular e-book vendors.

Printed digitally

Library of Congress Cataloging-in-Publication Data

Names: Bauman, Robert, 1964– author.
Title: Fighting to preserve a nation's soul : America's ecumenical
war on poverty / Robert Bauman.
Description: Athens : The University of Georgia Press, [2019] |
Includes bibliographical references and index.
Identifiers: LCCN 2018036558 | ISBN 9780820354873 (hardcover : alk. paper)
Subjects: LCSH: Economic assistance, Domestic—United States—
History—20th century. | Economic assistance, Domestic—
Moral and ethical aspects—United States. | Shriver, Sargent, 1915–2011.
Classification: LCC HC110.P63 B38 2019 | DDC 362.5/575097309046—dc23
LC record available at https://lccn.loc.gov/2018036558

For Stephanie

The War on Poverty is fundamentally
a nation fighting to preserve its soul.

—R. SARGENT SHRIVER, May 25, 1965

CONTENTS

List of Illustrations   xi

Acknowledgments   xiii

Organizational Abbreviations   xvii

INTRODUCTION
Setting the Context for the Struggle
Religion and the War on Poverty   1

CHAPTER 1
"Kind of a Secular Sacrament"
The Catholic War on Poverty   12

CHAPTER 2
The Conscience of the Church
*The National Council of Churches
and the War on Poverty*   36

CHAPTER 3
Creating an Ecumenical Antipoverty Coalition
IFCO, Black Power, and the War on Poverty   67

CHAPTER 4
The Black Manifesto
Challenging the Ecumenical Antipoverty Coalition   87

CHAPTER 5
Fracturing the Antipoverty Coalition
The Aftermath of the Black Manifesto   120

CONCLUSION

"To Become as Radical as Christ"

*Faith-Based Activism and the Long War on
Poverty in the Twenty-First Century* 147

Manuscript Repositories and Collections 159

Notes 161

Bibliography 185

Index 199

ILLUSTRATIONS

1. Sargent Shriver with children and President Lyndon Johnson at swearing-in ceremony 8
2. Mathew Ahmann at the Conference on Religion and Race 16
3. Martin Luther King Jr., Andrew Young, and members of the Holy Child Jesus Mission in Canton, Mississippi 17
4. Father Jack Egan 24
5. Sister Audrey Kopp and the black power insignia 30
6. Sargent Shriver at Methodist Board of Missions meeting 66
7. James Forman presents the Black Manifesto to the NCC 93
8. James Forman burns a restraining order 97
9. Obed Lopez, Eliezer Risco, and James Forman 100
10. James Forman addresses the American Baptist Convention 103
11. James Forman speaks to the United Methodist Church Board of Missions 104
12. Cain Felder speaks to the United Methodist Church Board of Missions 107

ACKNOWLEDGMENTS

The History Department at Washington State University has provided me with support, both financial and moral. Department chairs Ray Sun and Steve Kale both approved research funds for my travel to archives across the country. In addition to Ray and Steve, a number of faculty members in the department have supported my work in one way or another. In particular, I would like to thank Jeff Sanders, Matt Sutton, Rob McCoy, and Peter Boag on the Pullman campus; Sue Peabody and Laurie Mercier on the Vancouver campus; and especially Brigit Farley on my home campus in the Tri-Cities. Administrators in the Tri-Cities, in particular Michele Acker-Hocevar, Michael Mays, and Allan Felsot, supported my research endeavors, and some administrative staff on the Tri-Cities campus were especially helpful to me over the years. Joanne Baker made my job so much easier when I took on interim administrative duties in the early part of this process. She helped make the beginnings of this project possible. Maggie Sisseck provided invaluable technical and administrative support near the end of this long journey. Library staff Steve Bisch, Cheryl Farrabee, and Harvey Gover located and processed innumerable books and journal articles for my research, always with professionalism and a smile.

In addition to librarians on my home campus, archivists and librarians on university campuses and at repositories across the country provided vital assistance. In particular, Cassie Brand and Frances Bristol at the United Methodist Archives at Drew University; Dana Bronson at the John F. Kennedy Presidential Library; Philip Runkel at the Marquette University Archives; Kathleen DeMerritte and staff at the National Archives in College Park, Maryland; and archivists and staff at the University of Notre Dame Archives, the American Catholic History Research Center and University Archives at the Catholic University of America, the Presbyterian Historical Society, and the Schomburg Center for Research in Black Culture all contributed to making this volume possible through their efforts and professionalism. Thanks to all of you!

xiv Acknowledgments

This book was made possible by generous research grants and funding from several institutions. I was fortunate to receive a Franklin Research Grant from the American Philosophical Society, which made research trips to the National Archives, the John F. Kennedy Presidential Library, and the United Methodist Archives possible. Institutional grants from the Presbyterian Historical Society and the Cushwa Center for the Study of American Catholicism at the University of Notre Dame, as well as a Dorothy Mohler Research Grant from the American Catholic History Research Center and University Archives at the Catholic University of America helped fund critical and fruitful research visits to those archives and repositories. A faculty travel grant from the Washington State University College of Liberal Arts helped fund a research trip to the Marquette University Archives. An Ashby-Armitage Grant from my home history department made the completion of this manuscript possible. The generosity of all of these institutions is much appreciated.

I would like to thank Mick Gusinde-Duffy, Thomas Roche, and Beth Snead at the University of Georgia Press. Mick was an enthusiastic supporter of this project from early on. Beth and Tom helped make the manuscript better and guided it to completion. Merryl Sloane's expert copyediting greatly improved this work. Many thanks to all of you!

A number of colleagues and fellow War on Poverty scholars have provided inspiration, constructive critiques, and innumerable productive conversations in the time that I have been working on this book. The research of Annelise Orleck, Wes Phelps, Rhonda Williams, Julia Rabig, Tamar Carroll, Susan Ashmore, Daniel Cobb, Bill Clayson, Martin Meeker, Marisa Chappell, Gordon Mantler, and Emma Folwell has inspired and influenced my own, and discussions during and after conference panels with each of these scholars over the years have greatly informed my work. I would like to especially thank Tom Kiffmeyer and Marc Rodriguez for their extensive conversations about the War on Poverty, community activists, and countless other topics, some scholarly and some not, over the years at conferences and at restaurants and pubs in various cities. Their scholarship and friendship have been vital to this project.

My family, both nuclear and extended, has been tremendously supportive. My parents-in-law, Ben and Rosie San Miguel, provided a place to stay when I had research to conduct in southern California and have been excited about this project from the beginning. My mother, Betty Enserink, and sisters, Beth Nishida and Betsy Bauman, have offered support and encouragement along the way. My wife, Stephanie San Miguel Bauman, and our children, Robert and Rachel, have provided inspiration and encouragement, as well as much-needed distractions from research and writing. In the years since I began this project, Robert has grown from a high school freshman to a college graduate and VISTA participant, working for AmeriCorps. He is among the newest generation of those continuing the fight against poverty. Rachel has grown from a fifth-grader to a college freshman and has developed into an amazing, intelligent, talented human being. I am incredibly proud of Robert and Rachel and the people they have become. Their examples give me hope for America's future.

This book is dedicated to Stephanie, without whom I would have accomplished very little. She has inspired me and listened to my ideas about theology, activism, poverty, and related topics with thoughtfulness and considered conversation. Her love and support over this long process, including challenges both professional and personal, have been vital to the completion of this book. The thirty-four years I have known her have been the best years of my life.

ORGANIZATIONAL ABBREVIATIONS

AJC   American Jewish Committee
BEDC   Black Economic Development Conference
BERC   Black Economic Research Center
BMCR   Black Methodists for Church Renewal
CBL   Contract Buyers of Lawndale (later known as Contract Buyers League)
CCCO   Catholic Committee of Community Organization
CCUM   Catholic Committee on Urban Ministry
CDGM   Child Development Group of Mississippi
CHD   Campaign for Human Development
CIC   Catholic Interracial Council
COPS   Communities Organized for Public Service
CSA   Community Services Administration
CSAC   Chicana Service Action Center
FCC   Federal Council of Churches
IAF   Industrial Areas Foundation
ICAP   Interreligious Committee against Poverty
IFCO   Interreligious Foundation for Community Organization
NBCCC   National Black Catholic Clergy Caucus
NBEDC   National Black Economic Development Conference
NBSC   National Black Sisters Conference
NCBC   National Committee of Black Churchmen
NCC   National Council of Churches in Christ
NCCB   National Conference of Catholic Bishops
NCCC   National Conference of Catholic Charities
NCCIJ   National Catholic Conference for Interracial Justice
NCWC   National Catholic Welfare Conference
NWRO   National Welfare Rights Organization
OEO   Office of Economic Opportunity

xviii Organizational Abbreviations

SATC   Social Action Training Center
SNCC   Student Nonviolent Coordinating Committee
TELACU The East Los Angeles Community Union
USCC   United States Catholic Conference
WICS   Women in Community Service
WLCAC   Watts Labor Community Action Committee

Fighting to Preserve
a Nation's Soul

INTRODUCTION

Setting the Context for the Struggle
Religion and the War on Poverty

In May 1965, the charismatic, energetic Sargent Shriver spoke to the General Assembly of the United Presbyterian Church, one of the key members in the National Council of Churches (NCC). From the beginning of his appointment to head the War on Poverty, Shriver had thrown himself fully into the fight against poverty, not only as the director of the government program but as a man of faith. Shriver believed that the powerful and influential NCC and its member churches, as well as other religious agencies and organizations, were important allies in this fight. His speech to the General Assembly of Presbyterians reflected both his Christian faith and his deep-seated belief in the importance of churches and synagogues to the War on Poverty. Echoing his essential argument that the War on Poverty was at heart a moral issue, Shriver opened his speech by quoting from the Presbyterian Standing Committee report on the War on Poverty: "When a nation fights for its soul, who but the Church should set the context for that struggle?" For Shriver, the church had a central and integral role to play in the War on Poverty.[1]

In this book I explore efforts by churches, synagogues, and ecumenical religious organizations and agencies to join the nation's War on Poverty in the 1960s. I examine the theological and moral underpinnings of antipoverty efforts by religious agencies and individuals, how those ideas and theories were implemented in governmental antipoverty programs and religious antipoverty efforts, and how the relationship between religious and government agencies in the War on Poverty evolved over time. I detail the creation, development, and fracturing of an ecumenical antipoverty coalition. In addition, I demonstrate that the long War on Poverty has continued into the twenty-first century.

In 2014, the Council of Economic Advisers and the House of Representatives Budget Committee issued dueling interpretations of the War on Poverty fifty years after its creation. That they did so reflects two important developments. First, it indicates that both major political parties view the War on Poverty as significant, although Democrats view it much more positively than Republicans do. Why commemorate or discuss a fifty-year anniversary of something you see as insignificant? It should be noted that the GOP followed up its House Budget Committee report with a second report on "poverty, opportunity, and upward mobility" as part of House Budget Committee chair (and later, Speaker) Paul Ryan's A Better Way initiative. Second, both the congressional Republican and the Democratic presidential administration reports viewed the War on Poverty as ongoing. Beyond those two similarities, though, there was not much agreement in the reports.

The Council of Economic Advisers argued that the War on Poverty has had "significant success in reducing poverty" over the past fifty years and made a convincing case for a continuation and expansion of antipoverty programs, while the Republican report argued that federal policies for the most part (other than the earned income tax credit and tax cuts, which they claim encourage work) have contributed to ongoing poverty. Ryan's Budget Committee report cited Daniel Patrick Moynihan's *The Negro Family*, published in 1965 and popularly known as the Moynihan Report. Ryan argued that *The Negro Family*, written by Moynihan in part to convince President Lyndon Johnson to adopt stronger antipoverty measures, supported the House report's contention that "the single most important determinant of poverty is family structure." Ryan and House Republicans used the Moynihan Report as support for their claim that antipoverty policies cause poverty, while liberals have tended to argue that the key legacy of the Moynihan Report is its focus on the underlying problem of black male unemployment. The two major political parties differ both in their perspectives on the War on Poverty and on the Moynihan Report. Indeed, both the Moynihan Report and the War on Poverty remain contested terrain for debating and understanding the continued racial and economic inequality in the United States. In addition, the two parties used two different poverty measures in their reports—the Republicans incorporated the official poverty measure and the Democrats the supplemental poverty measure, which utilizes a post-tax, post-transfer metric that includes all cash transfers and in-kind transfers (SNAP, housing vouchers, etc.) and deducts expenditures for child care and medical out-of-pocket and other expenses. As a result, the supplemental poverty measure shows a much more significant drop in poverty (26 to 16 percent) than does the official poverty measure (17 to 15 percent), and it attributes that drop, rightly I believe, to antipoverty programs.[2]

While my definition of the War on Poverty differs somewhat from that of both the Republicans and Democrats (I view the War on Poverty as the programs, policies, and agencies initiated and/or initially funded by the Office of Economic Opportunity and/or its successors), I agree with both parties that the War on Poverty, whether defined narrowly or broadly, has been fundamentally significant and is still being fought. I argue, though, that it is being fought by an antipoverty coalition of government agencies, community groups, and ecumenical religious organizations that formed initially in the 1960s but carries on in an evolved form in the twenty-first century. I believe that recent scholarship on the War on Poverty has been moving in directions that demonstrate those developments. For the best and most thorough review of the scholarship on the War on Poverty, I recommend Tom Kiffmeyer's article in the June 2015 issue of *Reviews in American History*.[3] Here, I briefly highlight some of the exciting avenues of War on Poverty scholarship that have developed in recent years. This book builds on that dynamic and evolving work.

Historical scholarship of the War on Poverty has flowered in recent years after decades of neglect on the part of historians. Studies by several scholars have challenged the way historians have thought and written about the War on Poverty, particularly in terms of race, ethnic identity, gender, and sexual orientation. A number of those works have explored linkages between the War on Poverty and social movements, including the African American and Mexican American civil rights movements, the Chicano/a and black power movements, and feminism. In addition, some of that work has sought to expand scholars' thinking about the time frame of the War on Poverty. Most early scholars of the War on Poverty discussed its beginnings in the early 1960s and its end in the mid- to late 1970s. More recent authors, though, have argued that the War on Poverty lasted much longer than that and, indeed, that it continues today. Adapting Jacquelyn Dowd Hall's term "the long civil rights movement," a few scholars have used "the long war on poverty" to describe the antipoverty efforts that continued beyond the 1970s.[4]

Many of the early works on the War on Poverty, including those by Daniel Moynihan, Charles Murray, Allen Matusow, and others, argued that it was a dismal failure. The work of those scholars created a success/failure paradigm for interpreting the War on Poverty. One of the first books to challenge

4 Introduction

and begin to change that paradigm was Annelise Orleck's *Storming Caesars Palace*. Orleck's brilliant work argued for lengthening the War on Poverty; emphasizing the activism of people at the grassroots, particularly women of color; and linking that antipoverty activism to feminism and civil rights. Orleck's book remains one of the seminal works on the War on Poverty, both for its exploration of the central role of black women in shaping the course of their local War on Poverty and for demonstrating that the War on Poverty lasted much longer than early scholars suggested. Others followed Orleck, demonstrating a long War on Poverty and unraveling intricate connections between antipoverty efforts and various social movements: civil rights, black power, the Chicano/a movement, feminism, and gay rights. Some of the key works in this wave of scholarship include Marc Rodriguez's exploration of the antipoverty activism of Tejanos in Wisconsin; Crystal Sanders's and Emma Folwell's examinations of links between civil rights and African American antipoverty efforts in Mississippi; books by Bill Clayson and myself that explored relationships between African American and Chicano/a antipoverty activism in Texas and Los Angeles, respectively; Daniel Cobb's work on Native American antipoverty activism; Christina Hanhardt's exploration of gay activism and the War on Poverty; and Tamar Carroll's work linking AIDS, antipoverty, and feminist activism. These works collectively demonstrate the ways that Native American, black, Chicano/a, and feminist activists shaped the direction of the War on Poverty in their communities and show that the War on Poverty lasted well past the 1970s and continues in many communities today.[5]

One aspect of the War on Poverty that has been little explored to this point, despite this flowering of historical scholarship, is the central role of religion. Some historians, like Bettye Collier-Thomas, Betty Livingston Adams, Nancy Robertson, and Judith Weisenfeld, have brought to light black women's religion-based social activism primarily in the first half of the twentieth century. Other scholars, such as James Findlay, David Chappell, and Carol George, have deftly explored the fundamental role of religion in the civil rights movement.[6] In his foundational work, *Church People in the Struggle*, Findlay brilliantly analyzes the involvement of the National Council of Churches in the civil rights movement, its response to the Black Manifesto, and its relationship with black power organizations — but he pays little attention to the War on Poverty.

Scholars like John McGreevy have examined the complex relationship between Catholicism and the black freedom movement.[7] Catholics have often been left out of narratives of the War on Poverty and the 1960s. In addition to writing that "one of the deafening silences in the scholarship on the

1960s . . . is the history of religion," noted historian Thomas Sugrue has argued that the lack of incorporation of Catholicism into broad national narratives of the period is "primarily the result of the blindness that most nonreligious historians have to lived religion, spirituality, theology, and institutional history." Sugrue says that this is also a result of the "largely internalist orientation" of scholars of twentieth-century American Catholic history, much of which "remains largely trapped in the Catholic ghetto."[8] In this book, I include Catholic antipoverty activism alongside that of Protestant and Jewish individuals and organizations. The Catholic antipoverty activists in this story were central to economic and racial developments in the United States in the 1960s and 1970s and worked closely with Protestant and Jewish groups in ecumenical organizations.

The vital, complex, and often conflicted role of religious organizations and agencies in the War on Poverty has for the most part remained unexamined. Some exceptions to this scholarly void are Kenneth Heineman's 2003 article in the *Historian* on Catholic social activism in the War on Poverty in Pittsburgh; Susan Ashmore's 2003 essay on Catholic antipoverty efforts in Mobile, Alabama; Ashmore's 2008 book; Martin Meeker's excellent 2012 *Pacific Historical Review* essay on the involvement of a coalition of ministers and gay activists in the War on Poverty in San Francisco's central city; and Wesley Phelps's book on the War on Poverty in Houston.[9]

The work of Marisa Chappell and others in exploring the roots of opposition to the War on Poverty and social welfare programs in general has helped us better understand both the failures of liberalism and the growth of conservatism in the 1960s and beyond with more nuance. In many ways, that opposition to the War on Poverty and related programs played a fundamental role in galvanizing conservatives in the 1960s, helped lead to the election of Ronald Reagan in the 1980s, and remains central to conservatism today. Indeed, the report on the fiftieth anniversary of the War on Poverty from Paul Ryan's A Better Way uses the ubiquitous Ronald Reagan quote—"We fought a War on Poverty in the 1960s and poverty won"—to begin its contention that many government antipoverty programs create poverty, an argument first made by Charles Murray in *Losing Ground* in the 1980s. Importantly, A Better Way incorporates Murray's language of "poverty traps" to argue that government antipoverty programs create poverty.[10] Fifty years later, conservatives still rally around opposition to the War on Poverty. The Trump administration's first budget proposal targeted many antipoverty programs initiated as part of the War on Poverty. The opposition to the War on Poverty and the influence and significance of that opposition remain fertile ground for additional scholarship.

6   Introduction

This book addresses the important role religion played in the War on Poverty in terms of support and activism as well as division and opposition. While focused on religion, this project also explores themes of race by analyzing the creation and development of a primarily black antipoverty organization, the Interreligious Foundation for Community Organization (IFCO). IFCO highlights the move toward ecumenism among American religious organizations and the significance of black power to the evolving War on Poverty. The Black Manifesto, issued by civil rights and black power activist James Forman in 1969, plays a central role in this story. Forman's manifesto challenged American churches and synagogues to donate resources to IFCO as reparations for those institutions' participation in slavery and racial segregation. The manifesto linked black power and the War on Poverty and reshaped ecumenical antipoverty efforts. In this book, then, I explore the often intricate and fundamental connections between religious organizations, social movements, and community antipoverty agencies, and I expand the argument for a long War on Poverty.

America's War on Poverty officially began when President Lyndon B. Johnson signed the Economic Opportunity Act (EOA) on August 20, 1964. The War on Poverty had emerged out of concerns over juvenile delinquency, which garnered significant national attention in the 1950s and early 1960s. Research into that subject had begun as early as the 1920s, when University of Chicago sociologists Robert Park and Ernest Burgess used their theories about urban ecology to address the issue of juvenile delinquency and argued that delinquency was related to the failure of community organizations. To deal with juvenile delinquency, then, community institutions needed to be reorganized through community action. Their work influenced the research of Columbia University sociologists Richard Cloward and Lloyd Ohlin, who in their opportunity theory argued that juvenile delinquency was caused, at least in part, by societal structures—unresponsive city governments, school systems, and welfare administrations—that blocked opportunities for inner-city youth. In response to these concerns, President John F. Kennedy created the President's Committee on Juvenile Delinquency to explore remedies to what some perceived to be a national crisis. When Kennedy ordered committee staffers to seek out ways to combat poverty, one of the options involved adapting Ohlin and Cloward's opportunity theory for an antipoverty program. Kennedy also was influenced by his chief economic advisor, Walter Heller, who argued that the administration's tax cut would not do enough to help the poor, and by Michael Harrington's *The Other America*, published in 1962, and an article by Dwight MacDonald in the *New Yorker*, published in early 1963, both of which highlighted the persistence of poverty in America and both of which Kennedy read.[11]

The effort to tackle poverty was still evolving when Lee Harvey Oswald assassinated President Kennedy on November 22, 1963. When White House staffers informed Johnson about the idea, the new president reportedly replied, "that's my kind of program." Johnson established a new task force, which led to the EOA and the creation of the Office of Economic Opportunity (OEO). The EOA incorporated a number of programs designed to address poverty—Head Start, Upward Bound, Legal Services, and so on—and also provided federal funds to community action agencies (CAAs) that fought poverty at the local level. Johnson chose R. Sargent Shriver, the director of the Peace Corps and a brother-in-law of John and Robert Kennedy, to head the War on Poverty. Shriver was a Catholic whose religious devotion would be important in his efforts to incorporate churches, synagogues, and religious organizations into the War on Poverty. Community action was the key strategy of the legislation; communities were to include the "maximum feasible participation of the poor" in their local antipoverty efforts. The inclusion and empowerment of poor people were two of the most controversial aspects of the War on Poverty and key elements for the involvement of religious social activists in antipoverty efforts.[12]

While many of the CAAs established, particularly early in the War on Poverty, were created and developed by city and county agencies, OEO officials specifically targeted nonprofit agencies and organizations created outside of traditional government entities as a way to avoid established bureaucracies, which antipoverty program planners saw as blocking opportunities for poor and minority individuals and communities. For instance, while the OEO funded a city-county government-led antipoverty organization in Los Angeles, the Economic and Youth Opportunities Agency, following the uprising in Watts in 1965, it also provided funds to community-based agencies like the Watts Labor Community Action Committee (WLCAC) in South Central Los Angeles and the Chicana Service Action Center (CSAC) in East Los Angeles. As the War on Poverty evolved over time, funding community-based organizations, particularly in black and brown communities, became a more typical practice. That practice also led to increased OEO funding of church- and religion-based antipoverty organizations in communities across the country.[13]

It is important to understand that the War on Poverty was not a static policy. It evolved over time to meet changing demands and needs expressed by ordinary people in communities across the United States and to meet challenges and opposition from Congress and government officials. It also

FIGURE 1. Sargent Shriver and children Maria, Robert, and Timothy (*left to right*) with President Lyndon Johnson at Shriver's swearing-in ceremony as director of the new Office of Economic Opportunity, the agency created to lead the War on Poverty. Cecil Stoughton, photographer. R. Sargent Shriver Personal Papers, John F. Kennedy Presidential Library and Museum, Boston.

responded to requests from churches, synagogues, and religious organizations that expressed support for the War on Poverty. Some of those organizations reduced their antipoverty efforts or removed themselves completely from the War on Poverty as criticisms, particularly of community action programs, mounted in the mid- to late 1960s. Other religious groups helped reshape and remold OEO policies, leading to the evolution of a church-state antipoverty effort and the creation of an ecumenical antipoverty coalition. In this book, I demonstrate that these efforts remain in place today through faith-based and racially distinct community organizations that carry on the work begun by activist priests, nuns, ministers, rabbis, and religious laypeople in the mid-1960s. I particularly focus on efforts by Catholic and Protestant national organizations that were involved from the beginning and have continued their dedication to the War on Poverty despite reduced funding and attacks from conservatives in their own religious traditions.

Religion and the War on Poverty

These battles over the War on Poverty in part highlight the ongoing struggles between the Christian left and the Christian right. Scholars have written seminal accounts in recent years about the role of religion, particularly evangelicalism, in the ascendancy of conservatism in post–World War II America.[14] This book complements those works by exploring the decline in support for antipoverty programs and in efforts by some religious organizations in the 1970s. At the same time, this story adds to that narrative by demonstrating that some liberal religious organizations have continued to support the long War on Poverty and helped to reshape the relationship between public and private antipoverty efforts in the process. In other words, the rise of the religious right has not meant the disappearance of the religious left.

As the first broad, national account of efforts by organized religion to fight the War on Poverty, this book necessarily focuses on key religious groups and leaders, rather than the laity or church congregants, although chapter 5 does delve into the ways that people in the pews viewed the churches' antipoverty efforts and their responses to the Black Manifesto. That focus is, in large part, informed by which religious organizations and individuals actively participated in antipoverty efforts. The Catholic Church, the American Jewish Committee, and mainline Protestant denominations, mostly those affiliated with the National Council of Churches, were the religious groups most active in the War on Poverty. As a result, my research focused on repositories that house the collections of individuals and groups related to those significant religious organizations.

A wealth of underappreciated sources awaited me at those repositories. For Catholic antipoverty efforts, the National Catholic Conference for Interracial Justice records at Marquette University, the papers of Monsignors Geno Baroni and John Egan at the University of Notre Dame Archives, and the records of the National Conference of Catholic Charities at the American Catholic History Research Center and University Archives at the Catholic University of America, among others, offered a comprehensive view of Catholic involvement in the War on Poverty. The National Council of Churches records at the Presbyterian Historical Society and the United Methodist Archives at Drew University supplied the fundamental story of the mainline Protestant antipoverty efforts. The American Jewish Committee records provided the important history of that group's efforts. Finally, Sargent Shriver's papers at the John F. Kennedy Presidential Library were vital to demonstrating the ways in which his religious faith informed much of his work fighting poverty.

Chapter 1 begins with an exploration of Catholic antipoverty efforts, in part because OEO director Shriver was an active and devout Catholic who encouraged the church's involvement in antipoverty programs. I argue that

10   Introduction

social activist Catholic priests like John (Jack) Egan and Geno Baroni created a Catholic War on Poverty through Catholic civil rights organizations, like the National Catholic Conference for Interracial Justice (NCCIJ), and the development of community antipoverty organizations. Informed by the theology and social teachings of Vatican II, Egan, Baroni, Shriver, and other Catholic activists saw the national War on Poverty as an extension of the civil rights movement. Their efforts led to the eventual formation of the Campaign for Human Development, the Catholic Church's official antipoverty organization, which continues to fight poverty in the twenty-first century.

Chapter 2 shifts to mainline Protestant antipoverty efforts and explores the relationship between the National Council of Churches in Christ (NCC) and the War on Poverty. I argue that the NCC and its member churches saw the War on Poverty as fundamentally a moral and spiritual issue and, despite some internal debates about how to enact that vision, were involved integrally in fighting the War on Poverty. Indeed, the leadership of the NCC made the War on Poverty a central part of its social action agenda through the 1960s and into the 1970s, initially through its own departments and agencies and eventually through interreligious cooperation with Catholic and Jewish institutions. The NCC saw the War on Poverty as a battle for the soul of the nation.

Chapter 3 explores the interfaith antipoverty efforts created through the Interreligious Foundation for Community Organization, which became the focus of leading Protestant, Catholic, and Jewish religious organizations, like the NCC, the NCCIJ, and the American Jewish Committee (AJC), that were involved in the War on Poverty. The creation of IFCO reflected both the movement toward ecumenism among leading Protestant, Jewish, and Catholic organizations in the 1950s and 1960s and the emphasis on community action in the War on Poverty. The influence of black power and black theology, reflected in the creation of organizations like the National Committee of Black Churchmen (NCBC) and the National Black Catholic Clergy Caucus (NBCCC), shaped IFCO and its antipoverty activism. IFCO's support of religious antipoverty organizations that were controlled by African Americans indelibly linked the black power movement, religion, particularly religious ecumenism, and the War on Poverty. IFCO also reflected the creation of an ecumenical antipoverty coalition.

Chapter 4 centers on the Black Manifesto issued by James Forman in May 1969, which demanded that churches and synagogues pay reparations for their role in slavery to black antipoverty organizations through IFCO. I place Forman's manifesto in the context of the black power movement and earlier efforts at reparations. I argue that the manifesto further linked black power and the War on Poverty and fundamentally shaped religious organizations' antipoverty efforts through IFCO. In addition, the Black Manifesto and its demand for reparations, in part through black community antipoverty organizations, challenged the racial and religious status quo and raised important questions about race and religion in American society. It also challenged the ecumenical antipoverty coalition.

Chapter 5 explores the responses of members of that antipoverty coalition to the Black Manifesto. I argue that the manifesto fractured the antipoverty coalition of Protestant, Jewish, and Catholic organizations over issues of race and the War on Poverty. The negative responses of some congregants to the demands of the Black Manifesto led to declining support of the War on Poverty by many religious denominations, while other denominations and ecumenical organizations continued their support but reshaped their antipoverty efforts. The ecumenical antipoverty coalition that had formed around IFCO splintered but never completely disappeared. In addition, religious organizations' responses to the manifesto highlighted the evolving church-state antipoverty effort.

I conclude by examining the continued faith-based antipoverty efforts in the twenty-first century. I describe how both the religious right, most of which had opposed the initial War on Poverty in the 1960s, and the religious left, which largely supported federal antipoverty efforts from the beginning, have engaged in the church-state antipoverty efforts that have characterized the evolving War on Poverty for the past several decades. In many often-contested ways, these faith-based organizations represent the clearest examples of the continuation of an ecumenical antipoverty coalition and of the long War on Poverty in America. That coalition has reformed and evolved, but it demonstrates that some religious individuals and organizations continue the fight against poverty and the fight to preserve the nation's soul to which Sargent Shriver called America in 1965.

CHAPTER ONE

"Kind of a Secular Sacrament"
The Catholic War on Poverty

In May 1966, more than three hundred poor people, mostly black women and children along with a number of priests and antipoverty workers, marched up Madison Avenue in New York demanding more money for the poor from the Office of Economic Opportunity (OEO). The demonstration was organized by a coalition of community antipoverty groups, many of them with religious affiliations, to protest new budget limits that the federal government had placed on the city of New York's antipoverty programs. Carrying signs that read "OEO, We've Got the Poverty, Where's the Dough?" the protestors faced hostility from some passersby. One woman angrily told a reporter, "Those priests should be in their churches instead of out here demonstrating on the streets." Some people in the offices of Young and Rubicam, a prestigious advertising agency, hit the demonstrators with water bombs made of water-filled paper bags. The television show *Mad Men* portrayed this incident in an episode of the series. In this episode, one of the Young and Rubicam employees says of the protestors, "That's all there is—cops and Negroes and priests."[1]

This moment highlights the central role that Catholic priests and other religious figures played in many aspects of the War on Poverty, including actively supporting the Economic Opportunity Act and antipoverty programs and challenging the Office of Economic Opportunity to meet the needs of the poor. It also demonstrates the debates about the proper role of religious lead-

The Catholic War on Poverty

ers and organizations in the War on Poverty and the related deep societal divisions that it at times created. It highlights the central relationship between race and the War on Poverty, and it shows that by 1966, the once-popular federal antipoverty effort, with its community action focus, had become the most controversial program in Lyndon Johnson's Great Society.

Several months prior to the Madison Avenue protests, in September 1965, Sargent Shriver, the director of the Office of Economic Opportunity, prepared to speak to the Ohio Catholic Education Association convention. He exuded a natural energy and enthusiasm, despite regularly working eighteen- to twenty-hour days, and the confidence of a man for whom things were going well. Shriver directed both the Peace Corps and the OEO, arguably the two most popular federal agencies at the time. Shriver was a devout and faithful Catholic from an early age, and his religious beliefs integrally informed his leadership of both programs. His biographer, Scott Stossel, believed it was "impossible to overstate the presence of religion in Sargent Shriver's childhood." Shriver's grandfather had almost joined the priesthood, and his seminary roommate, James Gibbons, later became the archbishop of Baltimore. Gibbons spent summers at the Shriver family home in Union Mills, Maryland, during Sargent Shriver's boyhood and had a profound and fundamental influence on the young Shriver. Various Catholic religious officials and seminary students regularly visited the Shriver home. Discussions at meals generally centered on religion, theology, and philosophy. As Stossel writes, "The Catholic religion was woven into the fabric of Shriver's daily life." It remained central to Shriver in his adult years as well. Shriver was not an occasional Catholic. He read, discussed, and lived religion and theology his entire life. Shriver continued attending daily mass, reading Catholic and other religious literature, and engaging in vibrant theological discussions well into his eighties, until Alzheimer's disease began its destructive path in 2003. His friend and colleague Bill Moyers wrote of Shriver, "He is the Christian who comes closest, in my experience, to the imitation of Christ in a life of service."[2]

It was that Catholic faith and the desire to be more like Christ that most informed Sargent Shriver's vision of the War on Poverty and how he directed his new agency. For Shriver, it was a Christian's duty to live an active life of social justice, to care for and serve the poor and needy wherever they lived. Shriver had ardently supported a central role for religious organizations in the War on Poverty from the beginning, believing that they were vital to the creation and development of a community-based attack on poverty. Shriver met early and often with Catholic, Protestant, and Jewish leaders and encouraged their development of church- and synagogue-based antipoverty

14   Chapter One

programs. As one scholar has noted, Shriver "successfully instilled spiritual values in a societal response to the problem of poverty."[3]

Shriver believed the activism and commitment of religious individuals and organizations were central to the success of the War on Poverty and to his ultimate goal of eliminating poverty from American life. Speaking at the Ohio Catholic Education Association convention, Shriver focused on Catholic antipoverty efforts. He lauded a number of individual Catholic parishes, priests, including Father Geno Baroni from Washington, D.C., and nuns who had created or led antipoverty programs. He chided those who had questioned the involvement of religious organizations in federal antipoverty programs and praised ecumenical efforts, noting that religious groups were ready "to put aside denominational differences in order to concentrate on one job and one job only—eradicating poverty!" He praised the Catholic Church for its "willingness, daring and boldness . . . to seek new ways, as it has always done . . . in order to speak with relevance and mission to every age."[4]

This chapter explores some of those daring and bold efforts by Catholic priests, nuns, and organizations. Building on the work of Kenneth Heineman, Susan Ashmore, and others, I discuss the development of a national Catholic War on Poverty from its beginnings in the National Catholic Conference for Interracial Justice (NCCIJ) through its maturation in the Catholic Campaign for Human Development (CHD). I examine the Catholic War on Poverty through the evolution of the NCCIJ and the careers of two priests, Geno Baroni and John Egan. Fathers Baroni and Egan were the most significant of a group of activist clerics whom one scholar has referred to as "community organization priests."[5] Exploring Baroni's and Egan's activism demonstrates the connections between the civil rights/black power movement and the War on Poverty; the influence of an evolving Catholic theology on Baroni, Egan, and the organizations they created; and the ways in which Catholic social activism and the War on Poverty intertwined.

Many Catholic social activists had been involved in civil rights efforts prior to their engagement with the new federal fight against poverty. Some of them had formed the NCCIJ in 1959 as a way to bring together the Catholic Interracial Councils (CICs) that liberal Catholics had created in major cities in the North and West, like Chicago, Pittsburgh, New York, and Los Angeles, in the 1930s and 1940s. Father John LaFarge, a friend of Sargent Shriver's parents, had formed the first CIC in New York in May 1934 following an ideological division in the Federated Colored Catholics between those who wanted to focus on black identity and those, like LaFarge, who promoted interracialism. Arguing that racism was a sin, CICs, which by 1955 numbered twenty-four local chapters, particularly focused on segregation in schools, both public and parochial.[6]

Sargent Shriver joined the Chicago CIC in the early 1950s. The Chicago CIC, founded in 1943 by Father Reynold Hillenbrand, had a reputation for being bolder and more activist oriented than its New York counterpart. Chicago CIC leaders quickly appointed Shriver to head the organization's school committee with the goal of integrating Chicago's Catholic high schools. In 1955 Shriver was elected chair of the board of the CIC and president of the Chicago school board. Those positions enabled Shriver to address the issue of Chicago's segregated public schools in particular.[7]

The success of the Chicago CIC in challenging officially sanctioned school segregation led to a meeting in that city in 1958 of more than four hundred delegates representing thirty-six CICs nationwide, which pledged to work to end racial discrimination. Father LaFarge gave the keynote address at that formative conference, arguing that "the teaching of interracial justice was firmly grounded in Church doctrine." That meeting resulted in the creation of the NCCIJ in 1959 with Mathew Ahmann, a sociologist and dedicated civil rights activist, as executive director. Ahmann had been a graduate student in sociology at the University of Chicago, where he had become familiar with theories about community action and began working on issues of social justice with activist priests like John Egan. Headquartered in Chicago with a field office in New Orleans, the NCCIJ promoted itself as working "to end racial discrimination and prejudice and to foster interracial justice in all areas of life." Led by such prominent liberals as Shriver and Ahmann, the NCCIJ was at the forefront of connecting civil rights activism to the church by supporting open housing laws and civil rights legislation and by organizing the ecumenical national Conference on Religion and Race in Chicago in January 1963.[8]

Ahmann, Rabbi Philip Hiatt of the Synagogue Council of America, and the Reverend Oscar Lee of the National Council of Churches planned the conference, which included more than 650 participants from sixty-seven national religious groups, to coincide with the hundredth anniversary of the Emancipation Proclamation. Ahmann and Hiatt invited Rabbi Abraham Heschel of the Jewish Theological Seminary to give the opening talk and the Reverend Martin Luther King Jr. to give the keynote address. Ahmann later wrote, "There was a conviction present in the Conference that religion should influence our society not only through the informed communicant, who acts on religious principle, but also through the proper exercise of institutional power. Religious groups bear institutional responsibility, too." In other words, the conference encouraged delegates to take action.[9]

In his keynote speech, King admonished the churches and synagogues for being "an echo rather than a voice, a tail light behind the Supreme Court and

FIGURE 2. Mathew Ahmann (*right*) at the national Conference on Religion and Race, January 1963. Ahmann, the executive director of the NCCIJ, was one of the key planners of the conference. Standing next to him is Stephen Gill Spottswood, a bishop of the AME Zion Church and chair of the board of the NAACP. Courtesy of the Department of Special Collections and University Archives, Marquette University Libraries.

other secular agencies, rather than a headlight guiding men progressively and decisively to higher levels of understanding." King told those gathered in Chicago that they had "an opportunity and a duty to lift up their voices like a trumpet and declare unto the people the immorality of segregation." King went further than racial integration, though, by focusing part of his talk on poverty, telling the delegates that churches and synagogues "must support strong civil rights legislation and exert their influence in the area of economic justice. Economic insecurity strangles the physical and cultural growth of its victims.... There are few things more thoroughly sinful than economic injustice." King, who saw economic justice as a central part of his civil rights activism, encouraged conference attendees to lead civil rights and antipoverty efforts.[10]

In addition to its leadership role in the Conference on Religion and Race, the NCCIJ lobbied strenuously for the passage of President Kennedy's civil

FIGURE 3. Martin Luther King Jr. (*third from left*) and Andrew Young (*far right*) with members of the Holy Child Jesus Mission in Canton, Mississippi, during the Meredith March against Fear in 1966. The march was begun by James Meredith in an effort to convince black Mississippians to register to vote. Many Catholics participated in the march. Photo by Father Luke Mikschl (1923-2007). Courtesy of the Department of Special Collections and University Archives, Marquette University Libraries.

rights bill and joined in the plans and coordination of the March on Washington later that year. Ahmann gave a speech and served as one of ten chairs of the march, and NCCIJ leaders were among those who met with Kennedy afterward to discuss his civil rights legislation. NCCIJ members, along with a significant number of priests and women religious, participated in the march from Selma to Montgomery in 1965 and in the Meredith March against Fear in 1966. Indeed, by the mid-1960s, Catholic interracialists had become central participants in the civil rights movement.[11]

18   Chapter One

Leaders of the NCCIJ argued for civil rights legislation from a moral per-spective: racism, discrimination, and segregation were sins or immoral actions against people, who were God's creations. The NCCIJ board of directors issued a statement in July 1963 insisting that civil rights was "a moral issue . . . of unique and decisive importance" and that support for the civil rights bill "should be uni-versal, at all levels of Catholic life." The NCCIJ admonished, "Catholics who fail to take a positive stand on this issue fail to meet their obligation as responsible citizens." Essentially the members of the NCCIJ thought and acted as theolog-ical neo-abolitionists, arguing that the United States needed to purge itself of the immorality of racism and segregation and create an interracial, socially just society. As outliers among Catholics in the early 1960s, the NCCIJ pushed for change in the church. The NCCIJ created interracial Conferences on Religion and Race in several communities to "touch the conscience" of the faithful and persuade them to "work to eliminate the sin of discrimination and social injus-tice." In addition to participating in marches, lobbying for civil rights legislation, and organizing community protests, NCCIJ activists joined and used similar moral arguments to support President Lyndon Johnson's War on Poverty.[12]

Father Geno Baroni, the pastor of Saints Paul and Augustine Parish in Washington, D.C., and an NCCIJ leader and civil rights activist who partici-pated in the March on Washington and in the Meredith March against Fear, told a *Washington Post* reporter that social issues like poverty, civil rights, jobs, and housing were "moral issues" and were "the proper and vital busi-ness of the church." Baroni claimed that a split had developed in the Catholic Church between the middle class and the poor—as middle-class Catholics moved out of the city, the religious connection between the social classes was lost. Baroni argued that affluent, middle-class Catholics did not see "poverty, housing, civil rights as moral issues." For Baroni, it was a "great scandal . . . that the church has lost the poor. . . . And if we are not the church of the poor, we are in trouble."[13]

Baroni, who served on the NCCIJ board of directors from 1965 to 1978, was an outspoken advocate for African Americans and the white ethnic poor who stands as a prime example of Catholic clerical social activism in the twentieth century. Born in Pennsylvania to Italian immigrant parents (his father was a coal miner) in 1930, Baroni graduated from Mount Saint Mary's College and Seminary prior to his ordination as a Catholic priest in 1956. He initially served in white ethnic working-class parishes where he clashed with the highly orthodox and conservative pastor Father John Manning. Baroni's feelings of inadequacy as a priest, particularly his ability to deliver hom-ilies, led him into a period of depression, and he spent several months in 1959–1960 recovering at the Seton Institute outside Baltimore.[14]

The Catholic War on Poverty 19

When he recovered from his depression, he jumped at the chance to relocate to Washington, D.C., where he could study at Catholic University while serving as a parish priest. That led him in 1960 to Saint Augustine's Parish, an all-black congregation established during the Civil War. While serving as parish priest at Saint Augustine's, Baroni's interest in the realities of the African American urban experience and the emerging civil rights movement crystallized. Shortly after Baroni's arrival in D.C., Saint Augustine's merged with Saint Paul's, an all-white parish. Baroni saw this merger as a tremendous opportunity to address issues of racial and economic inequality. His bishop in Washington, D.C., was Patrick O'Boyle, a theological conservative who was a liberal on social issues; O'Boyle also hailed from a working-class background in Pennsylvania. O'Boyle had desegregated parishes and Catholic schools in the D.C. area and openly advocated for civil rights. He urged the passage of the Civil Rights Act of 1964 and participated in the March on Washington, although he generally discouraged priests and nuns under his direction from participating in public demonstrations. Baroni, with the support of O'Boyle, spearheaded NCCIJ civil rights and antipoverty efforts and became one of the leading voices of Catholic social justice activism. O'Boyle, at Baroni's urging, created the Office of Urban Affairs, with Baroni at the helm. Through that office, Baroni led community antipoverty efforts.[15]

Baroni's activism included publishing a number of articles in religious journals expounding on the theology behind Catholic involvement in civil rights efforts and the fight against poverty as well as the practical implications of those beliefs. In an article titled "The Church and the War on Poverty," Baroni explained the fundamental significance of the Second Vatican Council to the expanding involvement of Catholic priests and parishes in social justice causes. Baroni argued that Vatican II urged Catholics to take on the causes of the poor and underprivileged as their own. For him and other Catholics, the joining of Vatican II with the civil rights movement and antipoverty efforts had profound meaning. According to the Second Vatican Council, the church most resembled Christ when it revealed "a predilection for the poor, the outcast, the injured, and the despised." Vatican II influenced countless Catholic agencies and individuals, including Baroni, to be more involved because it located the church in the people, not in the hierarchy of the institution. For example, Vatican II inspired participants in Catholic charities "to reconstruct themselves as 'justice' workers, committed to advocacy and service to the poor." In addition, liberation theology, which had become influential in the United States by the 1960s, emphasized the role of the church in assisting the poor in their struggle for liberation. In testimony to the House Subcommittee on Appropriations for the District of Columbia,

20   Chapter One

Baroni said, "religion must provide a voice for the poor of the community." Thus, for Baroni, participation in a government program to aid the poor was not optional, but a requirement for those Catholics who desired to be more like Christ.[16]

But how to implement the theology of Vatican II and liberation theology? How to use the War on Poverty for the church's ends? For Baroni, the answer was the parish. He argued that since the parish was "traditionally the central force in the Church's network of bringing spiritual and material support to the person of the culture of poverty" and was an integral part of the local community, it could play a significant role in the new federal fight against poverty. Through activist antipoverty efforts, inner-city parishes could "demonstrate a new relationship to the poor in the community."[17]

Catholics could implement that new relationship through the parish Neighborhood Center. The center, housed in parish buildings, would provide assistance to the poor in the community through education, housing referrals, employment services, health and welfare referrals, and a "community action volunteer program" aimed at bringing in volunteers "from middle income and suburban parishes who are anxious to participate in an active program that promises assistance to the less fortunate." In addition, the center involved poor people themselves in planning and delivering the programs. Baroni stated that the volunteering of the more fortunate to work with the poor "underlies the essential commitment of the laity to the war on poverty."[18]

Baroni posited that the Neighborhood Center could become "a vital force" in the creation of community action programs, which he clearly saw as central to the War on Poverty and as an extension of the civil rights movement. For Baroni, the community action aspect of the War on Poverty represented "a new phase in the civil rights struggle—a switchover from a decade in which the concentration was on breaking down legal barriers to one in which the excluded seek genuine equality in jobs, education, and housing." This phase of the extended civil rights movement would give "the poor of the city the power to solve their own problems. It means giving them a collective voice to be heard when their garbage is not picked up, when the landlords cheat them, and when their elected officials refuse to listen to them."[19] For Baroni, the community action approach of the War on Poverty continued the democratization of the civil rights movement and empowered the poor.

Baroni saw a direct connection between poverty and racism. In another publication, "The Church and the Inner City," Baroni asserted that poverty and racism were dual sins in American society. He argued that while racism was "a radical distortion of the relationship between man's body and his social life," poverty was "a radical distortion of the relationship between man

The Catholic War on Poverty   21

and the goods that he needs for social life." Baroni maintained that "to deny men goods, property, the means to sustain life, is to deny them the right to participate in creation. . . . The poverty of the exploited is a denial of their spiritual function in the world, which is to participate with Him in creation. As racism denies man's bodily integrity, poverty denies his spiritual integrity." It was a Christian's duty, then, to work to expunge poverty and racism from society in order to improve both the economic and spiritual life of the poor.[20]

While community action programs would aid and empower the poor, they would also enable individual Catholics to live out their faith. The War on Poverty provided a vehicle for Baroni to continue his activism, his efforts at social justice, and his attempts to be more like Christ. Indeed, Baroni noted that "many of the same priests and ministers so recently involved in the struggle for civil rights now find themselves brought together to assist in developing community action programs in our poor center city neighborhoods."[21]

But Baroni also recognized that not all priests and ministers saw themselves as activists. In a 1966 article, he noted "a serious division of views" among priests at a joint meeting of the NCCIJ and the National Catholic Social Action Conference in 1965 between those who wanted "the church to play its customary role as guardian of the past" and those who insisted that "the Church should play a more direct role in social change." Baroni acknowledged that these different approaches had always been present among priests, but he observed that "recently a strong and young group of clergies within the Church have gained momentum because of their involvement in the civil rights movement. . . . At any gathering of clergy, there seems to be a clear demarcation between those who have participated in direct action and those who have not." Experience in civil rights direct action led many priests, including Baroni, to advocate for parishes' involvement in community action and the War on Poverty.[22]

Father Baroni wrote this article from experience. Although it was published in September 1966, just two years after the creation of the Office of Economic Opportunity (OEO), by then Baroni had already established a parish Neighborhood Center at Saints Paul and Augustine with the active participation of residents of the area, complete with a volunteer program, employment services, job opportunity workshops, a parish credit union, and a summer youth educational and job training program. Indeed, Baroni had established the Neighborhood Center, the employment services program, and the summer youth program in 1963, prior to the creation of the federal legislation establishing the OEO. Baroni and members of Saints Paul and Augustine Parish were already fighting their own Catholic War on Poverty prior to the federal government declaring one.[23]

A colleague of Baroni who also served as a leading voice of Catholic social activism, John Egan was one of the foremost advocates for Catholic involvement in the War on Poverty and a prominent community organizer. Born in New York in 1916 to Irish immigrants, Egan and his family moved to Chicago when he was a young boy. The city of Chicago and the Catholic Church became Egan's true passions. Egan attended DePaul University and Saint Mary of the Lake Seminary and served as a priest in several of the city's parishes. Monsignor Egan's involvement in social action began during his seminary years while studying under Monsignor Reynold Hillenbrand, who had formed the Young Catholic Workers movement geared toward economic and social activism during the Great Depression. Hillenbrand trained a number of priests in Catholic social reform and was responsible for Chicago's reputation as the center of Catholic social activism in the United States. Hillenbrand's theology was informed by the idea of the laity as equal members of the mystical body of Christ, a notion promoted by Dorothy Day and the Catholic Worker movement that led its followers to work toward the democratization of the church and society. For Hillenbrand and Egan, racism was divisive to that mystical body. Egan's involvement in and commitment to community organization began in 1954 when he met Saul Alinsky, who had authored *Reveille for Radicals* (1946), a blueprint for community organizing. Alinsky had attended graduate school at the University of Chicago and was well versed in the school's theories about community organization. Alinsky, though, argued for a more directly political approach by community residents to organize to demand better services and urban reform. Three years after their first meeting, Egan became Alinsky's first priest intern. The famed organizer of the Back of the Yards Chicago neighborhood and founder of the Industrial Areas Foundation (IAF) connected with Egan's own commitment to the dignity of each human being. Their friendship lasted until Alinsky's death in 1972. Alinsky, whose emphasis on community mobilization influenced Lloyd Ohlin and Richard Cloward's opportunity theory, trained Egan on the dynamics of power, leadership development, and "the skills of democratic organization."[24]

In the 1950s, Egan had the support of Samuel Cardinal Stritch, the archbishop of Chicago, who gave Egan leave from his regular priestly duties and issued Egan and the IAF a grant of almost $120,000. Egan used that money for his first foray into community organizing with the Latin American Committee of the Woodlawn Organization—the community organization Alinsky started in the Back of the Yards neighborhood—and for canvassing black neighborhoods on the South Side of Chicago to determine how the construction of the Dan Ryan Expressway had impacted black residents. In the process, again with the support of Cardinal Stritch, Egan established the first diocesan Office of Urban Affairs in the nation, which "gave community organizing a Catholic mantle of credibility . . . and articulated the theological premises for church involvement in community organization." Those experiences led him to further involvement in social justice organizing and demonstrations, including participation in the Selma to Montgomery march in 1965 and in open housing and employment campaigns in Chicago. His activism against urban renewal in Chicago created enemies in the political, economic, and religious power structure there. The new cardinal of Chicago, John Patrick Cody, who took office in 1966, was no fan of "troublemakers" who advocated for social justice. Indeed, when priests in Chicago first learned who would be their new boss, one activist priest noted that "a malaise" infected the archdiocese. Cody represented the older, more conservative wing of the Catholic Church and opposed many of the causes that Egan and his activist friends supported. Shortly after he arrived, Cody attempted to silence Egan by appointing him pastor of Presentation Parish in the all-black neighborhood of Lawndale in 1966. Instead of being silenced, Egan helped form the Contract Buyers of Lawndale (CBL), an effort led by residents of the area to challenge unfair housing contracts. Banks had redlined certain neighborhoods and refused to provide traditional loans to black home buyers in those areas. As a result, blacks had been forced to buy their homes "on contract," which meant that the seller kept the deed until the contract was paid in full. Missing a single house payment could mean losing all of their previous payments and the home itself. From 1966 to 1969, Presentation Parish was the center of activity for the CBL, and Egan was an integral part of it, participating in picket lines and barricading himself in the homes of people scheduled for eviction. Cody's effort to remove the troublemaker had backfired.[25]

Egan continued his efforts outside of Chicago as well, despite Cody's opposition. In February 1966, Egan spoke at the Fifteenth Street Presbyterian Church in Washington, D.C., on the topic of Saul Alinsky and community organization. Baroni had helped arrange Egan's address and wrote a memo to his boss, O'Boyle, outlining the significance of Egan's speech and the need to establish and support community organizations in D.C. Baroni wrote to O'Boyle, "The serious question of the role of the priest and the parish in community organizations needs urgently to be discussed."[26]

Egan's involvement in civil rights and antipoverty community organizations seemed natural as he, like Baroni, saw the War on Poverty as an extension of the social justice goals of civil rights. Egan, who served on the NCCIJ board of directors from 1967 to 1971 and again from 1972 to 1974, had given a speech at the Conference on Religion and Race in 1963 in which he outlined

FIGURE 4. Father Jack Egan in 1965. Egan was a leading Catholic social activist deeply involved in the civil rights movement and the War on Poverty. Courtesy of the United Methodist Archives, Drew University.

his thinking on the connection between religion and racial justice. Egan stated that Catholics, Protestants, and Jews shared a belief "that all men, as special creatures of God, possess a unique dignity by virtue of their creation." This notion of "kinship in God" led Egan to argue that it was "the people of God" who bore "the responsibility for racial intolerance."[27]

Egan's speech, though, went beyond addressing civil rights and segregation and focused largely on poverty. For him, the poor were also special creatures of God with innate dignity because of their relationship to God. Thus, Egan argued that Catholics, Protestants, and Jews could not expect "to be taken seriously on the question of race relations" if they did not "insist on being taken seriously on the question of the poor." Egan further stated that America would never be successful "in eliminating the cancer of racial intolerance" until it had also eliminated "the cancer of intolerance of the poor." For him, removing intolerance of the poor meant loving the poor, and love of the poor necessarily implied active involvement in civil rights and anti-poverty efforts. Importantly, Egan's speech advocating for the commitment of people of faith to issues of the poor took place prior to the official federal

The Catholic War on Poverty 25

War on Poverty. While Egan was not involved directly in the planning for the War on Poverty, he and Shriver worked together in the civil rights efforts of the Chicago CIC and the NCCIJ.[28]

Egan already had years of involvement in community organizing with the poor in Chicago prior to President Johnson's declaration of the war against poverty in 1964. For Egan, community organization was almost a holy method of ministry, a "kind of secular sacrament . . . [through which] the weak can get power to make their lives whole." Egan connected the sanctity of community organization to Catholic involvement in civil rights and antipoverty efforts.[29]

Baroni and Egan were active in the NCCIJ, which had begun its own antipoverty efforts prior to 1964 and by the mid-1960s had become the center of the Catholic antipoverty campaign. As an organization, the NCCIJ first started discussing poverty at a February 1963 meeting, when the group's board of directors initiated a study to determine, in part, the relationship between race and poverty. Later that year, the board directed NCCIJ staff to "study and make recommendations for a program concerning economic and other socio-economic problems" that were slowing progress in race relations.[30]

The theme of the 1963 NCCIJ convention, "Poverty, Race and Religion: Challenge to a Catholic Community," reflected its commitment to both civil rights and ending poverty. Mathew Ahmann wrote that the convention theme "was developed to explore the socio-economic problems which limit advances to interracial justice and love, and to explore program ideas which would enable the Catholic community to meet more adequately the needs of poverty stricken people." Delegates highlighted the convention's focus on poverty when they passed a resolution to remove poverty from America. In November 1963, just a week before his assassination, President Kennedy sent a telegram to Raymond Hilliard, chair of the NCCIJ, commending the organization for focusing on poverty. Kennedy wrote to Hilliard that while it was "vital that the basic civil rights of all our citizens" be protected, poverty and full employment were also important issues.[31]

Two years later, the theme of the NCCIJ convention in Omaha, "Poverty's Challenge to Interracial Action," continued the NCCIJ's understanding of the relationship between race and poverty. The conference theme and the resolutions passed by the delegates demonstrated the connection the NCCIJ had made between the civil rights movement and the War on Poverty. In planning the 1965 conference, Ahmann recommended that "a theme should be selected which relates problems in race relations to the economic life of this country, again pursuing the poverty question raised at the 1963 Conference convention." Ahmann went on to say that "effort should be made to explore the relationship which Catholic institutions might have in meeting problems of race and poverty." The prelude to the conference resolutions highlighted Ahmann's suggestions and his racialized conceptualization of poverty: "if it is not painfully obvious in 1965 that poverty and racial tensions are inextricably intertwined we affirm it again: at every turn in their unending struggle for participation in the responsibilities and the benefits of the free society, Negroes, Indians, and the Spanish-speaking feel the effects of generations of weakening destitution." Importantly, for the NCCIJ, antipoverty efforts needed to be multiracial to reflect the diversity of the American people and the poverty that informed the experiences of many of America's minority groups. For Catholic clergy in America, poverty was not just a story of black and white. Although Catholic programs had been established earlier in the twentieth century that attempted to address the economic and spiritual concerns and needs of Native Americans and Mexican migrants, race had never been the focus of a concerted Catholic battle against poverty.[32]

The NCCIJ supported the federal government's antipoverty efforts, but also criticized its "defects and omissions." The War on Poverty's key shortcoming, according to the NCCIJ, was a lack of participation of the poor in most community action programs. As the result of conflicts and tensions in some major cities in the United States over the meaning of the "maximum feasible participation of the poor" in community action programs, the U.S. Conference of Mayors had passed a resolution earlier in the summer of 1965 attempting to limit the participation of the poor. The NCCIJ responded to that action by passing its own resolution, which called for OEO director Shriver "to take prompt and realistic steps to insist on genuine participation in the decision-making process by poor persons in every War on Poverty program." Democratic participation in the War on Poverty was the primary way, NCCIJ members believed, that the civil rights movement could be expanded. The NCCIJ concluded its conference report by recommending that "the church dedicate its resources primarily to the poor of all races." Ahmann later reported that the 1965 conference was "designed to relate grass roots leaders in the War on Poverty and the local Catholic human relations organizations more effectively" to the OEO and other governmental resources. Religious organizations, like the NCCIJ, not only supported the War on Poverty and served as an important ally for the OEO, but they also pushed Shriver and his agency to live up to the maximum feasible participation mandate.[33]

The NCCIJ's support for the War on Poverty included active lobbying efforts. In 1967, amid concerns over the costs of the Vietnam War and conflict in some cities over the maximum feasible participation of the poor, the OEO faced significant congressional opposition to its funding authorization. The

The Catholic War on Poverty 27

NCCIJ pressed hard for the OEO's continuation. Ahmann spoke in support of the War on Poverty at congressional hearings, and NCCIJ members sent thousands of telegrams and letters to members of Congress "urging them to vote adequate funds and to oppose any dismantling of OEO."[34]

Baroni, Egan, and other NCCIJ members continued their support of the War on Poverty as the civil rights movement shifted to more of an emphasis on black power. The NCCIJ supported the movement both ideologically and practically through its backing of the Interreligious Foundation for Community Organization (IFCO).[35] Formed in early 1967, IFCO sought to coordinate religious organizations' efforts at supporting community action programs, arguing that there were "limits on the degree to which Federal and city governments can support community action programs." IFCO's top priority, according to its bylaws, was "to implement common programs and strateg[ies] among religious groups for the development of community organizations among the poor . . . as part of the urban mission, ministry and program of such religious groups." In August 1967, NCCIJ joined the board of the newly formed IFCO. At the same time, it issued a policy statement that addressed common misunderstandings about the meaning of black power, noting that civil rights groups "which are predominantly Negro in membership are in fact black power organizations dedicated to full citizenship and full partnership in our society for all men."[36] That same month, the NCCIJ board, with Baroni and Egan playing key roles, passed a resolution calling on "the white community to accept the primary responsibility for the presence and atmosphere of violence found in the cities of our country. . . . We resolve that funds be used positively to alleviate poverty and build self-sufficient communities. . . . We resolve that the Church support the efforts of the Negro, Puerto Rican, Mexican American and other minorities to attain necessary power to achieve political, social and economic equality."[37]

Early in 1968, the NCCIJ celebrated black power, stating that "the terms of the struggle for racial justice and equity" were "happily being dictated by the Negro community itself." It also maintained that "the primary task" of the NCCIJ was "in the white community . . . and the white church." As a result, the NCCIJ looked for ways to direct "white resources to the . . . requests of the Black community." One way NCCIJ demonstrated its support of black power was through its creation of the Department of Urban Services, which became the organization's institutional and financial link to IFCO.[38]

Some activist priests incorporated black power into civil rights and antipoverty agencies not directly related to IFCO. In Milwaukee, Father James Groppi was the parish priest at Saint Boniface in the African American community in the central city. Groppi participated in the March on Washington,

28   Chapter One

the march from Selma to Montgomery, and other civil rights demonstrations and became an integral part of a black power group, the Commandos, which marched for fair housing laws. Groppi worked with the leadership of the Commandos, taught the tenets of black power (self-definition and community control) to neighborhood children, and wore black instead of colorful vestments during mass as a way of showing solidarity with the Commandos and the wider movement. In Pittsburgh, Catholic priests and lay activists were members of the city's CIC and saw the War on Poverty as "an opportunity to forge ecumenical and interracial alliances and eradicate discrimination." Activist priests, like Father Donald McIlvane of Saint Richard's Parish and Father Charles Owen Rice of Holy Rosary Parish, used OEO funds for education and job training programs and to promote civil rights and black power. Groppi's relationship with the Commandos, McIlvane's and Rice's activities in Pittsburgh, and the involvement of Baroni and the NCCIJ with IFCO demonstrate both the varieties of black power and the importance of activist Catholics in some of those organizations.[39]

The ideology of black power evident in IFCO and Catholic War on Poverty efforts also infused the development of black nationalist Catholic organizations in the late 1960s and 1970s. In 1967, black Catholics formed the Council of Catholic Negro Laymen, which a year later became the Council of Black Catholic Laymen. In 1968, in what one scholar has called "a milestone in the history of the black Catholic community," black clergy formed the National Black Catholic Clergy Caucus (NBCCC) at a meeting of the Catholic Clergy Conference on the Interracial Apostolate, the theme of which was "Black Power and the White Church." At its first meeting, the NBCCC issued a statement saying that the American Catholic Church was "primarily a white racist institution" and demanded the hiring of more black priests, the training of white priests working in black communities, and the inclusion of black clergy in decision making at the diocesan level. The same year, black women religious created the National Black Sisters Conference (NBSC) to address the needs of black Catholics and "to confront individual and institutional racism and injustice found in society and in the Church." The first president of the NBSC, Sister M. Martin de Porres Grey, invited black nuns "to meet to become attuned to the plight of our people, to reevaluate our role as black religious women, and to determine more effective ways of combating racism and liberating our people." In October 1971, de Porres Grey held the Institute on Black Sister Formation to create racial unity among black religious women. In 1970, lay Catholics had created their own black nationalist organization, the National Black Lay Catholic Caucus. All of these organizations, to one degree or another, espoused the ideas of self-definition and community

The Catholic War on Poverty 29

control, which formed the core of IFCO's message and the central ideology of black power, and the principle of maximum feasible participation of the poor in community action.[40]

The advent of black power in the Catholic Church in part reflected the realities of a growing black Catholic population. In 1940, black Catholics totaled fewer than three hundred thousand. By 1970, that total had risen to almost a million parishioners. The number of black priests also rose during this period from 120 in 1961 to more than 200 by 1970. When black priests and nuns advocated for increased black power in the Catholic Church, the numbers supported their arguments.[41]

The ideology of black power, though, challenged the core message and philosophy of the NCCIJ. As an explicitly interracial civil rights organization, the NCCIJ struggled to adapt to black power ideas, which some members saw as separatist and in opposition to the central principles of the organization. Following intense internal debate on the direction of the NCCIJ, Ahmann resigned as executive director in July 1968. James T. Harris replaced Ahmann in January 1969. In announcing the appointment, NCCIJ chair Rawson Wood wrote that Harris would work "to channel the full resources of the white community to meet Black Power's legitimate demands towards the creation of that humane one society which is the very essence of Christianity."[42]

The advent of black power, combined with declining membership and financial troubles, challenged the NCCIJ's ability to stay relevant for the next several years. In August 1969, Harris notified the board of directors of extremely low registration numbers for the conference to be held later that month in Los Angeles. Harris told the board that the organization was "entering a most turbulent and delicate period, when world and national circumstances have conspired to present a whole new set of challenges to which NCCIJ must respond or wither away." In addition, Harris reported a significant reduction in the number of active NCCIJ affiliates. When Harris resigned in 1971 due to the illness of his daughter, the NCCIJ remained in serious financial trouble and continued to debate its future direction.[43]

Under its new director, Sister Margaret Ellen Traxler, the NCCIJ continued to attempt to redefine its identity and purpose. An internal committee established by Traxler to discuss possible organizational directions reflected on the NCCIJ's role in a changing world. It concluded that the NCCIJ "should not try to compete with the new wave of black and brown Catholic organizations and institutions which are seeking to formulate and express the rights, needs and contributions of particular black and brown ethnic strains in the Catholic mosaic." Instead, the report recommended that the "NCCIJ should

FIGURE 5. Sister Audrey Kopp, director of research and curriculum for the NCCIJ, with black power insignia behind her, talks to other nuns about the centrality of black power to the NCCIJ and the Catholic Church. Courtesy of the Department of Special Collections and University Archives, Marquette University Libraries.

seek friendly relations with these groups, cooperate on reform issues of mutual concern, and perhaps most important, seek to play a bridge role between these groups and white Catholics." One of the ways in which Traxler and the NCCIJ implemented this recommendation was by offering educational talks by priests and women religious to parishes and Catholic organizations on the history and significance of black power. For instance, Sister Audrey Kopp of the NCCIJ regularly spoke to Catholic groups, particularly women religious, about the black power movement.[44]

In addition, Traxler explored the possibility of sponsoring a new Conference on Religion and Race. She queried Ahmann, the organizer of the original conference, about the possibility, but he replied, "that kind of meeting would be impossible now." He claimed that agendas had changed since the original Conference on Religion and Race in 1963, due to "the rise of ethnic pluralism and the demolishment of the ideal of assimilation." Traxler and the NCCIJ agreed with Ahmann's conclusions and never pursued another Conference on Religion and Race. The NCCIJ spent the next several years

The Catholic War on Poverty   31

trying to reestablish itself as a significant player in debates on religion, race, and poverty in the United States, but it never succeeded. In 1975, the NCCIJ moved its offices to Washington, D.C., where it worked quietly in the shadow of the United States Catholic Conference (USCC) until it suspended operations in 2002. The NCCIJ had lost its prominence in the late 1960s and early 1970s to ecumenical and black power antipoverty organizations like IFCO.[45]

Some NCCIJ members were actively engaged in IFCO. The individual Catholic who provided the most significant support for IFCO was Monsignor Egan. For him, IFCO represented a way for socially activist Catholic priests to be involved in a national antipoverty community organization and to live out that secular sacrament. In March 1967, Egan, Baroni, and a number of other priests formed the Catholic Committee of Community Organization (CCCO) at NCCIJ's "The Church and the Urban Racial Crisis" conference to provide the official Catholic link to IFCO. The formation of CCCO was based on a variety of influences, but primarily the establishment of diocesan Offices of Urban Affairs in the late 1950s and early 1960s and the experiences of priests in civil rights and antipoverty community organizing. It was the community organizing experiences of priests like Father Egan in Chicago, Father Groppi in Milwaukee, and Fathers McIlvane and Rice in Pittsburgh that led the members of the CCCO to desire to be a part of IFCO. The CCCO stated that its "highest priority" was "the development of mass-based, self-determined organization of the urban poor to effect direly needed social change." The first item on the new organization's agenda was an official association with IFCO. Egan and Baroni were chosen to represent the CCCO on the IFCO board. Egan wrote to Baroni following the July 1967 IFCO board meeting that the "enthusiasm . . . was evident and the national response to IFCO has been somewhat overwhelming." Egan later wrote his friend and colleague at the NCCIJ Emil Seliga that the organization needed "to decide how we can substantially help IFCO. . . . I am more convinced than ever of the rightness of our direction."[46]

Later that year, the CCCO priests met with the NCCIJ (most of them were members of both organizations) and changed the CCCO's name to the Catholic Committee on Urban Ministry (CCUM) to reflect the notion that while community organizing was still central, they wanted to be involved in all types of urban ministries. Many Catholic priests, like Francis X. Walter, who founded the Selma Interreligious Project, had developed or been involved in urban ministry programs, which grew in popularity in the 1960s. The NCCIJ and the CCUM were closely linked. Noting that the CCUM could provide "a strong, heavily clerical organization of those involved in race" and poverty work, Ahmann wrote to Seliga that it was "imperative that the NCCIJ be

32   Chapter One

closely related to CCUM, and CCUM requires NCCIJ energy and staff services." Ahmann proposed that Egan remain "the Charismatic leader" of the CCUM, with the NCCIJ actively involved in providing all staff services and serving as the coordinator of interracial activities.[47]

Egan's role as "the charismatic leader" of the CCUM, though, became more difficult as his continual clashes with Cardinal Cody began to take their toll on Egan's physical and emotional health. In the spring of 1970, Egan ran into his friend Father Theodore Hesburgh, president of the University of Notre Dame, in O'Hare Airport in Chicago. Noticing that Egan "looked awful," Hesburgh invited him to join the Theology Department at Notre Dame. Egan readily accepted and, with Cody's permission, left the Archdiocese of Chicago in the fall of 1970. He would not return until 1983, after Cody had passed away and had been replaced by Joseph Bernardin. Egan spent much of his time at Notre Dame continuing to lead the activist members of the CCUM.[48]

The members of the CCUM "were at the forefront of Catholic activism and had experience in organizations focused on self-determination: community organizations, economic development organizations, . . . housing initiatives, and neighborhood associations." In addition, the CCUM was a way for Egan to continue community organizing after he left Chicago and a way to provide "ministry to the ministers, ministry to those empowering the poor." The CCUM served essentially as a network for priests, community organizers, and others interested in addressing causes of social justice. The CCUM held a four-week program every summer where, according to Egan, it trained "a whole generation of priests, Sisters, and lay people" in community organization.[49]

The CCUM received money from the Raskob Foundation for Catholic Activities, the Schubert Foundation, and other religious grant-making organizations. Egan wrote annual reports to the Raskob Foundation highlighting the CCUM's accomplishments. In his 1973 report, Egan noted that almost five hundred people had attended the CCUM's annual meeting, the largest group to date. Egan wrote, "CCUM has become a network which is widespread and essential. It is the only coalition which enjoys the support of every Catholic and many Protestant and secular organizations." Lucius Walker, the director of IFCO, wrote on his copy of Egan's report, "This is a report to a foundation from a group (one of the church groups) we relate to—Fr. Egan is one of our big supporters." By 1975, the CCUM had grown to more than three thousand members. It used the money from the Raskob Foundation and others and developed diocesan urban ministry programs, created the National Center for Urban Ethnic Affairs (headed by Geno Baroni), and helped

The Catholic War on Poverty 33

create the Campaign for Human Development, the Catholic Church's official antipoverty program.[50]

The Campaign for Human Development had its immediate origins in the creation in the summer of 1968 of the USCC Urban Task Force headed by Baroni with Egan and other CCUM members participating. The task force began exploring ways to coordinate diocesan antipoverty efforts in urban centers. Following a year of long-distance discussions, Baroni called the group together in Combermere, Canada, in August 1969, partly in response to James Forman's Black Manifesto and the formation of Catholic black power organizations like the Council of Black Catholic Laymen and the NBCCC.[51] While most mainline Protestant churches had committed funds to Forman's National Black Economic Development Conference (NBEDC), the Catholic Church had not. At the meetings at Combermere, this group of social activist priests, who had long been involved in War on Poverty projects, created what they called at the time the Catholic Crusade against Poverty. The task force report called on the church to commit $50 million to community organizations of "white and minority poor to develop economic strength and political power in their own communities" and to "self-help funds for voter registration . . . seed money to develop non-profit housing corporations, community-run schools, minority-owned cooperatives and credit unions, capital for industrial development and job training programs." In other words, they recommended that the Catholic Church create its own War on Poverty, based on the antipoverty and urban community organizing experiences of Baroni, Egan, and other members of the NCCIJ and the CCUM and spurred on by the Black Manifesto and groups like IFCO and the NBCCC.[52]

Baroni and the Urban Task Force then took the resolution to the November 1969 meeting of the National Conference of Catholic Bishops (NCCB). The bishops discussed Baroni's proposal in smaller sessions at the meeting. From those sessions, the bishops identified two priority courses of action: the "education of the total Catholic community in terms of a more generous, sympathetic and Christ-like attitude toward the poor and minority groups" and the establishment of a "special poverty collection." The final resolution approved by the bishops stated: "There is an evident need for funds designated to be used for organized groups of white and minority poor to develop economic strength and political power in their own communities. . . . Therefore, be it resolved that the National Conference of Catholic Bishops establish a National Catholic Crusade Against Poverty." Community organization remained central to the Catholic War on Poverty.[53]

Over the next year, as the OEO faced mounting challenges from the new administration of President Richard Nixon, who had promised to dismantle the embattled organization, the NCCB plotted strategy for its antipoverty campaign. In March 1970, a memo from Baroni and his Urban Task Force to Bishop Joseph Bernardin, the first general secretary of the NCCB, which had been founded in 1966, recommended that the USCC Crusade against Poverty focus on educating Catholics on the extent of poverty in the United States and on providing funds to community organizations, many of which had received OEO funding in the past. Clearly influenced by the language and goals of the War on Poverty, the task force argued that the crusade "could be a national conduit of funds for self-help development projects . . . to develop economic power and organization among groups living in poverty and dependence."[54]

In November 1970, just prior to the NCCB annual meeting, the CCUM had held its own meeting. Father Egan reported on the CCUM meeting to Bernardin, writing that the CCUM members "support and strongly endorse" the bishops' antipoverty campaign. Egan added that the bishops' action had "given renewed hope to many in the Church and a new promise to the poor." A few days later, on November 16, 1970, the NCCB adopted the resolution establishing the Campaign for Human Development (CHD; the new and permanent name for its antipoverty campaign). The official Catholic War on Poverty had begun.[55]

The Campaign for Human Development underscores the significant relationship between the evolving, long civil rights movement and the War on Poverty. The careers of priests like Geno Baroni and John Egan demonstrate the connection that social activists saw between the civil rights movement and antipoverty efforts. The priests' involvement and leadership in groups like the NCCIJ, the CCUM, and IFCO and their experience in community organization prior to 1964 led them to an understanding of the connection between race and poverty. The development of these Catholic civil rights and antipoverty groups also reflects the changing nature of the long civil rights movement. Beginning with the NCCIJ, an organization focused on interracialism, Fathers Baroni and Egan moved to groups like the CCUM and IFCO, influenced by the increasing emphasis on black power. By the late 1960s, the community groups that Baroni, Egan, and their organizations sponsored were highly influenced by the ideas of self-definition and community control of the black power movement. In many ways, the eventual creation of the CHD was the church's response to the increasing focus on community economic power.

Baroni's and Egan's significant involvement and leadership in the Catholic Church's antipoverty efforts reflects a number of influences, including their experiences as urban priests and their own theology, much of which was formed or confirmed by Vatican II. With a theology that emphasized the centrality of the church's commitment to the poor, the sanctity of each individual, and a desire to emulate Christ, a cadre of socially active priests, like Baroni, Egan, Groppi, and McIlvane; women religious, like Sister Margaret Ellen Traxler; and lay activists, like Mathew Ahmann, spearheaded Catholic civil rights and antipoverty efforts. Both Baroni and Egan continued organizing communities around issues of poverty and social justice well beyond the 1960s and 1970s. The Catholic War on Poverty was an essential part of the long War on Poverty.

The antipoverty activism of Egan, Baroni, Ahmann, Traxler, and other Catholic individuals, as well as groups like the NCCIJ, the CCUM, and the CHD, complicate our understanding of the Catholic Church as a conservative force in American politics. While popular and many scholarly accounts highlight the Catholic Church's conservative stance on issues like abortion and other reproductive rights and same-sex marriage, it is important to understand that the church has often taken a much more progressive stand, both politically and financially, on issues related to poverty. Indeed, as demonstrated in this chapter, devout Catholic individuals, like Shriver, Baroni, and Egan, and organizations, like the Campaign for Human Development, have not just led the Catholic War on Poverty but challenged America to continue its long War on Poverty through combined church and state efforts.

Catholic activists were not the only religious individuals to see the War on Poverty as a moral issue in which people of faith should participate. Key Protestant and Jewish organizations, like the National Council of Churches and the American Jewish Committee, which were active participants in the civil rights movement, also engaged in the War on Poverty. Like the Catholic activists discussed in this chapter, Protestant and Jewish organizations and individuals also connected civil rights and antipoverty efforts and used their experiences in civil rights efforts to inform their participation in the War on Poverty. Some of those Protestants and Jews helped form an ecumenical antipoverty coalition with Catholics in support of agencies like IFCO to fight an interreligious War on Poverty. And many of them agreed with Father Egan that participation in the War on Poverty was a sacred and holy cause.

CHAPTER TWO

The Conscience of the Church
The National Council of Churches and the War on Poverty

In his speech to the General Assembly of Presbyterians in 1965, Sargent Shriver told the delegates, "We need the conscience of the Church in our War on Poverty because the War vs. Poverty is fundamentally a nation fighting to preserve its soul." Like Shriver, the National Council of Churches (NCC) and its members saw the War on Poverty as fundamentally a moral and spiritual issue and, despite some internal debates about how to enact that vision, were involved integrally in fighting the War on Poverty. The leadership of the NCC made the War on Poverty a central part of its social action agenda, initially through its own departments and agencies and eventually through interreligious cooperation with Catholic and Jewish religious institutions. The NCC did indeed see the War on Poverty as a battle for the soul of the nation.[1]

The NCC's history began in 1908 when thirty-two Protestant denominations joined together to form the Federal Council of Churches (FCC). This ecumenical organization aimed to help churches respond more effectively to the problems of a modern industrial society and saw its members as "guardians and advocates of the Social Gospel," an early twentieth-century movement of liberal Protestants who argued that Christianity should be focused on social justice issues. The FCC first turned its attention to race in the late 1940s when it began issuing amicus curiae briefs to the U.S. Supreme Court in support of some desegregation cases and created a Department of Racial and Cultural Relations, which had a "cautious, evolutionary, go-slow approach to the solution of racial problems." The FCC changed its name to the National Council of Churches in 1950, and in 1952 it issued a statement on churches and segregation supporting, but not insisting on, desegregated churches.[2]

The NCC more actively engaged with the civil rights movement in the 1960s. It was involved significantly in planning the Conference on Religion and Race in January 1963 and later that year formed its own Commission on Religion and Race, which was enthusiastically supported by NCC leadership. According to historian James Findlay, NCC leaders "sought to forge a new public stance for the mainstream churches regarding racial issues" so that African Americans could "be given long-denied political and economic rights and be fully admitted into the mainstream of American life." NCC members participated prominently in the March on Washington and other civil rights events during the 1960s. A delegation of church leaders met with President Lyndon Johnson in March 1965 to advocate for voting rights legislation, and the president invited organization officials to be guests in the Johnson family box at his speech before a joint session of Congress announcing the Voting Rights Act. Their presence gave a clear message of mainline religious support of the civil rights movement. Later in 1965, Edwin Espy, general secretary of the NCC, wrote Johnson that the "policies and the concerns of the National Council of Churches have on the whole reflected parallel positions [to those of the Great Society] to a remarkable degree." That certainly included NCC support of the federal fight against poverty.[3]

While the national War on Poverty began officially in August 1964 when Johnson signed the Economic Opportunity Act (EOA), the National Council of Churches had begun addressing the issue of poverty as early as 1955. In July of that year, Shirley Greene, director of the NCC Division of Christian Life and Work proposed a consultation (a term the NCC gave to institutional conferences held on specific topics) on persistent poverty in America. According to Greene, the idea for addressing the issue of poverty developed from a consultation earlier in 1955 on stewardship of the land. Participants in that meeting had concluded that "the National Council of Churches would do well to arrange a conference or consultation which would inquire into both the economic and moral issues presented by the persistence of a hard core of poverty in the midst of our generally prosperous American economy." Greene further noted what he saw as a link between race and poverty, arguing that the NCC should address the issue of poverty as it related to "special groups," whom he identified as "American Indians, Negroes, and Spanish Americans." From an early period, then, the NCC linked race and poverty.[4]

The NCC leadership took Greene's proposal seriously. The executive board of the Division of Christian Life and Work approved Greene's idea at its Jan-

38   Chapter Two

uary 1956 meeting. Tackling poverty, though, did not become an immediate priority for the NCC. As civil rights moved to center stage in the late 1950s and early 1960s, NCC leaders focused more on that movement and less on poverty directly. As a result, Greene's recommended consultation did not happen for six years.[5]

Not until January 1962 did Greene hold his conference, "Consultation on the Churches and Persistent Pockets of Poverty in the USA," which was convened by the Divisions of Home Missions and Christian Life and Work in Washington, D.C. Discussion groups at the consultation focused on defining poverty, identifying its causes and consequences, and determining possible programs for ameliorating or eliminating it. The final report of the conference noted that the churches had been "confronted by undeniable and shocking evidence of continuing massive poverty in the midst of a national economy which boasts of its affluence and which possesses technological skills and productivity capable of providing adequate levels of living for our total population." The report, reflecting a connection to the Social Gospel prominent in the FCC's early years, continued with an explanation of the importance of social action on the part of churches: "while the Church must forever seek effective ways of bearing relevant witness to the poor through the word, the sacraments and the works of Christian charity, such ministries may never be the substitutes for vigorous and imaginative support of public policies and programs designed to remove the causes of poverty." In addition, the publication of Michael Harrington's *The Other America* in the same year likely influenced NCC leadership. So, almost two years before Johnson declared a federal War on Poverty, Greene and others at the National Council of Churches began addressing the issue of poverty in the midst of plenty and committed the NCC to supporting programs designed to tackle poverty.[6]

The NCC also engaged in another issue related to poverty that drew national attention during the late 1950s and early 1960s—juvenile delinquency. The postwar rise of juvenile delinquency led to a Senate subcommittee investigation headed by Senator Estes Kefauver in 1955 and the President's Committee on Juvenile Delinquency in 1961. During this period (again, prior to the creation of a federal program), the NCC began plans for juvenile delinquency programs in local communities. Based on the opportunity theory of sociologists Lloyd Ohlin and Richard Cloward, who argued that juvenile delinquency and poverty resulted from societal structures that blocked opportunity for the social mobility and advancement of youth, particularly minority youth, both the President's Committee on Juvenile Delinquency and the NCC's involvement in juvenile delinquency programs served as precursors to the War on Poverty. The NCC demonstrated the influence of Ohlin

The National Council of Churches 39

and Cloward and a connection between juvenile delinquency and poverty in its "Consultation on the Church and Youth Employment," which was held in January 1964.[7]

In 1963, the NCC began planning a film about poverty in America. Noting that 1962 was "the year that poverty was rediscovered in America," the NCC Poverty Film Production Committee cited the examples of the CBS News report *The Harvest of Shame*; Harrington's *The Other America*; and its own poverty consultation as it developed a film focused on poverty. They tentatively titled it "The Captives—The Story of People in Depressed Areas" and sought to reflect prominent theories about the culture of poverty. The NCC filmmakers planned "to communicate the overtones of the total reaction of people deeply and emotionally involved in poverty; to picture the people themselves caught in the web of poverty."[8]

Inspired by events both internal (the consultation report and the film) and external (President Johnson's announcement in January that his administration would wage a War on Poverty), on February 26, 1964, the general board of the NCC approved a resolution engaging its full efforts in the battle against poverty. Calling poverty "ethically intolerable" and humans "morally responsible" for the persistence of poverty in the midst of plenty, the general board called for all of its units "to give priority and creative thought to the development of programs and procedures . . . directed towards the elimination of the evil of poverty from an otherwise affluent society." Importantly, the NCC saw and described poverty not just as a social problem, but as morally reprehensible, as an evil. And who was more qualified to address evil than churches and other religious institutions?[9]

The NCC followed its antipoverty statement with institutional action. Representatives of fourteen different council units (including the Division of Christian Life and Work, the Division of Home Missions, the Department of Church and Economic Life, and the Commission on Religion and Race) organized into a Staff Anti-Poverty Committee in March 1964. Their first meeting consisted primarily of discussing the ways in which NCC member churches could contribute to the War on Poverty. That meeting resulted in a list of action objectives to "be considered as common ground for a cooperative program directed toward the elimination of poverty . . . upon which the churches—locally, denominationally, and ecumenically—may concentrate." The action objectives focused on areas such as job training, education, housing, and income maintenance programs. A special emphasis of the action objectives was recommending ways in which the local churches and congregations could participate directly in the federal attack on poverty. The NCC emphasized that the action objectives were "designed to stress the

40 Chapter Two

prime responsibility of Christian men and women throughout the nation for 'front line service' in the War on Poverty."[10]

Following the identification of action objectives, the Anti-Poverty Committee met with the newly appointed director of the Office of Economic Opportunity (OEO), Sargent Shriver, in April 1964 to discuss ways in which the NCC could participate directly in the War on Poverty. Following the meeting with Shriver, the NCC determined that it could contribute to federal antipoverty efforts by developing church members' support for them. In addition, Greene proposed that the Department of Church and Economic Life "initiate a process of study, discussion and publication on the basic economic and ethical issues involved in a national policy geared to the elimination of poverty from the United States." As part of this process, Greene created task forces to write papers on specific topics related to poverty. Those papers led to the publication of a number of pamphlets urging churchgoers to support the federal antipoverty efforts—again, before the EOA had been passed and before the War on Poverty was operational. One of the pamphlets urged church members to meet "the Christian Challenge—JOIN the National Council's Anti-Poverty Task Force in the Church's War on Poverty." The Staff Anti-Poverty Committee also created the *Anti-Poverty Bulletin*, a periodical circulated to local and state leaders of the various denominations within the NCC, encouraging their support of the antipoverty efforts of the Johnson administration and the churches.[11]

Published quarterly beginning in September 1964 by the Department of Church and Economic Life, the *Anti-Poverty Bulletin* served as a means of "coordinating the efforts of the various units of the National Council of Churches toward poverty and its elimination." The *Bulletin* kept readers informed of developments in the national War on Poverty and OEO programs. For example, an article in the second issue of the *Bulletin*, published in January 1965, highlighted the Job Corps, a War on Poverty program designed to train mostly at-risk young people for industrial jobs, and volunteer opportunities for church members at Job Corps centers. The following issue, published in March 1965, provided a detailed description of Project Head Start, a program providing early childhood education to low-income children, and suggested opportunities for churches and individuals to initiate or participate in Head Start programs in their communities. The *Bulletin* also regularly focused on specific examples of member churches' and local councils' participation in the War on Poverty. One story centered on the Greater Newark (New Jersey) Council of Churches' creation of the United Community Action Corporation, which became the city-wide community action agency in Newark. Another story noted how the Decatur (Illinois)

Council of Churches had instituted a Head Start program. In other words, local churches and individual church members heeded the call of the NCC and quickly and actively engaged on the ground in the War on Poverty. And the NCC, and the *Anti-Poverty Bulletin* in particular, enthusiastically championed the national effort to tackle poverty.[12]

The March 1965 issue of the *Bulletin* also announced the appointment of Shirley Greene to the positions of coordinator of the NCC's antipoverty program and associate director of the Department of Church and Economic Life. A minister with a history of social activism, Greene had previously chaired the NCC's Department of Migrant Work and the joint "Consultation on the Churches and Persistent Pockets of Poverty in the USA." In these early years of the War on Poverty, Greene served as the NCC's point person on all things related to poverty.[13]

The NCC demonstrated its support of the War on Poverty through the successful application for OEO funds for NCC antipoverty programs, particularly its Migrant Ministry program, which had a long history. An ecumenical group of Protestant women in the Federal Council of Churches, inspired by the Social Gospel, founded the Council of Women in 1908. By 1913 the council had begun focusing on the working and living conditions of agricultural laborers in the West. In 1920, the council changed its name to Migrant Ministry, and by the 1960s the Migrant Ministry program was one of the most developed of the NCC antipoverty efforts. NCC officials saw the War on Poverty as a way to expand its Migrant Ministry efforts. The NCC Migrant Ministry programs in New Mexico, Arizona, and North Carolina received significant OEO grants to support their efforts to alleviate poverty among migrant workers.[14]

In addition to encouraging its members' participation in War on Poverty programs, the NCC demonstrated its active support of the EOA through congressional testimony. The NCC president, Reuben H. Mueller, a bishop of the Evangelical United Brethren Church, was the first NCC representative to provide a statement of support to the House Committee on Education and Labor on the pending antipoverty legislation.[15] In his statement, Bishop Mueller noted that an essential element of Christianity was a "deep and abiding concern for those among us who are poor and without access to adequate food, clothing and shelter." Mueller saw the continuation of poverty in an affluent society as "essentially a moral issue." In addition, his statement highlighted what he saw as the direct connection between poverty and race: racial discrimination was "inextricably embedded in and is in fact a major basis for the persistence of poverty." Mueller and the NCC clearly saw their efforts against the twin sins of racism and poverty as intimately related and central

42   Chapter Two

to their mission, while the Johnson administration tried to downplay race in these hearings to avoid the opposition of southern congressmen. In the conclusion of his statement, Mueller noted that churches had already been involved in efforts "to *relieve* the effects of poverty." Reflecting the rhetoric of the Johnson administration and Shriver in particular, he also said that the NCC was convinced that "it is now possible to speak hopefully in terms of *eliminating* it from our midst."[16] Mueller left no doubt that the NCC was fully ready to engage in the administration's all-out battle against poverty. If fighting poverty was a moral cause, who better than the churches to help lead the fight?

The NCC threw its full institutional weight behind the War on Poverty. In October 1964, twenty NCC leaders met with Sargent Shriver and key OEO staff to discuss the institution's relationship to the federal antipoverty effort. According to an NCC staffer, Shriver expressed a "clear desire for the help of the churches and church people" with the Job Corps and Volunteers in Service to America (VISTA), in particular, and "the direct involvement of poor people for the community action organization and projects, and [with] providing leadership and facilities for the special program [Head Start] envisaged for children in the crucial years from three to five." Shriver and the OEO, then, envisioned the full support and involvement of the NCC and its affiliate churches in the War on Poverty, particularly in OEO programs directed toward children and young people, like Head Start and the Job Corps, even before the OEO had launched some of those programs. Indeed, the NCC proved very useful to Shriver and the OEO, especially in the early months of planning and implementation of the EOA.[17]

The NCC leadership demonstrated the centrality of the administration's War on Poverty to its own mission by holding a special staff meeting on that topic less than a week after the conference with Shriver and OEO officials. Working from the thesis that "the elimination of poverty is basically and primarily a moral issue," the staff members at the meeting concluded that the time had come for the churches to expand on their traditional concern for the poor and develop "a new social imagination and sense of social responsibility." Echoing the argument of Father Geno Baroni about neighborhood parishes, NCC staff members said that because local churches were based in communities, they were especially qualified to enact and participate in some of the OEO's community-based programs.[18]

Even before Congress passed the Economic Opportunity Act, NCC staffers saw the proposed community action programs as the part of the War on Poverty most appropriate for NCC member churches' focus. Staffers noted that "state and city councils of churches should be assisted to help set up these new organizations, or to arrange for appropriate representation on the board of the community action organization in their state or community." In addition, NCC staff recommended that member churches establish "a close working relationship to these organizations, both for sharing and for possible development of church-related service[s] which might qualify for poverty bill funds contracted through the state or local community action organization." The NCC's Commission on Religion and Race quickly established a director of community action, the Reverend James Moore, to connect churches to community action agencies.[19]

For many in NCC leadership, as evidenced by Bishop Mueller's congressional testimony and the creation of the position of director of community action in the Commission on Religion and Race, economic justice involved connecting antipoverty efforts with race and civil rights. Indeed, the NCC and its member churches had issued statements in favor of civil rights as early as the 1950s. For instance, the United Methodist Church, inspired by the antisegregation stance taken by its women's organizations, stated in 1956 that "there must be no place in the Methodist Church for racial discrimination or enforced segregation." The NCC had been involved centrally in the March on Washington and formed the Commission on Religion and Race in 1963 to highlight its view of civil rights as a moral issue. As the NCC began to fight in the War on Poverty, members linked the two causes of racial and economic justice. In November 1964, just a few months after Johnson signed the Civil Rights Act, Thomas Kilgore, a member of the Commission on Religion and Race, noted that "the next step for the administration seems to be to push the concerns of poverty and race. Poverty in the U.S. is a real moral issue along with race. . . . As poverty is inherently tied to the racial problem, they cannot be separated." Kilgore and others at the NCC clearly saw the War on Poverty and civil rights as "a coalescing of moral issues." The Commission on Religion and Race made plans for a summer program in 1965 in northern cities to "emphasiz[e] voter registration and other civil rights issues, including poverty."[20]

Kilgore's perspective on the morality of poverty and civil rights represented the central belief of the NCC leadership as a whole. Indeed, the theology of the NCC inherently perceived poverty as a moral issue. The Anti-Poverty Committee reflected this view when it argued that "the responsibility of church people toward helping make ours a poverty-less nation . . . is theologically grounded in God's redemptive work on behalf of the physical as well as the spiritual well-being of people." For the committee members and most of the NCC leadership, "underlying all the churches' anti-poverty programs is the need for communication and interpretation of the moral as well as the

44 Chapter Two

practical dimension of the problem." The church had a moral obligation to end poverty, and the War on Poverty, particularly its community action programs, provided the vehicle through which the church could work to attain that goal.[21]

The NCC espoused the moral reasons for member churches to support the War on Poverty in three missives published as books: *The Christian Case against Poverty* by Henry Clark and *One-Fifth of a Nation* and *How Churches Fight Poverty*, both by Elma Greenwood, director of the Women's Division of the Department of Church and Economic Life. Clark's book, published in 1965, argued that the idea of the common good had been central to much of historical Christian thought. Clark posited that "for the Christian, property rights always exist only in the context of the common good, and are always subordinate to it." This recognition of the centrality of the common good was a "moral imperative of the Christian life." As a result, Clark argued, both individual giving to the poor and large-scale government programs like the War on Poverty were "necessary and good." Clark concluded that given "the imperatives of Christian faith," poverty was a moral issue, and Christians could no longer rationalize "about why poverty is inevitable, necessary, or just. . . . The Christian must be honest . . . in acknowledging that poverty need no longer exist in twentieth-century America, and in admitting that so long as it continues to exist he is, to a greater or lesser extent, guilty before God for the moral outrage of its continued existence." Fighting in the War on Poverty, then, was for Christians not just recommended, but a required duty and responsibility. Christians should not be supporting the War on Poverty as cheerleaders on the sidelines. Instead, they should be active participants in antipoverty programs. Anything less than full engagement on an individual level would make one guilty before God for the continuation of poverty in America.[22]

In *One-Fifth of a Nation*, Greenwood noted that the War on Poverty was "closely linked" with the civil rights movement as part of a "revolutionary war" that would require the "mobilization of the churches" with the goal of eliminating poverty. Arguing that the War on Poverty was a struggle that "Christians can engage in with zest and enthusiasm," Greenwood explained some of the specifics of poverty in America and what churches could do about it. Emphasizing that poverty was a moral issue, Greenwood instructed churches to mobilize their resources to "inform and inspire their members" to fight in the War on Poverty. She reminded church members that "the primary emphasis in the President's War on Poverty is on action at the community level" and encouraged them to participate in antipoverty projects in their communities. In addition, Greenwood pressed readers of her book to support legislative proposals that would create more jobs, stimulate local development, improve education and job training, and challenge racial discrimination. If Clark's book provided Christians with the theological imperatives for why they should join the War on Poverty, Greenwood's book gave them the information on how to fight in it.[23]

A year later, the NCC published Greenwood's *How Churches Fight Poverty*. This book resulted from an assignment the NCC Anti-Poverty Task Force had given Greenwood—to study religion-based antipoverty projects across the United States. From June to November 1966, she investigated sixty antipoverty projects—mostly Protestant, but some Catholic or Jewish and some interfaith. Greenwood visited, among others, the Westminster Neighborhood Association (WNA) in Watts, which was funded by the Presbytery of Los Angeles and the Presbyterian Board of National Missions and directed by the Reverend Archie Hardwick; the East Central Citizens' Organization in Columbus, Ohio, funded by the Lutheran Board of American Missions and directed by Pastor Leopold Bernhard; and the Church Community Action Program of Portland, Oregon, funded by the Oregon Methodist Women's Society and the Presbyterian Commission on Religion and Race. All of these projects received some of their funding from the OEO and the rest from religious organizations. In addition, religious leaders or individuals connected to faith-based groups directed or operated the programs. For Greenwood and the NCC, these projects provided concrete examples of NCC and other religious groups' active engagement with the War on Poverty.[24]

The work of the Westminster Neighborhood Association provides insight into the ways in which the maximum feasible participation of the poor and community action in the War on Poverty transformed religious organizations' activism. The Presbyterian Church founded the WNA in the Watts neighborhood of Los Angeles in 1961 as a social service agency primarily providing services to single mothers and impoverished children. Following the creation of the War on Poverty in 1964 and the violence in Watts in 1965, the WNA shifted its methodology from service provider to community organization through the creation of neighborhood block councils composed of local residents. Those block councils determined what antipoverty programs the residents wanted in their neighborhoods. The Presbyterian Church, the NCC, and the OEO funded the programs, and the Presbyterian Church provided staffing and facilities for them. Thus, the WNA exemplified the NCC antipoverty activities highlighted by Greenwood, and it demonstrated the joint church-state funding and support of antipoverty programs that developed during the War on Poverty.[25]

A central vehicle of NCC antipoverty activism was its Unified Field Program. The Staff Anti-Poverty Committee created the Unified Field Program

46   Chapter Two

in April 1965 following a year-long study of how to implement the February 1964 general board resolution for NCC direct involvement in the War on Poverty. The Anti-Poverty Committee designed the Unified Field Program "to sensitize the churches to the realities of persistent poverty . . . and its moral evil, to muster the resources of the churches in a sustained major effort for the elimination of poverty, and to coordinate those resources for maximum effectiveness." Staff for the Unified Field Program came primarily from the Division of Christian Life and Mission and from local and state councils; some were denominational members of the NCC. The Unified Field Program's responsibilities included "to arouse awareness of the facts about poverty, . . . to sensitize church people to their moral responsibility toward the elimination of poverty, to encourage in all anti-poverty programs the inclusion of the poor themselves at all levels of planning and implementation, . . . to provide information regarding resources available, . . . to aid in the fight against poverty."[26]

The NCC's Anti-Poverty Committee and staff from the Unified Field Program also outlined specific opportunities for the participation of local churches and church members in the War on Poverty. For instance, following a thorough discussion of the Job Corps, staffers suggested that individuals and churches could recruit potential trainees for the Job Corps, and church camps could be made available for parts of the year to serve as Job Corps centers. The NCC Anti-Poverty Committee staff provided a detailed assessment of opportunities for participation in community action programs. Staffers envisioned churches and church schools operating Head Start centers, work-training programs, work-study programs, and legal service programs for neighborhood residents. These recommendations went beyond merely supporting the War on Poverty by lobbying legislators. They encouraged the active involvement of churches and churchgoers in the War on Poverty. As the Anti-Poverty Committee and Unified Field Program staff saw it, the NCC, its member churches, and the people in the pews of those churches would be engaged in hand-to-hand combat against poverty.[27]

Many NCC member congregations followed its lead. The Board of Social Ministry of the Lutheran Church, for example, issued a publication, "The Church and Office of Economic Opportunity Programs," both to explain the theological foundations for its support of the War on Poverty and to encourage local congregations to engage in the antipoverty battle. The Lutheran Church also adopted a statement on poverty in 1966 in which it committed itself "to the struggle against poverty in full continuity with the biblical testimony about concern for the poor." The statement also encouraged individual congregations "to be open to the kind of cooperation with public and volun-

The National Council of Churches 47

tary agencies which as a part of the church's witness to God's love in Jesus Christ will enable them to participate in the struggle against poverty." The Lutheran Church insisted that any Lutheran congregation or social service agency "enlist in some way in the battle against poverty."[28]

The Lutheran Church argued that church-state relationships called for church participation in the War on Poverty. Noting that churches often had access to the poor, buildings in areas where the poor lived, and volunteers, the Lutheran Board of Missions maintained that the churches thus were "a factor of real importance to the anti-poverty program." Lutheran Church publications also noted that involvement in OEO programs should not lead to the financial benefit of the church or its members and that the programs needed to be nonsectarian. Concluding that "the participation of the church in the efforts of government which are aimed at improving the conditions under which men live can be a valid way of testifying to the church's faith," a Lutheran publication noted that service "must constitute a *ministry* of love and justice expressing the church's own God-given responsibility to society."[29] The Lutheran Church, then, and other NCC member churches expressed an allegiance to the War on Poverty that reflected the commitment of their parent organizations.

While the NCC and at least some of its member churches committed to antipoverty efforts, Shirley Greene expressed concern about challenges to the War on Poverty, particularly to community action programs and the idea of the maximum feasible participation of the poor. In June 1965, the U.S. Conference of Mayors had passed a resolution, introduced by Mayors Samuel Yorty of Los Angeles and John Shelley of San Francisco, attacking community action for inciting conflict between the poor and city governments and for threatening mayoral control of community action programs. In addition, Bureau of the Budget director Charles Schultze kept the OEO's budget well below what Shriver requested, in part because of the Conference of Mayors' resolution and growing concerns about community action. The NCC demonstrated that it was an ally for Shriver and the OEO. Noting "controversy over participation of the poor in the War on Poverty," in November 1965 Greene encouraged Unified Field Program staff to send him "stories of successful participation of the poor in projects related to Community Action Programs" and to "publicize this issue in meetings." In a later memo, Greene said that "the Community Action Program of OEO has fallen far short of its goal of maximum feasible participation of the poor," and he encouraged the NCC to support its development. In other words, Greene believed that the NCC needed to not just champion the OEO, but critique it when it fell short of its duties.[30]

48   Chapter Two

Greene and the Anti-Poverty Task Force publicly advocated for the expansion of the War on Poverty and the centrality of community action and maximum feasible participation of the poor. In early 1967, Larold Schulz, a member of the task force, reported that two years of the War on Poverty had created some staunch opposition. He encouraged task force members to continue their commitment, insisting that they needed to continue to engage "actively in the struggle to change the structural systems of society which prevent full participation by powerless people. . . . we must make it clear that the poor and powerless are our first-line concern." Schulz further encouraged members to challenge congressional cuts to the OEO, arguing that "the federal poverty program in all its facets is a minimal effort. Now is the time to make it clear that we will not accept a minimal effort." Later that year, task force members heeded Schulz's call, demanding that Congress "end its unconscionable delay" in renewing the EOA and urging it "to provide more funds, strengthen community action and re-affirm the principle of maximum feasible participation of the poor."[31]

Active and continued NCC support for the maximum feasible participation of the poor, even after this principle had come under fire from mayors, congressmen, and others, demonstrates the fundamental commitment of the organization to the War on Poverty and its central strategy. That commitment seems to have been the result of at least a few influences. First, the NCC's predecessor, the FCC, had been greatly inspired by the Social Gospel and its emphasis on working with the poor. The NCC saw its Migrant Ministry program as an example of the possibilities of community-based antipoverty programs. Second, the experiences of many NCC leaders and staffers, such as Thomas Kilgore, in civil rights efforts and demonstrations had taught them the importance of community organizing. Third, similarly to how Father Baroni saw the neighborhood parish as the place for antipoverty activism, many NCC leaders, like Schulz and Greene, saw local churches as the central locations for community antipoverty efforts. Indeed, J. Edward Carothers, chair of the NCC Anti-Poverty Task Force, claimed that it was "likely that local churches will determine whether the war against poverty will end in victory or defeat for the nation." Finally, the Unified Field Program staff emphasized that local churches should incorporate the maximum feasible participation of the poor at all levels of program development and implementation. For many involved in antipoverty efforts at the NCC, full inclusion of the poor was fundamental to fighting poverty.[32]

In 1967, Schulz sent a memo to Morris Leibman of the National Advisory Council on Economic Opportunity, an advisory board to the OEO, both highlighting the NCC's commitment to the War on Poverty and expressing concern over what he saw as the government's lagging commitment to the OEO and its programs. Noting that the NCC and its member denominations had been "deeply engaged in efforts to eradicate poverty for a number of years" and had developed "programs to assist the poor in beginning to make decisions regarding their own identity," Schulz chided the federal government and private agencies for not "doing enough to deal with the real root causes of poverty." Schulz closed his memo by encouraging the federal government to make "the eradication of poverty and its related effects" the top national priority and by assuring the National Advisory Council of the NCC's "commitment to this cause."[33]

Thus, the NCC's dedication to the War on Poverty continued beyond the initial stages of the implementation of the EOA and despite growing congressional opposition. The general board of the NCC had issued one of its clearest statements in support of the War on Poverty and the need for NCC involvement in December 1966. At a time when the national War on Poverty, particularly community action programs, faced some difficult congressional attacks, the NCC general board unanimously adopted a statement, based in large part on a resolution passed by the NCC Division of Christian Life and Mission earlier in the year, unequivocally supporting the War on Poverty. Once again highlighting that poverty in the midst of plenty was a moral issue, the NCC argued that "in an economy which has developed the capacity to abolish poverty, no lesser goal than its total abolition can satisfy the moral demands of the Christian faith." In addition to expressing general support for the War on Poverty as a whole, the NCC general board's statement gave special attention and support to the inclusion of the poor in community action programs. Arguing that the principle of the maximum feasible participation of the poor supported the Christian principle of the inherent worth of every human being, the general board urged "the churches to support this principle in all public anti-poverty programs and to embody it in their own anti-poverty efforts." In its statement, the general board recommended types of participation and action in antipoverty programs for both local churches and churchgoers. The general board encouraged the use of church facilities for antipoverty programs and the participation of clergy and laity on community action boards and in leadership positions in antipoverty programs.[34]

The general board's statement in support of the principle of maximum feasible participation of the poor was in part a response to requests from poor people, who had presented a statement to the meeting of the general board in February 1966. Noting that the organizations they represented had been "inspired by church leaders" and that poor people were "members of many churches," the representatives of the poor asked the general board to

50 Chapter Two

investigate the implementation of OEO programs. Specifically, the group charged that the OEO was giving funds to "controlled, existing institutions" instead of to programs designed and implemented by poor people. The representatives asked the general board to fund projects "sponsored by the people themselves." The general board's statement in support of community action and the maximum feasible participation of the poor, then, reflected both its stated principles and the requests of the representatives of poor people, who effectively served as watchdogs from the grassroots ensuring that the OEO live up to the principles of community action.[35]

While its public statements and some of its actions suggested that the NCC was committed fully to fighting the War on Poverty, Shirley Greene, chair of the Staff Anti-Poverty Committee, had expressed some concerns about that commitment. In his October 1965 report, Greene noted that about thirty individuals were only working part time on the Unified Field Program while spending the rest of their time on other duties, and the NCC had not hired any full-time employees to work exclusively on the War on Poverty. Greene reported, "In view of the rising tide of interest in the war on poverty at all levels of Protestantism and the vast proliferation of church activity . . . I would be less than responsible if I did not state here my deep concern for the future of the National Council's anti-poverty program." Greene argued that without a significant commitment of funds, "I fear we may well be missing an opportunity to involve . . . the whole NCC meaningfully in one of the greatest moral issues of our time."[36]

Others in the NCC also expressed doubt about its institutional commitment to the War on Poverty. In November 1966, J. Edward Carothers wrote to Dr. Jon L. Regier, head of the NCC Division of Christian Life and Mission, asking that the Anti-Poverty Task Force be renewed for three more years, that more money be allocated for the task force, and that it be allowed to start new initiatives. Carothers closed his memo by arguing, "The church should assume a basic responsibility for new objectives and fresh motivations in the effort to make certain that our nation does not fail in this solemn moral obligation."[37]

Carothers did not receive the approval from Regier that he wanted, however. In February 1967, he went above Regier's head and wrote to the NCC general secretary, Edwin Espy, asking him to "renew the mandate for the Anti-Poverty Task Force," which had, "despite its budget and staff limitations," been "a useful channel for coordinating the efforts of the denominations and for initiating action programs through the church." Espy approved Carothers's request, but Carothers remained unhappy about what he saw as a lack of support from the NCC.[38]

The National Council of Churches 51

As a result, Carothers, who also served on the Board of Missions of the Methodist Church, resigned as chair of the Anti-Poverty Task Force in June 1967. In his resignation letter, Carothers told Espy that he was leaving due to "the failure of the National Council of Churches to register its support through some token of financial support. . . . When our first support was made of the Anti-Poverty Task Force it was with the agreement that this work would be regarded as a continuing responsibility of the National Council's program and would be accorded support."[39]

At least some of Carothers's concerns about the NCC's commitment to antipoverty efforts were about developments related to the Child Development Group of Mississippi (CDGM). The CDGM was a Head Start program largely run by African Americans in rural Mississippi, which provided free preschool to children. The NCC was an early and important supporter of the CDGM. As a program that largely benefited African American children and families, the CDGM came under intense scrutiny from Mississippi's conservative segregationist senator, John Stennis, who accused the organization of promoting black power and who pressured Shriver and the OEO to investigate the CDGM for fraud and misuse of funds. At that time, in 1966, Shriver was facing challenges from Republican congressmen, who accused community action programs of fomenting rebellion and who pushed to dismantle the OEO and move its programs into other cabinet-level departments, like Health, Education, and Welfare. Under pressure related to both the War on Poverty in general and the CDGM in particular, Shriver bowed and proposed replacing the CDGM with a multicounty Head Start program in Mississippi that would take control away from the African Americans in the CDGM. In October 1966, seventy clergy from NCC denominations protested at the OEO offices, and NCC leaders, including Jon Regier, led a group calling itself the National Citizens Committee for the Child Development Group of Mississippi, which placed a full-page ad in the *New York Times* castigating Shriver for his decision. NCC leadership proved crucial in convincing Shriver and the OEO to continue to fund the CDGM. That funding, though, was short-lived. After Shriver left the OEO and was replaced in 1968, the NCC and the CDGM no longer had a sympathetic ear, and the CDGM program ended. Despite Regier's support of the CDGM, Carothers believed that the organization had not done enough financially to support its own Anti-Poverty Task Force.[40]

Five days after Carothers's resignation, Espy responded. Writing that "it was a blow" to receive the letter, Espy tried to convince Carothers to stay on. Acknowledging "some of the frustration in connection with National Council participation in the Anti-Poverty Program, including the problem . . . of lack of financial support from most of the member denominations," Espy informed Carothers that there was a "good prospect for more backing and participation in the future," and he hoped Carothers could withhold his "final decision about resigning until there has been opportunity for a further effort to improve the situation." Espy further acknowledged Carothers's critique: "I realize . . . that your own [United Methodist] Board has provided most of the support thus far, and I am not surprised that you should be concerned." Espy urged Carothers to talk with Regier, telling the Methodist minister, "I can't help believing that an issue of this kind can be resolved if reasonable men are prepared to sit down and work it through."[41]

The meeting between Carothers and Regier either did not happen or it was not successful at convincing Carothers that funding for the task force would increase substantially. By January 1968, James McDaniel was serving as the acting chair of the task force. Though he was no longer directly involved in the daily operations of the task force, Carothers still remained concerned about it and its mission. Shortly after stepping down as the task force chair, Carothers wrote to Espy complaining about "the kind of confusion which takes place when a task force suddenly suspends operations and its concerns have to be distributed throughout an entire division." It appears that rather than increase funding for the task force, the NCC, specifically Regier, had instead decided to end the task force and shift its responsibilities to others. Carothers worried that the units with those new responsibilities would be "so deeply involved in other things that the references by the dissolved task force will be dropped or largely ignored."[42] Clearly, significant divisions existed within the NCC about its level of commitment to the War on Poverty and how that commitment would be carried out.

Greene and Carothers were not the only critics of the churches' commitment to the War on Poverty. In 1967, Lyle Schaller, a minister and church consultant who visited thousands of congregations during his lengthy career, published *The Churches' War on Poverty*, a detailed examination of the types and extent of church participation during the first two years of the War on Poverty. While generally positive in his assessment of churches' commitment to and engagement with the War on Poverty (he concluded that there was "good reason to expect that the churches will carry their share of the load"), Schaller did see uneven contributions from churches and religious organizations. According to Schaller, the organizations that had most quickly and effectively mobilized in the antipoverty war were the state councils of churches that had active migrant worker programs, groups that had been previously involved in civil rights efforts, those that had been operating social welfare programs, and the Catholic Church and the United Presbyterian Church. In other words, groups that had already been engaged actively in social welfare

The National Council of Churches 53

or social justice issues simply incorporated the War on Poverty into their efforts. Schaller explained the more active involvement of the Catholic Church and the United Presbyterian Church by highlighting their more developed and centralized organizational structure, which enabled them to mobilize their resources more quickly. He also credited the involvement of young, activist clergy among both Catholics and Presbyterians.[43]

Schaller also commented on what he saw as "considerable resistance within the churches to the war on poverty," noting that most churches had not "joined in the mobilization." Some of this was outright resistance to a program some saw as directed at helping blacks. Other resistance he saw primarily as apathy. Regardless of the reason, Schaller stated, "the vast majority of the individual congregations in America, most of the denominational agencies, and a large proportion of the councils of churches" had not committed themselves to the War on Poverty. Indeed, Schaller argued, "only a very few religious institutions" had dedicated "a substantial proportion of their resources to this effort to eliminate poverty." The lack of commitment by the NCC that concerned Greene and Carothers, which was highlighted by the dissolution of the Anti-Poverty Task Force, was reflected in the uneven commitment by many other religious institutions.[44]

While the NCC had dissolved its own Anti-Poverty Task Force, it had increased its commitment to and participation in the Interreligious Committee against Poverty (ICAP). ICAP originated after members of the National Catholic Coordinating Committee on Economic Opportunity inquired about the possibility of religious agencies receiving War on Poverty grants. OEO staff members told the committee they would be "reluctant" to make a grant to a religious agency that served one distinct religious group, but they did indicate a willingness to explore the possibility of making a grant to an ecumenical organization that included representatives from Catholic, Protestant, and Jewish groups. This interest in the creation of an interfaith organization reflected a general move toward ecumenism and interreligious cooperation among mainline churches and synagogues in the 1950s and 1960s.[45]

At about the same time, the Reverend Sheldon Rahn of the NCC proposed to Raymond Gallagher of the National Catholic Welfare Conference (NCWC) and Phillip Bernstein of the Council of Jewish Federations and Welfare Funds the formation of an interfaith antipoverty group. Representatives from those organizations met in February 1965 to discuss the possibility of establishing a joint corporation to facilitate communication between them on antipoverty efforts, to assist each of the major religious faiths in organizing their antipoverty activities, "to assist in the organization and development of interfaith councils for the War on Poverty," and to aid religious bodies in the evaluation

54 Chapter Two

of antipoverty programs. All parties at the February 5 meeting agreed to discuss the proposal with their own organizations before moving forward with the proposed interfaith antipoverty agency. According to Gallagher, discussions about obtaining OEO funds "met a slight roadblock here because of the strict policy of the National Council of Churches with regard to violation of church-state separation."[46]

The NCC Anti-Poverty Task Force recommended that the NCC join in the interfaith antipoverty organization "to contract with appropriate governmental agencies regarding programs related to poverty, manpower training, juvenile delinquency and other major social problems in the United States." Among the reasons the task force listed for supporting the new interfaith organization were that the War on Poverty called for "new forms of cooperative endeavor by both public and private segments of society," that an interfaith national service corporation could be "a helpful part of the churches' total anti-poverty program," that an arrangement between religious and governmental agencies on nonreligious activities represented "a valid part of the mission of the churches in the world," and that the proposed organizations represented "a promising way of increasing inter-religious activity." The task force further noted that while interfaith activity was often discussed, it rarely happened in practice. An interfaith antipoverty group offered the NCC and other religious organizations the opportunity to implement ecumenical cooperation, something that many leading Catholic, Protestant, and Jewish organizations supported. The NCC task force also argued that an interfaith organization could offer the War on Poverty "a special kind of motivation and empathy, a vast reservoir of organized . . . volunteer help and a highly strategic middle-class access to power structures."[47]

In addition, the Anti-Poverty Task Force memo raised the issue of church-state relationships. Noting that the NCC did not have a policy statement on the use of tax funds by a church-related agency, the memo highlighted church-related projects that did use government funds, including the Arizona Council of Churches' Migrant Ministry contract with the Department of Labor and the Michigan Migrant Ministry's contract with the OEO. The memo also cited an NCC conference on church and state in February 1964 that had determined that "under some well-defined circumstances, government may legitimately support specific programs of church-affiliated health and welfare agencies." The task force concluded that "the *service* interests of church bodies *can* be financed in part by tax funds (1) provided the service purpose and function is free from the distinctly religious group functions of worship and sectarian religious instruction and (2) provided the service function is administered under a separate legal entity." The task force stated that an interreligious antipoverty organization should not "administer state or local service or action projects, but should limit its function in the main to field service and information exchange." Many of these conditions for OEO grants to religious organizations had been determined when NCC and OEO representatives met in early 1964 to first discuss the NCC's participation in the War on Poverty. In December 1964, the OEO finalized its position on grants to church-related schools by stating that the money could not be used for religious instruction, proselytizing, or worship, but grant-funded activities could be held on a religious school's property. Two sections of the EOA opened the door for direct funding of church-related antipoverty programs. Section 113 of the legislation provided that federal funds could be used for local projects sponsored by nonprofit organizations, and section 203 authorized grants for community action programs to private organizations.[48]

The church-state issue created apprehension among certain church members and people involved in church-related social service agencies. Some were bothered by the alliance between the churches and the OEO and worried that it broke down the separation of church and state and would lead to the domination of the church by the state. They feared agency autonomy, possible absorption by the government, and the secularization of religious antipoverty agencies. Certain Protestants believed the War on Poverty was an effort by Sargent Shriver and the Catholic Church to get federal aid for Catholic schools. Most Protestants, though, ignored such conspiracy theories and supported, to a greater or lesser extent, church involvement in the War on Poverty. The passage of the Elementary and Secondary Education Act of 1965 created the child-benefit doctrine, which enabled private agencies to spend federal money if it was for the benefit of the child. A number of churches and religious agencies began Head Start programs with the child-benefit doctrine in mind.[49]

Dean Kelley, a Methodist minister and head of the NCC's Commission on Religious Liberty, who had gained notoriety in 1964 for leading the NCC's opposition to a constitutional amendment allowing prayer in schools, was one of the few NCC leaders who objected to the churches receiving OEO money. Warning against becoming "advance men for the government," Kelley suggested that rather than becoming OEO subcontractors, churches and religious organizations should remain free from government control so that they could preach the Gospel and critique governmental antipoverty efforts. Kelley worried that running War on Poverty programs would inhibit the freedom of religious institutions.[50]

Kelley, though, remained largely an exception in terms of his level of concern about NCC involvement in the War on Poverty. Following meetings of the various religious bodies in March and April 1965 and a clarification of the church-state issue, representatives of the groups met with Sargent Shriver on May 6, 1965, still less than a year into the War on Poverty. Shriver enthusiastically encouraged the groups to form an interfaith committee. Immediately after the meeting with Shriver, the representatives decided to establish the interim Interreligious Planning Committee on Poverty with three representatives from each group on the committee.[51]

The interim committee held its first meeting three weeks later. Representatives of the NCC presented a staff paper, "A Proposal for Inter-Religious Cooperation towards the Elimination of Poverty," which suggested the creation of an interreligious body "composed of the highest possible stature and responsibility for the purpose of symbolizing, expressing and implementing the commitment of the religious communities of the United States to the early elimination of poverty from this nation." After a discussion of the NCC paper, the representatives met separately with their religious organizations to gain support for the proposed alliance. On June 3, 1965, the NCC general board authorized its general secretary "to explore with suitable Roman Catholic and Jewish bodies the creation of an inter-religious committee." Later in June, the representatives of the religious groups approved a revised NCC proposal and established the Interreligious Committee against Poverty, an important step in the ecumenical movement, a successor to interfaith cooperation on civil rights, and the beginning of an ecumenical antipoverty coalition.[52]

The agreement reached between the interfaith organizations that created ICAP included a statement of purpose that noted, "the problem of poverty and its solution have been the concern of Judaism and Christianity through the ages. Deeply imbedded in the prophetic literature of our religious heritage are the moral imperatives calling for the elimination of poverty." Given the affluence of postwar American society, the statement argued, the persistence of poverty was "morally indefensible." The purposes of the committee would include communicating to each constituency the immorality of persistent poverty, applying ethical insights from the represented religious traditions to the War on Poverty, stimulating and coordinating the antipoverty efforts of religious groups, providing facilities for those groups to combat poverty, and encouraging the creation of interreligious efforts against poverty.[53]

While ICAP garnered attention as an ecumenical antipoverty agency, it was not the first such organization. As early as the summer of 1963, members of the National Council of Catholic Women, the National Council of Jewish Women, the National Council of Negro Women, and United Church Women (the women's social service organization of the NCC) had met secretively

The National Council of Churches 57

to discuss issues related to racial discrimination and poverty. Those groups joined forces and formally created Women in Community Service (WICS) in 1964. The WICS board of directors included Dorothy Height of the National Council of Negro Women and Theressa Hoover of the United Methodist Church. With the federal declaration of the War on Poverty, WICS focused on OEO programs, particularly the Women's Job Corps, geared toward young women. Jeanne Noble, the director of the Women's Job Corps, encouraged the active involvement of WICS. Her encouragement worked as more than ten thousand WICS members volunteered to work with the Women's Job Corps, and WICS became the official recruiting and screening organization for women applicants to Job Corps centers. In 1966, WICS established 150 recruitment centers and interviewed more than sixty thousand young women, ultimately approving thirteen thousand for inclusion in the Job Corps.[54]

Additionally in 1966, WICS expanded its involvement in the War on Poverty to provide services through community action programs. Its efforts focused on women aged sixteen to twenty-one who were living in poverty, including those who had not qualified for the Job Corps. The WICS program began in ten cities in early 1966 with an expansion to fifty cities by the end of the year. Representatives from both WICS and United Church Women testified in support of the OEO and the Job Corps in 1966 and 1967, in part due to encouragement from Shriver. WICS served as a functioning ecumenical antipoverty agency impacting the lives of young women and demonstrated the reach of the War on Poverty through religious groups and institutions.[55]

While WICS began operating its Job Corps recruitment centers, ICAP held its first meeting in Washington, D.C., on January 18, 1966. In addition to electing officers, the thirty-eight participants from the NCC, the NCWC, and the Synagogue Council of America formalized the new organization through a memorandum of understanding. The members also held a press conference with Shriver and Vice President Hubert Humphrey. At the press conference, Dr. Eugene Carson Blake, the general secretary of the NCC and newly elected chair of ICAP, stated that the new organization supported "increased efforts by Congress to eradicate poverty." Humphrey thanked the committee for "translating their faith into resounding action that will transform America." He linked the War on Poverty with the civil rights movement by stating that civil rights legislation would not have succeeded "without the clergy bringing their moral persuasion to bear"; he believed that the clergy's support of the War on Poverty would bring similar success. Both Shriver and Humphrey saw churches and synagogues as valued allies in the War on Poverty. Interreligious groups like ICAP helped provide some legitimacy for the OEO as it faced constant congressional scrutiny and pressure.[56]

58 Chapter Two

ICAP members issued a statement following their meeting, emphasizing their continued commitment "to the proposition that the persistence of massive poverty in our society is a moral blight which can and must be eradicated." ICAP noted that America's "military commitments in Vietnam [had] led some to suggest reduction or holding the line on the domestic antipoverty and health, welfare and educational programs," but ICAP rejected those suggestions "as a major retreat in the war on poverty, and a major defeat for America." In addition to encouraging increased support for the War on Poverty in general, ICAP, like the NCC Anti-Poverty Task Force, specifically focused on community action programs and the strategy of the maximum feasible participation of the poor as necessary and central to the War on Poverty. Indeed, ICAP called the maximum feasible participation of the poor "an integral part of the religious and democratic commitment to help people help themselves" and urged "a redoubling of the efforts to encourage the full involvement of the poor in anti-poverty programs." The ICAP statement concluded that the War on Poverty "must not only be maintained, but must be increased to achieve its noble purpose—the development of a just society."[57]

ICAP representatives regularly made statements to congressional committees and subcommittees to advocate for the continuation and expansion of the War on Poverty. In July 1966, ICAP issued a statement to the Senate Sub-Committee on Employment, Manpower and Poverty, asking for increased appropriations for the War on Poverty "to strengthen and broaden the nation's programs to eliminate poverty." Expressing concern that the $1.75 billion funding requested by the Johnson administration was "insufficient" to fight the War on Poverty, ICAP asked the subcommittee to appropriate "substantially more" than that, arguing that if the United States was serious in its "determination to eradicate poverty, to wage a total War on Poverty, this substantial increase in funding is absolute[ly] necessary." In addition, ICAP once again reiterated its support for the centrality of maximum feasible participation of the poor and community action programs to the success of the War on Poverty.[58]

In September 1966, ICAP issued its most complete rationale for support of the War on Poverty and the need for an interfaith effort in that battle. The ICAP statement noted that its members' involvement in an interfaith antipoverty organization was "rooted in theological convictions" shared by all three religious traditions. Those convictions included the principle that the existence and perpetuation of poverty in an affluent society was not only an indignity to human beings, it was "evil in the sight of God." As a result, ICAP declared that "the minimum goal of the United States must be adequate food, clothing, housing, medical care, education and social security for every

The National Council of Churches 59

individual and family." ICAP argued for full employment, adequate wages, unemployment insurance, and the end of racial discrimination as important elements in tackling poverty, and the continuation and expansion of the War on Poverty was central to meeting those goals. With poverty identified as an evil, it was the duty of Protestants, Catholics, and Jews to end it.[59]

ICAP provided congressional testimony in support of the OEO and the War on Poverty again in July 1967. The OEO faced growing opposition from congressional Republicans and continued budget challenges from Schultze. The Bureau of the Budget director regularly denied Shriver's requests for budget increases, and in March 1967, when Shriver had asked to shift $20 million from Head Start summer programs to full-year programs, which had proven to be more effective, Schultze refused. At the same time, Republican House minority leader Gerald Ford had threatened to end the War on Poverty and dismantle the OEO. As a result, the budget hearings lasted several months and were the most difficult Shriver and the OEO had faced. Indeed, the length of the hearings caused the OEO to run out of money, and the agency had to cancel some projects and stop paying some local staffers. The OEO budget hearings were so challenging that one historian has called the survival of the agency in that year the "administration's greatest legislative achievement in 1967."[60]

So, testimony in support of the OEO was more crucial than ever. In July 1967, in its official statement to the House Committee on Education and Labor, ICAP stressed the continued need for OEO programs, particularly in light of the urban unrest earlier that summer. ICAP strongly defended the OEO, which was under attack from conservatives for doing too much and from liberals for not doing enough, arguing that the agency should remain the single coordinator of the federal government's War on Poverty because it was "a champion for the poor" and much more likely "to attempt new and innovative programs than older established agencies." ICAP continued its support of the principle of maximum feasible participation of the poor, noting that it was the element of the War on Poverty that recognized "the humanness of the poor." Shriver had earlier expressed his appreciation of ICAP's support in a letter to Thomas Hinton, executive secretary of ICAP and executive director of the National Catholic Community Service. Shriver thanked Hinton for ICAP's support and said he was "especially pleased that the Committee is against the dismantling of OEO. The war on poverty cannot be successful if there is no command post."[61]

Shriver suggested to ICAP members that they explore the possibility of creating a religious ministry to Job Corps participants. But due to differences of opinion on how the ministry would work (Catholic representatives wanted

60								Chapter Two

the government to handle the Job Corps ministry like it did chaplaincy in the military, while Protestants and Jews preferred voluntary participation), ICAP was unable to provide a Job Corps ministry, highlighting some of the difficulties with an ecumenical antipoverty organization. Instead, ICAP established community relations services at Job Corps sites and at residential communities and offered personal counseling to both men and women Job Corps workers. Following the example of WICS, ICAP also helped young men and women who had completed their Job Corps training to find jobs and locate places to live in new communities. It also provided financial guidance to corps members.[62]

While ICAP made an impact as a result of its work with the Job Corps and its support of the continuation of the OEO, it struggled throughout its existence to define its purpose and objectives. At the November 1967 meeting, committee members discussed a statement by Shirley Greene that despite its significant congressional testimony in support of the OEO and its well-received "Statement on Poverty," "in terms of operation or as a significant educational force in the national community ICAP has not been effective and to do this would require considerable financial assets for staff and programs." Greene was right. ICAP had less than $250 in its bank account at the time of the meeting. Following a lengthy discussion, ICAP members decided to keep the organization active but focus on communicating the moral and ethical imperatives of ending poverty and not involve itself significantly in operating antipoverty programs.[63]

A year later, much of ICAP's meeting again focused on its own purpose and existence. Thomas Hinton, chair of the committee, raised the issue of the "future and usefulness" of the organization. Some members felt there remained a definite role for ICAP in providing information and interpretation for religious groups about the War on Poverty and in continuing to provide congressional testimony supporting the OEO. Others were not so sure. They felt that other organizations had provided more services of relevance, especially in terms of actual antipoverty programs. The overall purpose of the organization was left undetermined at the end of the meeting, other than to lobby whoever won the presidential election in November 1968 for the continuation and expansion of the War on Poverty.[64]

Two months after the meeting, Hinton authored a memo outlining the activities, strengths, and weaknesses of ICAP. According to him, the major strength of ICAP was "that it brought together for the first time the three national religious organizations in a formalized way" to address poverty, particularly concerning legislative issues and with governmental agencies. Hinton noted several weaknesses, including "no full-time staff or a budget to support an operational program" and the fact that it had played no role in the urban unrest following the assassination of Martin Luther King Jr. earlier that year. Despite these shortcomings, Hinton saw a role for ICAP in communicating "to the nation the immorality of poverty" and applying "the common ethical insights of the major religious bodies to the formulation and the application of goals and standards for the nation's anti-poverty efforts." Writing at the end of 1968, Hinton, hinting at the possibility of an ecumenical antipoverty coalition, saw a continued role in the coming year for ICAP "to stimulate and assist in coordinating the anti-poverty efforts of religious groups, agencies and institutions." But exactly what that meant was not clear.[65]

It is true that by the end of 1968, ICAP had done little concretely, other than to offer testimony in support of the OEO and the War on Poverty and to provide funding and programs for the Job Corps. It seemed that ICAP was most effective as a symbol of the churches' and synagogues' vision of the War on Poverty as a moral issue and as an effective lobbying agency for continuing the OEO. But it would be left to another interreligious organization to demonstrate the full possibilities of an ecumenical antipoverty coalition— one that would link the War on Poverty with black power, create significant divisions among and within religious organizations, and highlight the local focus of community action in the War on Poverty.

From the beginning of the Office of Economic Opportunity, the NCC had engaged with the War on Poverty, particularly on a moral and theological level. The NCC clearly saw poverty as a moral wrong, an evil, much like racism, that those of faith needed to expunge from American society. To the NCC leaders, the War on Poverty was in many ways an extension of the civil rights movement, and they actively supported both through congressional testimony, publications, directives to member churches, participation in civil rights marches, and the development of and engagement with church-based antipoverty programs. In both civil rights and antipoverty efforts, they saw themselves as allied with the federal government.

At the same time, the NCC struggled internally with exactly what its role and responsibilities were in terms of the implementation of the War on Poverty. How much should it spend on antipoverty programs? What was the correct relationship between church and state on antipoverty efforts? How should those programs and efforts be coordinated? As the civil rights movement shifted toward black power, what did that mean for the churches and their antipoverty activism? And to what extent should they be involved in a possible ecumenical antipoverty organization or coalition?

In March 1966, a CBS News program highlighted religious efforts and ecumenical cooperation in the War on Poverty. In *The Church and Poverty—A*

62   Chapter Two

One Hour Special, CBS correspondent Stuart Novins focused on three clergy-men, Bishop Paul Moore Jr., Rabbi Richard Hirsch, and Father Geno Baroni, whom Novins described as "three Washington [D.C.] clergymen who see as their most vital task the elimination of poverty." For these three and others like them, a clear moral imperative existed for their involvement in the War on Poverty. Novins noted that "beginning with the struggle for civil rights, the liberal church and synagogue began to emerge as a force for social and economic action." That involvement with civil rights led directly to antipov-erty activism for many of the religious leaders who saw their role as, in part, to effect social change.[66]

Novins made clear that the OEO also saw religious groups' involvement in the War on Poverty as important. Hyman Bookbinder, assistant director of the OEO, called the War on Poverty "the most moral, spiritual program in this country," and he welcomed the participation of churches and synagogues to provide "whatever religious impact" they could "on the things we do" in antipoverty programs. For Bookbinder, who was Jewish, and his Catholic boss, Shriver, ecumenical religious influence in the War on Poverty was a natural fit.[67]

But this did raise questions about the appropriate role of churches and synagogues in government programs. Baroni argued that "there are a lot of things that the Church could do in the area of social change that the govern-ment cannot do." At the same time, he questioned if participation in the War on Poverty might hamper the kind of antipoverty programs that religious institutions could create. Baroni asked, "Should the churches become part of the poverty program . . . or should the churches be independent?"[68]

The Church and Poverty did emphasize that not all Protestants were ac-tive in the War on Poverty. Indeed, while the NCC and its liberal member churches were involved as central participants, evangelicals were not so convinced of the moral rightness of the War on Poverty. As Novins noted, middle-class evangelical churches "as yet have had little to do with church efforts against the causes of poverty."[69]

That was not true for all evangelicals, of course. The leading evangelical preacher in the United States, Billy Graham, although he initially expressed uncertainty about the War on Poverty, demonstrated his support for it on more than one occasion. Graham toured Appalachia with Shriver to garner support for OEO programs there, recorded an interview in support of the OEO that was broadcast throughout the South, and helped produce a docu-mentary titled *Beyond These Hills,* which espoused the benefits of antipov-erty programs. Some of Graham's backing was no doubt a result of his close

The National Council of Churches 63

relationship with his fellow southerner President Johnson. At one point, Graham called for "a global version of Johnson's War on Poverty."[70]

Evangelicals on the left, though small in number in the 1960s, actively supported the War on Poverty. Rufus Jones, a leading leftist evangelical, argued that the Gospel called for believers to care for the poor and to address issues of economic and racial justice. Evangelicals for Social Action was a leftist organization founded in 1973 by Jones, Ron Sider, and others, which issued its Chicago Declaration of Evangelical Social Concern on Thanksgiving of that year. The declaration called evangelicals to action on issues related to poverty and racial and economic injustice. That group, though important, remained small. Most evangelicals were conservative in their politics and tended to either oppose or at least question the War on Poverty. By incorporating churches and religious organizations into the War on Poverty, however, the OEO began the process of connecting conservative religious groups to the state. Over time, some evangelical organizations would link themselves more directly to federally subsidized antipoverty programs.[71]

Novins's broadcast highlighted ecumenical antipoverty activism, especially the creation of ICAP, as evidence of "the real cooperation which exists among the churches in the area of social action." According to Rabbi Hirsch, religious groups involved in the civil rights movement recognized that "cooperation had been so fruitful in the area of race. . . . the religious groups recognize that we should be doing the same thing in the area of poverty." Bishop Moore argued that ecumenical cooperation had become almost second nature for many activist clergy members. According to Moore, the ecumenical movement had convinced those involved that "God wants us to be working together." In addition, they recognized that the church should use "whatever power she can for the kingdom." A cooperative ecumenical alliance or coalition brought more power.[72]

Religious organizations of various types had made an impact in the War on Poverty. Novins noted that at the time of the broadcast, over 10 percent of all OEO antipoverty projects were directed by churches or church-related organizations, and that did not include men and women motivated by their religious faith who were fighting the War on Poverty as individuals working on antipoverty projects. At the conclusion of the CBS program, Novins highlighted how religious organizations' and individuals' involvement in the War on Poverty was influencing both the War on Poverty and the institutions themselves: "The church and synagogue in America are moving forward in directions which would have astounded its members a generation ago. The church alone cannot win the war on poverty, but it is doing things, often, no

64   Chapter Two

one else can or will do. . . . [The churches and synagogues] see a need which they feel morally required to fill. To them it is rightfully their job."[73]

No one was more supportive of an ecumenical antipoverty coalition than Sargent Shriver. His emphasis on the potential role of churches and synagogues in the War on Poverty did indeed pay some dividends. Shriver's meetings with NCC leaders led to their development of a staff Anti-Poverty Task Force, and he actively supported ICAP. In April 1965, Shriver wrote to the Reverend Rodney Shaw of the Methodist Church Board of Social Concerns that "the response by the religious community to the war against poverty is one of the most gratifying developments to date. Religious leaders, both lay and clergy, have been most active and most helpful in the development and the implementation of many of the poverty programs."[74] Earlier that month, Shriver had emphasized the centrality of religion and his Catholic faith to his view of the War on Poverty in his testimony to a congressional committee. Shriver told the committee, "The ultimate dimension of this war is a spiritual dimension because, for us and all Americans, the war on poverty is a movement of conscience, a national act of expiation . . . of humbling and prostrating ourselves before the Creator."[75]

Shriver's passionate belief in the importance of religion in the War on Poverty remained central to him throughout his tenure as OEO director. In 1967, Shriver gave an interview to Walker Knight of the American Baptist Convention on the role of religious organizations in the War on Poverty. Shriver, exaggerating a bit, said that "from the beginning, nearly all religious groups have been overwhelmingly in favor of what we are attempting." He informed Knight that of all the institutions that supported the War on Poverty, "none . . . is more important [than] the religious groups." Shriver believed that "any religiously-motivated person—of any denomination, Christian or Jew—should be participating" in the War on Poverty. When asked to give examples of involvement by religious organizations, Shriver specifically mentioned ICAP, WICS, and migrant labor programs operated by the NCC. To Shriver, then, religious organizations were vital to the existence of the War on Poverty and to the operation of OEO programs in local communities.[76]

Shriver also made his case about the strong religious support for the War on Poverty to President Lyndon Johnson and his top advisors. In a May 1967 memo to the president, with OEO on the defensive from congressional attacks and amid concerns about the strength of the president's support, Shriver emphasized "the desirability" for Johnson "to speak out on the *moral* aspects of the War against Poverty. . . . It is not mere coincidence that even Martin Luther King and Dr. Eugene Carson Blake support OEO publicly, plus Billy Graham and Archbishop [Robert] Lucey, and Bishop Fulton Sheen, to mention only a few." To Shriver, the evidence that religious leaders from most leading denominations supported the War on Poverty meant that "no one could attack the moral rightness of this cause." In a separate memo, Shriver told presidential advisor Joseph Califano, "with Billy Graham on the right, and Martin Luther King on the left, OEO shall overcome!"[77]

Shriver expounded on his belief in the fundamental role of religion in the War on Poverty in speeches to religious gatherings. Shriver gave numerous talks every year to drum up support for the War on Poverty or to thank those actively involved in fighting poverty on the ground, like the one he gave to the Presbyterian General Assembly in May 1965. Less than a year after that speech, in an address to the United Church Women, Shriver extolled the organization and its efforts with WICS and the Job Corps. He also informed the group that WICS was one of hundreds of religious institutions and organizations that had received OEO money for antipoverty programs. Noting that prior to the War on Poverty, "it was practically impossible for a federal agency to give a direct grant to a religious group," Shriver argued that the principle of the separation of church and state "was put there to keep government out of the pulpit, not to keep the clergy away from the poor!"[78]

Shriver had made a similar argument about the role of church and state a few years earlier at the Conference on Religion and Race. Though he was talking about civil rights, not poverty, in 1963, the talking points were similar. He told the ecumenical audience in 1963 that he hoped "the traditional American regard for the separation of church and state will never be interpreted as an excuse for either to preempt, or ignore, the vigorous pursuit of human dignity and freedom which are the legitimate concerns of both church and state." He encouraged religious groups to throw themselves actively into efforts for civil rights. For Shriver, civil rights and the War on Poverty were both moral causes that required the direct engagement of religious institutions and individuals.[79]

In January 1968, near the end of Shriver's tenure as OEO director, he gave one of his last speeches on federal antipoverty efforts to the annual meeting of the Methodist Board of Missions in Denver. One more time, he reminded the attendees that the nation could not "win a War against Poverty without the help of the churches and of churchmen." Again, he hailed the efforts of the "thousands of ministers and priests and nuns and dedicated lay people . . . practicing their religion" through their activism in the War on Poverty. He even poked fun at the number of religious leaders involved in the OEO, saying, "there are now so many ministers and priests and nuns working at OEO . . . that somebody said we ought to change the name to

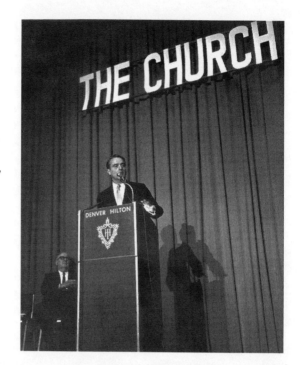

FIGURE 6. Sargent Shriver speaks at the Methodist Board of Missions annual meeting in Denver, Colorado, in January 1968. Courtesy of the United Methodist Archives, Drew University.

Office of Ecclesiastical Outcasts."[80] While some had expressed concern at the blurred lines between church and state that the hiring of clergy in the War on Poverty created, Shriver was thrilled. Even as he was about to leave office, he firmly believed that a coalition of ecumenical religious individuals and institutions remained central to leading America's War on Poverty and guiding America's moral path. He was excited about the possibility of an ecumenical antipoverty coalition.

CHAPTER THREE

Creating an Ecumenical
Antipoverty Coalition

IFCO, Black Power, and the War on Poverty

The Reverend Lucius Walker paced nervously in his office as he was on the telephone accepting congratulations on his new position. Walker had recently been appointed the executive director of the newly formed Inter-religious Foundation for Community Organization (IFCO). The energetic American Baptist minister had spent the previous six years as the director of Northcott House, a settlement house in Milwaukee established by the Wisconsin Annual Conference of the General Board of Ministries of the National Council of Churches in 1961 and supported by the Women's Division of the United Methodist Church. Born in Roselle, New Jersey, in 1930, Walker received a master's degree in social work from the University of Wisconsin and a doctor of divinity degree from Andover Newton Theological School and had developed a reputation as a first-rate preacher. Walker, known as "Lu" to his friends, had combined his interest in the teachings of Jesus with a passion for social justice and brought both to his leadership of Northcott House, where he emphasized community organization and neighborhood control. He brought that same ideology to IFCO.[1]

IFCO represented perfectly the coalescence of the War on Poverty, the black power movement, and religious organizations into an ecumenical antipoverty coalition. Formed by a broadly diverse group of individuals and organizations that had been involved in the civil rights movement and had actively supported the War on Poverty, IFCO was the vehicle through which

68   Chapter Three

these people and organizations could continue their support of black and brown antipoverty activism. IFCO demonstrated the shift in the 1960s from an interracial religious activism to an ecumenical activism centered on black power. Walker and IFCO were at the center of that transformation.

IFCO originated in meetings in 1965 where activist Catholic priests, like John Egan, and staff from the National Council of Churches (NCC) and the American Jewish Committee (AJC) who had been involved in the civil rights movement and community organization joined forces to discuss creating an ecumenical antipoverty agency. Catholic, Protestant, and Jewish community activists sometimes had found themselves working in the same urban areas, often with overlapping programs. IFCO was the result of discussions of ways to better coordinate the community organizing efforts of these denominational religious organizations. IFCO participants also believed that at some point, particularly as black community organizations grew in number and effectiveness, church and synagogue support would decrease. Thus, they saw a need for an organization like IFCO. In April 1966, the United Presbyterian Church Board of National Missions directed its Division of Church Strategy and Development to "pursue cooperation with other interested denominations in establishing and funding enabling structures for training organizers . . . and for united support of local community organization projects." By late 1966, plans for IFCO had been finalized. The original founders of IFCO included the American Baptist Home Mission Society, the Board of Missions and the General Board of Christian Social Concerns of the United Methodist Church, the executive council of the Episcopal Church, the Board of Ministries of the United Church of Christ, the Board of National Missions of the United Presbyterian Church, and, thanks to John Egan, the National Catholic Conference for Interracial Justice (NCCIJ) and the Catholic Committee on Urban Ministry (CCUM). Each member agency was required to contribute $1,000 but could contribute more.[2]

Like the Interreligious Committee against Poverty (ICAP), IFCO was truly an ecumenical agency with a wide range of religious denominations participating. But rather than functioning primarily as a symbolic representative of the major religious organizations and their vision of the War on Poverty, IFCO actively channeled funds from those organizations to local community antipoverty groups, particularly those that emphasized community action and the maximum feasible participation of the poor. And IFCO was truly ecumenical, with no one denomination or religious organization dominating the agency. Representatives from various churches, synagogues, and other religious organizations could give financial support to IFCO, but all of the projects funded were community-based and community-controlled. IFCO's

IFCO and Black Power   69

founders clearly stated that the organization's purpose was "to implement common programs and strategy among religious groups for the development of community organizations among the poor . . . as a part of the urban mission, ministry and program of such religious groups." IFCO was an active participant in the War on Poverty, fundamentally engaged in community action.[3]

IFCO's founding initially created some confusion and consternation among ICAP members and the religious organizations they represented. ICAP officials were concerned about the possible overlap of ICAP and IFCO, while they also wondered why official church organizations had not been asked to participate in IFCO. Walker met with Shirley Greene of the NCC and Maurice Bernstein of ICAP in December 1967 to explain IFCO's purpose. Walker explained that IFCO desired flexibility and latitude in its organizational structure, which might not be possible if official church organizations were directly involved. In addition, IFCO was focused on giving more control to community antipoverty organizations. IFCO and ICAP staff met a month later to discuss their organizations, and they determined that no real conflict existed. IFCO was involved in directly funding antipoverty community action programs, while ICAP was focused on lobbying and overall policy development around the War on Poverty for church- and synagogue-related organizations.[4]

The AJC and its director of interreligious affairs, Rabbi Marc Tanenbaum, were key players in the formation and operation of IFCO. Founded in 1906, the AJC was the leading Jewish advocacy organization in the United States. The AJC had initially hesitated at openly supporting civil rights initiatives amid internal debates over how much effort the organization should expend on issues that did not directly impact Jews. In 1947, however, following President Harry Truman's Committee on Civil Rights' report, "To Secure These Rights," which advocated for federal government action related to civil rights issues, a majority of the AJC's executive committee determined that any human rights issue was of concern to them. The executive committee issued what became known as the Chicago Mandate, which declared that the AJC would "join with other groups in the protection of the civil rights of the members of all groups irrespective of race, religion, color or national origin."[5]

The AJC's efforts in civil rights in the mid-twentieth century focused primarily on equality in four areas: housing, employment, public accommodations, and education. The group submitted an amicus curiae brief in support of the NAACP's *Brown v. Board of Education* arguments and participated in both the March on Washington in 1963 and the Selma March in 1965. The AJC emphasized its commitment to equality by honoring civil rights leaders with its American Liberties Medallion—Thurgood Marshall in 1962 and Martin Luther King Jr. in 1965. Like the NCC, the AJC created a commission on race relations, which promoted job training programs and finding summer jobs for black teenagers. The AJC president, A. M. Sonnabend, explained the organization's support of civil rights by noting the connection between all human beings: the AJC's "responsibility to the Negro is really no more or less than our responsibility to ourselves." Philip Hoffman, chair of the AJC's domestic affairs committee, stated, "If we can't achieve full equality for all Americans, it goes without saying that we can't achieve welfare and safety for the Jews." In other words, the cause of African Americans was the cause of all Americans, particularly Jews, who had also experienced discrimination and segregation.[6]

The AJC embraced the War on Poverty, seeing it as an extension of the civil rights movement. Indeed, in 1964, the AJC, at Tanenbaum's urging, passed resolutions affirming its concerns "with the problems of the poor" and calling on AJC chapters to support programs aimed "toward the elimination of the disabilities created by poverty." The following year, noting that it was "properly concerned with the effort to reduce or eliminate poverty," the AJC declared that its efforts toward that end would be focused on "understanding the racial and ethnic factors in poverty" and on community organization. As the War on Poverty unfolded, the AJC encouraged its chapters to join the fight. Many did, establishing Head Start centers and joining VISTA programs.[7]

Other Jewish organizations also actively joined the battle against poverty. In March 1965, the Religious Action Center of Reform Judaism, a Jewish social action organization founded in 1962 by Rabbi Richard G. Hirsch, who would be featured along with Father Geno Baroni in the CBS News program on the War on Poverty in 1966, held a national conference on poverty titled "Judaism in Pursuit of Economic Justice." Hirsch was an active participant in civil rights efforts, including advocating for the passage of the Civil Rights Act of 1964. Writing to Sargent Shriver in December 1964 to ask the OEO director to serve as the keynote speaker for the conference, Hirsch said: "We believe that active support and leadership by religious forces is essential to elevate the War on Poverty to a passionate moral crusade."[8] Hirsch's statement reflected much of Tanenbaum's thinking.

In many ways, IFCO was an ideal vehicle for the AJC and Tanenbaum, who served as the president of the board of IFCO from its inception. Tanenbaum had formerly served as executive director of the Synagogue Council of America, and civil rights and ecumenism had long been central to his faith. He served as program chair of the national Conference on Religion and Race in 1963, working closely with Mathew Ahmann, and he was the only rabbi in Vatican City at the issuing of the "Decree on the Jews," in which the Catholic Church acknowledged a shared spiritual heritage between Catholics and Jews and encouraged mutual respect and dialogue, at Vatican II in 1965. As the NCC and the Catholic Church emphasized social action and involvement in issues like civil rights and the War on Poverty, Tanenbaum saw them "increasingly as allies."[9]

For Tanenbaum, IFCO represented a coming together of civil rights and ecumenism, as well as a way to fight poverty. According to Tanenbaum, IFCO was "a coalition of black and brown militants who are cooperating with religious activists" whose goal was for the urban poor to "achieve self-determination." IFCO served as the vehicle for this "controlled transfer of power." Major religious organizations gave money to IFCO, and IFCO then distributed the money to community-action-oriented antipoverty agencies. This arrangement had a number of benefits for national religious organizations. It allowed them "to remain anonymous and protected from their white constituents who might object to the uses of their money for social change." By giving money through IFCO, the organizations could be a step removed from funding proposals they did not want to publicly support. It also allowed them to give some money with strings attached, if they so desired. IFCO acted as a broker between the institutional religious structures, which were largely white, and community antipoverty agencies, which were largely black.[10]

From the beginning, a division existed on the IFCO board between those who wanted to work on getting large sums of money from both private and public sources and those who wanted to start channeling the funds they did have immediately into active community antipoverty programs. In addition, some criticized the IFCO board for being too white. As a result, one of Walker's primary initiatives when he became executive director in September 1967 was redesigning the board to provide more representation for African Americans. By early 1969, IFCO's board consisted of twenty blacks, eighteen whites (including Father Geno Baroni), and one Mexican American. The black board members, including Albert Cleage, founder of Black Christian Nationalism and pastor of the Shrine of the Black Madonna Church; James Harris of the NCCIJ; Gayraud Wilmore of the NCC; James Lawson, a civil rights leader and head of Black Methodists for Church Renewal; and George Wiley and Beulah Sanders of the National Welfare Rights Organization (NWRO), joined with black staff members at IFCO to form a black caucus. That development caused some to criticize IFCO for focusing too much on black organizations and not enough on Latino and Native American communities. Walker and the IFCO board argued that the economic crisis was

72   Chapter Three

most severe in black urban neighborhoods, so they made those areas their "highest priority."[11]

Despite IFCO's focus on black community organizations, black churches had not joined the interreligious group during its first two years of existence. Walker and IFCO staff believed that this was because IFCO was still seen as a "white church operation" despite the changes in board representation and structure. IFCO began working with the National Committee of Black Churchmen (NCBC) to try to counter that perception by black churches. The NCBC had initially formed in 1966 as the National Committee of Negro Churchmen, reflecting the influence of black power ideology in religious institutions. Led by Benjamin Payton, a National Baptist minister who served as director of the Commission on Religion and Race for the NCC, the NCBC placed an advertisement in the *New York Times* shortly after its formation endorsing black power and urging solidarity among African Americans. In 1968, the organization replaced the word "Negro" in its name with "Black," further emphasizing its identity as a black power organization. The NCBC was ecumenical, with board representatives, including prominent clergymen like Cleage, from a number of Protestant denominations, and it hoped to "unite black churchmen in their aspirations for greater power and influence in the churches and in their communities." It was logical for IFCO to work with the NCBC as a way to counter perceptions by black churches that it was a white organization. Another way IFCO challenged that notion was by ensuring that no IFCO board member was an official NCC representative. Instead, IFCO board members represented specific denominations, not the NCC directly. Some black religious leaders saw the NCC as essentially a white organization, so Walker moved to ensure that blacks did not see IFCO as NCC's puppet.[12]

The creation of the NCBC was part of an evolution taking place in many religious denominations in the late 1960s. Reflecting national trends, some denominations had agencies that had shifted their focus from civil rights to black power. The Episcopal Church, for instance, had established the Episcopal Society for Cultural and Racial Unity in 1959 as an interracial organization, partly in response to the creation of the NCCIJ. In 1967, the society shifted its focus from integration to black power. Similarly, black evangelicals established the National Black Evangelical Association in 1963 as an evangelical civil rights organization. By the late 1960s, the association had moved away from a focus on civil rights and emphasized black power. Meanwhile, other denominations created brand-new black clergy organizations focused on issues of black power. Black Episcopal priests created the Union of Black Clergy and Laymen in 1968. That same year, black Methodists created

Black Methodists for Church Renewal (BMCR), arguing that the Methodist Church had ignored their economic needs. In a published statement, the BMCR argued, "we have too often denied our blackness (hair texture, color and other God-given physical characteristics) rather than embrace it in all its black beauty." The BMCR answered the question of how its members would respond to racism in the church and the wider world by "unashamedly" answering, "Black Power!" The BMCR further argued, "We, as Black Methodists, affirm the search for black identity. When we affirm and embrace our blackness we are acknowledging what God has done and we no longer wear our blackness as a stigma, but as a blessing." In 1969, the Presbyterian Church of the United States approved the creation of the Black Presbyterian Leadership Conference with the goals of recruiting black ministers and providing support for black antipoverty programs. IFCO's focus on antipoverty agencies with black power orientations reflected a trend happening throughout the religious world as well as the secular one.[13]

The decision to emphasize IFCO's focus on black communities extended to the creation of the IFCO logo. Walker and IFCO staff were determined to create an organizational symbol that would project an image of black consciousness and celebrate IFCO's role in effecting community organization in black communities. IFCO emphasized that its symbol would be rooted in the concepts of beauty, truth, and goodness. The chosen logo was green to represent life, hope, and fertility and black to represent dignity, strength, and beauty. Those colors intertwined into triangles representing the tripartite church and circles representing the interdependence of all people. The symbol ended with a black circle that embraced all it touched but also emerged as an autonomous entity. The logo represented IFCO as a coming together of black power, the War on Poverty, and religious ecumenism.[14]

IFCO is not the only example of the coalescence of the War on Poverty and community organizations rooted in black power. The Watts Labor Community Action Committee (WLCAC) in Los Angeles, for instance, combined community-based economic, political, and cultural empowerment programs and ideology with antipoverty activism. Other organizations, like The East Los Angeles Community Union (TELACU) and the Chicana Service Action Center (CSAC), which formed in the early 1970s and focused on Chicano/a economic, political, and cultural empowerment, serve as prime examples of the links between Chicano/a activism and the War on Poverty. These black and brown nationalist antipoverty agencies are also evidence of the long War on Poverty.[15]

But IFCO uniquely represented the confluence of empowerment movements, the War on Poverty, and interreligious activism. The development of

74   Chapter Three

IFCO as a black nationalist ecumenical religious organization reflected the growing influence of black power and black theology. Black nationalism—the ideology that African Americans should develop economic, political, and cultural power through their own community organizations—was not a new concept in the 1960s. Nor was a black religious nationalism completely new. Indeed, Marcus Garvey had preached a popular brand of black nationalism in the early twentieth century that argued that Jesus Christ was black and his suffering symbolized the sufferings of black people in America.[16]

Some proponents of black power in the 1960s, like the Black Panthers, saw black theology and the black church as irrelevant to the struggle. Maulana Karenga (also known as Ron Karenga), the son of a Baptist minister and the founder of the US organization, which focused on cultural nationalism, called Christianity "a white man's religion" and said that "any Negro who believes in it is a sick Negro." Many others could see no way to link religion and black power. To them, they were antithetical. But for some, religion, the black church, and black theology were the soul of black power.[17]

A formal black theology came to full fruition in the late 1960s in part through two sources that were directly connected to IFCO: the National Committee of Black Churchmen and the Reverend Albert Cleage Jr. The NCBC had formed as an ecumenical organization of black clergy with members including Roman Catholic priests and ministers in the Church of God in Christ. One of its stated purposes was to "unite black churchmen throughout the nation in order to effect strategies related to the empowerment of their communities." Shortly after its formation, the NCBC issued a statement on black power in which it "defended the right of black people to empower themselves against the encroachment of white racism." According to James Cone, the leading proponent of black theology, it was, in part, "the theological arm of Black Power with the responsibility to define the religious meaning of [African Americans'] prior political commitment to black liberation." To Cone, black theology was "the theological expression of a people deprived of social and political power." Black theology focused on black liberation from white oppression, and IFCO's emphasis on black community antipoverty organizations was one avenue to achieve that liberation.[18]

The Reverend Albert Cleage Jr. represented one of the other significant influences in the development of black theology. Cleage had founded the Shrine of the Black Madonna in 1953 as a black nationalist church. For Cleage, central to the theology of Black Christian Nationalism was the notion of a black Christ. In addition, a church could be black nationalist only if it accepted the idea that it needed to be a "place to which Black people [came] with pride, knowing that Jesus was Black, that the Nation of Israel was Black, and that [they were] following in the footsteps of a Black Messiah." Cleage developed the Black Christian Nationalist Creed, which stated in part: "I believe that Jesus, the Black Messiah, was a revolutionary leader, sent by God to rebuild the Black Nation [of] Israel and to liberate Black people from powerlessness and from oppression, brutality, and exploitation of the white gentile world." That liberation meant that black people needed to "control all the basic institutions" in black communities. "Self-determination and community control" had to become realities in all aspects of black life, as Cleage saw it. The War on Poverty, with its emphasis on community action and the maximum feasible participation of the poor, served as a perfect vehicle for black communities to focus on self-determination and community control. Cleage believed that prior attempts at maximum feasible participation had not been successful because they "failed to appreciate the distinction between black participation and black control or black direction." Cleage saw IFCO as the remedy to those shortcomings. Indeed, with its focus on funding black nationalist community antipoverty organizations, IFCO melded smoothly with Cleage's Black Christian Nationalist theology.[19]

Cleage's Black Christian Nationalism was one variation of black theology. James Cone helped define and explain this new phenomenon when he published *A Black Theology of Liberation* in 1970, highlighting the growing influence of black theology and black nationalism. For Cone, Christianity was "essentially a religion of liberation." He connected what he saw as Christ's story of liberation with the black experience. As he argued, "in a society where persons are oppressed because they are *black*, Christian theology must become *black theology*, a theology that is unreservedly identified with the goals of the oppressed and seeks to interpret the divine character of their struggle for liberation."[20] The black experience in America was directly connected to the ideology of liberation of the oppressed that Cone saw in the Bible. African Americans could only overcome that deprivation and oppression through their faith in black theology and through the activism of black nationalist community and religious organizations, like those funded by IFCO.

In its first two years of existence, IFCO allocated more than $1.5 million to about fifty community organizations, many of them in black neighborhoods. IFCO had received grant requests from almost three hundred community organizations during that period for a total of almost $25 million, but was restricted by its budget. Limited resources, in part due to the fact that IFCO had no endowment or capital reserves from which to draw, would plague the organization for much of its history. In addition, receiving consistent donations from more than twenty different church- and synagogue-based organizations would prove difficult for the multiracial ecumenical coalition

76   Chapter Three

intent on encouraging community organization and social change. Indeed, by the end of 1968, IFCO had received all but $15,000 from Protestant organizations, and most of its funds came from four primary sources: the Episcopal Church ($200,000 with $500,000 more promised), the Home Mission Societies of the American Baptist Convention ($200,000), the Board of National Missions of the United Presbyterian Church ($180,000), and the National Division of the Board of Missions of the United Methodist Church ($100,000).[21]

IFCO, though, did provide significant assistance to those organizations it was able to help. The largest IFCO grants were given either to special purpose groups, like the NWRO, which received a majority of its funding from IFCO, or to coordinating agencies, designed to eliminate overlap among existing community action projects in the same geographic area. One such regional group was the Southwest Georgia Project, which served as an umbrella agency for nine community organizations and provided training and support for black people campaigning for political office. IFCO also provided funding to the HOPE (Human, Organizational, Political, and Economic) Development Association, a community organization in Houston that incorporated a wide range of antipoverty programs determined by area residents; the Citizens Action Committee in Detroit; and the Deep South Education and Research Association in New Orleans, to name a few. IFCO's grants included church-related organizations, like the NCC's California Migrant Ministry, which provided aid to the United Farm Workers Organizing Committee through its worker-priest program; the Unitarian Black Caucus in Nashville; and the Interreligious Council on Urban Affairs in Chicago. Churches, synagogues, and religion-based organizations had contributed money to IFCO for these community antipoverty organizations, thus demonstrating the central link between religion and the War on Poverty.[22]

A number of IFCO grants went to black power organizations, like the United Black Community Organization in Cincinnati, a coalition of fifteen community groups working toward black economic development; the Afro-American Black People's Federation in Peoria, Illinois, which taught black history and culture and encouraged economic development; and the Los Angeles Black Congress, an alliance of black power organizations chaired by Walter Bremond. The Black Congress consisted of more than twenty black groups, most notably the Los Angeles chapter of the Black Panther Party and the US organization, an influential group focused on black cultural power and headed by Maulana Karenga. The Black Congress emphasized "operational unity" to promote cooperation among black community groups of varying ideologies, ranging from black capitalism to cultural power to political power to revolutionary Marxism. One of the more unusual IFCO grantees was the Suburban Action Centers in Philadelphia, which aimed to organize suburban whites to be "agents of social change" through supporting black community antipoverty organizations and working to change the racial attitudes of their white neighbors.[23]

Beginning in 1969, Walker began to address the accusations that IFCO was too focused on funding black antipoverty organizations and had not given enough money to community agencies organized by other people of color. By early 1970, IFCO's policy of reaching out to Latino and Native populations had become evident in its grant recipients. While black power community organizations, like the Black Economic Research Center, the National Black Sisters Conference, and Malcolm X Liberation University received grants, so did the Alaska Federation of Natives, American Indians United Conference, the American Indian Movement Center, the Latin American Union in Milwaukee, El Barrio Communications Project in Los Angeles, and Los Padres in San Antonio. IFCO grants clearly linked the War on Poverty to movements for cultural, political, and economic empowerment.[24]

Applicants for IFCO grants had to meet certain criteria. They needed to demonstrate that their agency supported community organization efforts with active training components, including indigenous leadership, that they were located in potential "crisis" areas, that they had plans for achieving self-support, that they had exhausted local resources, and that they had an evaluation component. While the board set policy for grants, Walker had the authority to make the grants.[25]

IFCO also provided training in proposal writing to community organizations. This included assistance in reworking proposals, reviewing budgets, and field evaluations. In addition, IFCO trained those desiring to be community organizers, including the leaders of the NWRO. IFCO had reached an agreement in 1967 with Saul Alinsky, the godfather of community organizing, and the Institute for Urban Affairs for the institute to provide training in community organizing to IFCO grantees. IFCO planned on creating the National Black Training Institute with Alinsky's help, so that leadership training and community organization funding would be more coherently linked. Reflecting IFCO's focus on black power and black community organizations, the institute would emphasize black cultural value systems as "the prime motivator of social change in black communities."[26] Plans for Alinsky's involvement with the institute, though, fell apart. Alinsky wanted to focus on interracial organization, while IFCO and its member organizations wanted the training to center on concepts of black power. Walker wrote to IFCO board member Trevor Austin Hoy that he was "afraid that Saul Alinsky . . .

78   Chapter Three

simply does not understand the depth of commitment behind the black community's thinking about the black nation concept. . . . Neither does he understand, or apparently appreciate, that IFCO could and would have funded his training efforts. The problem was that we could not agree on the terms which he demanded, which were total lack of accountability and blackmail." As negotiations broke down, Alinsky charged IFCO with being racist because of its emphasis on black power.[27]

Two days after that letter, Walker wrote to Walter Bremond, chair of the Los Angeles Black Congress and an IFCO grant recipient, about the urgency of establishing the National Black Training Institute even without Alinsky. Walker claimed that the famous community organizer would "not seek in any way to reach a rapprochement with the movement such as IFCO has encouraged or to submit himself to any measures of accountability." For Walker, this meant that any funding for the institute would be "outside of church sources except for specific contracts for training that any particular denomination may wish to negotiate with him personally." This was not going to work for IFCO, and Walker noted that it left "a vacuum which should be filled immediately."[28]

That vacuum was filled by Bremond and the Los Angeles Black Congress. In its 1968 annual report, IFCO commented that it would be "counterproductive to continue funding local community organizations without engaging in a serious national effort to train lay leadership and career organizers." As a result, IFCO reached an agreement with Bremond to train black organizers from across the country. Bremond, Karenga, and John Davis of the Social Action Training Center (SATC) joined together to create a training institute in Watts in 1968. The SATC incorporated both community organization and community development into its nonviolent training workshops. Sponsored jointly by IFCO and the NCC Department of Social Justice, the SATC incorporated theories of nonviolence along with Alinsky's methods of community organizing without Alinsky himself leading the training. The SATC and its IFCO funding represented another link between religion, black nationalism, and the War on Poverty.[29]

IFCO's basic policy was to support mass-based umbrella community organizations, like the Black Congress. IFCO assistant director Louis Gothard described IFCO's policy as seeking "to support . . . organizations with money from the churches [and] with the kinds of dollars that provide staff for them to fight the battles they have in their own communities." In other words, IFCO aimed to help antipoverty organizations achieve the maximum feasible participation of the poor in their local communities. The organization saw itself as a vehicle for transferring power from the powerful to the powerless by helping black, Latino, and indigenous community organizations continue to fight the War on Poverty in their neighborhoods.[30]

In its promotional literature, IFCO emphasized its War on Poverty roots. In a 1968 brochure, IFCO noted that its existence was "based on the premise that community organization, community development, and ghetto economic development . . . are essential to any lasting solution" to American poverty. IFCO described itself as "a unique coalition of *roman catholic, jewish, protestant, black and Mexican* organizations" that joined "*black-brown* militant spokesmen with religious, civic, and business spokesmen to coordinate financial support for community organization, community development, and indigenous economic development efforts." The brochure highlighted that IFCO funds enabled "indigenous groups to develop cooperative and self-determined programs in their communities." Marketing itself as an organization that "honestly implements the principle of 'maximum feasible participation of the poor,'" IFCO noted that its grantees were "empowered to define their own goals, select their own experts, set their own priorities, choose their own strategies." IFCO saw itself as a true manifestation of the community action goals of the War on Poverty, as a vehicle for the empowerment of people of color, and as an ecumenical antipoverty coalition.[31]

In May 1969, IFCO found itself in trouble as a result of its emphasis on community empowerment and its relationship with black and brown power organizations. The Los Angeles Police Department conducted an investigation of what it deemed militant organizations and their funding sources. IFCO was one of the targets of the investigation. LAPD chief Tom Reddin informed a Los Angeles City Council meeting that IFCO had given money to activists involved in confrontations with authorities and public school walkouts and that the NCC was one of the sources of IFCO funding. Reddin claimed that two NCC programs, the Delta Ministry and the California Migrant Ministry, were "engaged in militant, disruptive activities." The Reverend David R. Hunter, deputy general secretary of the NCC, noted that it had endorsed the goals of IFCO but had never contributed any money to it directly. Instead, some of NCC's denominational members had contributed to IFCO. The LAPD focused particularly on IFCO's $35,000 grant to the Los Angeles Black Congress, which the police deemed a dangerous, radical organization for participating in "demonstrations, walkouts and other disruptive activities in the city." According to IFCO, the grant was made to the Social Action Training Center led by Walter Bremond and Maulana Karenga of the Black Congress. The fact that the Black Congress included the Los Angeles chapter of the Black Panthers as one of its members was a primary reason that it was targeted by the LAPD. The Panthers were consistently targeted

80   Chapter Three

by police departments in cities throughout the country, but particularly in California.[32]

Walker responded to the LAPD charges, calling them "McCarthyite tactics" created "to purposely mislead the public." Walker noted that IFCO was "not supporting revolution, but viable efforts to effect change within existing democratic structures." To him, that made IFCO "a very American organization." Walker said that since IFCO money went to projects encouraging the maximum feasible participation of the poor, some of the groups "may well include black militants . . . but a community organization setting provides a healthy atmosphere where disenfranchised, powerless people may come together for justice." Walker ended his letter by saying: "Let me set the record straight: the claim that we are connected with the Black Panther Party is utterly ridiculous." Of course, while IFCO had not issued a grant directly to the Black Panthers, the party was a member of the Black Congress, which had received IFCO money. In the inflamed, tense atmosphere of the late 1960s, that indirect connection was enough to have IFCO investigated. And this would not be the last time that IFCO faced scrutiny for financing radical or militant organizations. During the late 1960s and early 1970s, black nationalist organizations of various ideologies, including the Black Panthers, the US organization, and the Black Congress, faced constant surveillance and persistent investigation by local police departments and the FBI.[33]

Indeed, one immediate result of the 1969 LAPD inquiry was the expansion of an FBI file on IFCO. The FBI investigation of IFCO was part of its domestic counterintelligence program COINTELPRO, begun in 1956 as an attempt to disrupt the activities of the Communist Party of America as part of the Cold War. COINTELPRO expanded in the 1960s to other domestic organizations determined by the FBI to be extremists, including the Ku Klux Klan and the Socialist Workers Party. That list also included civil rights leaders, like Martin Luther King Jr. and Malcolm X, and what the FBI termed "black nationalist hate groups," like the Black Panther Party, the Nation of Islam, and others. IFCO became one of the "hate groups" that the FBI monitored. The FBI's IFCO file may have been created in part as an expansion of its existing file on the NCC. Begun in 1961, that file was composed primarily of letters from citizens asking if the NCC was communist-infiltrated.[34]

The FBI file on IFCO began in August 1968 as a direct result of IFCO's funding of Albert Cleage's Citywide Citizens Action Committee in Detroit. Cleage was already under surveillance by the FBI for being a militant black power advocate. IFCO's funding of the Citizens Action Committee automatically opened the agency to investigation. The FBI file makes clear that the federal agency had an informant at IFCO. The FBI began its investigation through the pretext of an agent posing as a graduate student from Columbia University who was interested in joining IFCO. The bureau's surveillance of IFCO intensified in May 1969 shortly after LAPD chief Reddin handed over his files to the bureau. An FBI agent issued a report on May 8, 1969, and a week later he reported that IFCO had disbursed 85 percent of its funds to "black militant organizations." These reports came at more regular intervals following the LAPD investigation.[35]

By June 1969, the FBI had infiltrated IFCO and was receiving reports from a confidential source, likely the supposed Columbia University graduate student, within the organization. That source sent the FBI a list of all IFCO officers and board members, as well as a list of all organizations funded by IFCO. In addition, the source reported that IFCO was funding the Black Panther Party in New York, a clear sign of its radical intentions. Apparently, the FBI had contacted several IFCO staff members about serving as a confidential source. Shortly after the infiltrator's first report, IFCO's attorney Frank Patton contacted the FBI to request that any interviews of IFCO staff should take place in his presence. In July, Walker sent a memo to all IFCO staff about the FBI efforts and informed them that they should contact Patton if the FBI approached them. The agency's confidential source reported Walker's memo back to the agency a few days later. The FBI agent's surveillance and the confidential source's reports became more intense and frequent in 1969 as IFCO gained more visibility. Because IFCO regularly funded black nationalist antipoverty groups and supported black community empowerment, IFCO was perceived as a threat by the FBI and COINTELPRO. Indeed, FBI surveillance of IFCO increased with IFCO's relationship to the National Black Economic Development Conference (NBEDC) and the Black Manifesto.[36]

IFCO received additional attention from the FBI because of its continued funding of what the bureau determined to be "black nationalist hate groups." For example, in June 1969, IFCO issued a small grant of $5,000 to the Dodge Revolutionary Union Movement, a subsidiary of the League of Revolutionary Black Workers, a radical black union focused on organizing automobile plants in Detroit. The FBI planned to disseminate this information to the United Auto Workers and the Teamsters in hopes that those unions would attack the League of Revolutionary Black Workers for "operating as a labor union while being financed by a tax-exempt religious organization." COINTELPRO agents hoped this action would "serve to discredit IFCO with the white church groups which supply it with funds."[37]

The COINTELPRO investigation and surveillance led directly to an audit by the Internal Revenue Service. The IRS audit included the presence of

82   Chapter Three

IRS agents in IFCO offices for two years as the agents examined the organization's financial records, the financial records of half of the community organizations funded by IFCO, and the personal financial records of several IFCO board members. The audit ultimately revealed no financial wrongdoing by IFCO, and the FBI investigation ended in 1971 when the agency shut down COINTELPRO as the result of popular and congressional pressure.[38]

Meanwhile, religious organizations that supported IFCO responded to the LAPD and FBI investigations by noting their strong approval of IFCO's work. Although they made clear that they had not "authorized nor provided direct funding for the Black Panthers or any similar group," the United Methodist Church Board of Christian Social Concerns also issued a statement adamantly supporting IFCO. The statement noted that because IFCO was "dedicated to the democratic process for bringing about change," those efforts would "inevitably involve controversy as they confront social habits and systems marked by racism and narrow self-interest." The Methodist board affirmed both its support of IFCO and its "commitment to sustain its continued dedication to social change through democratic and non-violent processes."[39]

J. Edward Carothers, associate general secretary of the Board of Missions of the Methodist Church and the former chair of the NCC Anti-Poverty Task Force, took umbrage at the investigations of IFCO and what he described as "reckless and unfounded" charges that IFCO was "bent on destroying what Americans believe in." Issuing a statement in support of IFCO, Carothers argued that because IFCO had been "formed by religious bodies in order to help disadvantaged people help themselves," efforts to do so would necessarily meet with some social disturbance and controversy. Carothers anticipated "additional efforts to discredit and disqualify IFCO" but reaffirmed his and the Board of Missions' continued support of the beleaguered organization.[40]

The Board of National Missions of the Presbyterian Church conducted a study to determine the accuracy of the charges against IFCO and reported that any allegations of extreme militancy and disruptions were unfounded. The board had continued confidence in both IFCO and the leadership of Lucius Walker. The Presbyterian board saw the LAPD allegations as lacking any credibility or evidence, as there was no direct connection between IFCO and the Black Panthers.[41]

Hunter responded to the charges against IFCO by highlighting IFCO's raison d'être. To a concerned churchgoer, Hunter wrote that IFCO existed "to assist people who live in the ghetto to face their own problems, to become involved in meeting these problems, increasingly the better to be able to determine their own destiny." Hunter saw IFCO's efforts as "conducive to a growing sense of dignity, self-respect, social responsibility, and citizen power." Any allegations against IFCO could easily be dismissed by all the good it was doing, particularly in supporting community organization efforts in black neighborhoods.[42]

While community organizations continued to be the central focus of IFCO, beginning in mid-1968, Walker began showing interest in economic development initiatives. Community economic development had become the newest version of antipoverty work. Senator Robert Kennedy in 1966 had successfully advocated for amendments to the Economic Opportunity Act, which eventually led to the creation of community development corporations (CDCs) in the 1970s. CDCs emphasized community control and planned economic development strategies to tackle poverty. While CDCs did not officially come into existence until the early 1970s, some antipoverty agencies began to look into economic development as part of their poverty-fighting strategy. Economic development generally meant an emphasis on private enterprise and the coordination of business and neighborhood efforts in conjunction with government initiatives to create jobs in poor neighborhoods. Walker and IFCO saw the economic development approach as a way for black communities to retain community control of businesses and job growth, and they saw community organization and economic development as integrally related. Indeed, Walker and IFCO saw "community organization as a necessary precondition for black economic development."[43]

Walker and the IFCO board moved from discussions about economic development to proposing and planning a conference on black economic development. Indeed, as early as July 1968, Walker had proposed a national conference on that topic. Following the IFCO board meeting in September 1968, Walker and IFCO began making concrete plans. IFCO desired a broadly representative group not only at the conference itself, but also involved in planning it. Walker established a conference committee consisting of representatives from more than twenty black community organizations, thus ensuring that any plans determined at the conference would be decided *by* African Americans, not *for* them. As Walker and his associates planned the conference, they did so inspired by and infused with the concepts and language of black power and black liberation.[44]

Writing to the Economic Development Council of Greater Detroit to appeal for funds for the conference, Walker argued that "the most widely recognized need today for the liberation of the Black community is in the area of economic development." As he saw it, black capitalists had an important role in black economic development, but they needed to assume more responsibility for the people of the black communities in which their businesses

84 Chapter Three

operated. For Walker, this meant that "a new type of economics along cooperative lines, a wide indigenous base for community economic control" needed to be developed. Black capitalists needed to work closely with community activists in order to more fully incorporate community control of economic resources. As IFCO saw it, black economic development needed community action, the maximum feasible participation of the poor, and black capitalism and economic development. Walker's appeal to the Economic Development Council worked. The council agreed to fund about one-third of the costs of the conference. IFCO would fund another third, with the remainder of the conference costs coming from other black corporations and private sources.[45]

IFCO further elaborated on its position on black economic development in a brochure it produced to advertise the planned conference. IFCO explained that the organization regarded "Black Economic Development as one of the most vital and challenging concerns to which any total perspective of community organization must address itself." IFCO claimed a "strong commitment to economic development training and research" rather than to "specific economic projects and programs." The organization claimed to not have the answers to black economic development, but did believe it was fundamentally important for black people to come together to discuss, deliberate, and attempt to determine what those solutions might be. Or, as IFCO put it, "to define those values, to set those priorities, to assess those realities and to establish those goals to which we can commit ourselves as Black people, in the struggle for total liberation." For IFCO, a combination of community action, antipoverty activism, and community economic development would aid African Americans in their economic struggle. The discussions and deliberations at a conference devoted to black economic development would help determine the direction of that struggle.[46]

IFCO's planning led to the National Black Economic Development Conference in April 1969 in Detroit. Largely ignored in the scholarship on black power, the NBEDC was an important event that had a significant and long-lasting influence on black nationalism and the War on Poverty. In a press release issued a few days before the conference, the NBEDC asked the question that would drive the conference: "Is capitalism the only framework in which to organize for black liberation and economic development, or must black people repudiate all capitalism and organize independently in their own framework, in their own interest, and towards their own development?" In the same press release, Walker noted that the purpose of the conference was "to bring black persons together to develop economic concepts that reach beyond the current fad of black capitalism and envelop total community development." Again, Walker emphasized the need to link economic development and community control and activism. And he pulled no punches in his assessment of the reasons that black economic development was needed. As he saw it, the NBEDC approach would "not only be economic in nature" but would "include political and direct action activities needed to bring about the controls necessary to end the rape of black Americans."[47]

About eight hundred delegates from across the United States representing a variety of black power, antipoverty, black religious, and economic development organizations gathered on the campus of Wayne State University in Detroit from April 25 to 27, 1969, for the Black Economic Development Conference. In many ways, Detroit was an ideal location for a conference on black economic development. The city had long been the home of black nationalists like Cleage, Malcolm X, the Nation of Islam, and the League of Revolutionary Black Workers. The NBEDC delegates filled lecture halls at Wayne State to listen to a variety of prominent speakers, including Julian Bond, then a member of the Georgia House of Representatives; U.S. congressman John Conyers from Michigan; Fairleigh Dickinson economics professor Robert Browne; and James Forman, former director of the Student Nonviolent Coordinating Committee, present their perspectives on black economic development. Conference participants also met in workshops to discuss land, labor, capital, and other issues. The delegates passed a resolution defining the purpose and goals of black economic development and making recommendations for the comprehensive economic development of black communities. The resolution stated that the NBEDC "commits itself to the development of cooperative economic enterprises in the black communities in order to develop self-help and establish and perpetuate self-reliance in the black community." It went on to define the organization's perspective on the relationship between black capitalism, black community activists, and economic development. The delegates asserted that NBEDC had "no interest in developing individual black capitalists. It seeks to involve people who are poor in its program." The NBEDC chose a program of economic development that included the poor and antipoverty programs and activists, but did not include black capitalists. In that way, it represented a continuation of the community action directive in the War on Poverty of the maximum feasible participation of the poor. The NBEDC planned for poor blacks to help determine economic development projects in their own communities.[48]

The NBEDC was emblematic of the shift taking place in antipoverty activism across the country. By the late 1960s and early 1970s, a growing number of black and brown community-based and -controlled antipoverty agencies began to include economic development in their attempts to fight poverty in their communities. During that period, African American and Chicano/a

86 Chapter Three

communities in Los Angeles, for instance, developed antipoverty agencies like WLCAC and TELACU, which incorporated economic development into their antipoverty efforts. IFCO's creation of the NBEDC reflected that trend in the War on Poverty.[49]

What differentiated IFCO from those other antipoverty organizations was its ecumenical religious connection. Importantly, the NBEDC existed largely because of the confluence of the War on Poverty, black power ideology, and religious antipoverty activism in IFCO. While there certainly were other antipoverty organizations that had been funded and supported in large part by churches, synagogues, and other religious agencies, IFCO uniquely served as a national umbrella agency disbursing funds donated by religious organizations largely to community antipoverty agencies imbued with the rhetoric and strategies of black nationalism. The NBEDC reflected the coming together of all of those influences, plus the movement toward economic development as an antipoverty strategy.

Had the NBEDC resulted only in the resolution to support black nationalist antipoverty agencies focused on economic development, that would be enough reason to consider the conference seminal to the evolution of the War on Poverty and black power. But that was not the case. The highlight of the conference was the declaration of the Black Manifesto by James Forman, the former chair of the Student Nonviolent Coordinating Committee. Forman's manifesto, building on the ideas of community action, black theology, and black nationalism, fundamentally transformed the black power movement, black economic development, IFCO, and the ecumenical antipoverty coalition.

CHAPTER FOUR

The Black Manifesto
Challenging the Ecumenical Antipoverty Coalition

At 7 p.m. on April 26, 1969, an unassuming, middle-aged black man, his hair graying at the temples, approached the microphone at the National Black Economic Development Conference (NBEDC) on the campus of Wayne State University in Detroit. Briefly adjusting his horn-rimmed glasses, looking like a mild-mannered professor or businessman, James Forman addressed the throng of about eight hundred black attendees: "We have come from all over the country, burning with anger and despair not only with the miserable economic plight of our people, but fully aware that the racism on which the Western World was built dominates our lives." Forman spent the next several minutes connecting domestic racism and poverty with international events in Vietnam, the Middle East, and South Africa. He told the mostly rapt audience that their "seizure of power" at the NBEDC was "based on a program" that was contained in a manifesto. Forman's manifesto began: "We the black people assembled in Detroit, Michigan, for the National Black Economic Development Conference are fully aware that we have been forced to come together because racist white America has exploited our resources, our minds, our bodies, our labor. For centuries, we have been forced to live as colonized people inside the United States, victimized by the most vicious, racist system in the world." And then Forman got to the heart of his message: "We are therefore demanding of the white Christian churches and Jewish synagogues, which are part and parcel of the system of capitalism, that they

88   Chapter Four

begin to pay reparations to black people in this country. We are demanding
$500,000,000 from the Christian white churches and Jewish synagogues."[1]

With those words, Forman launched what he called the Black Manifesto,
one of the key documents in the history of the civil rights/black power movement and, of particular importance for this story, the evolution of the War on
Poverty. Most scholars on civil rights/black power have paid scant attention
to the Black Manifesto. Peniel Joseph, for instance, in his brilliant *Waiting
'til the Midnight Hour* did not mention the manifesto and discussed Forman
only in terms of his tumultuous relationship with the Black Panthers. Some
scholars, such as Robin D. G. Kelley, Rhonda Williams, and Michael West,
have spent several pages in larger works on black power writing about the
manifesto and the NBEDC and their importance to black power ideology.
Kelley called the Black Manifesto "the first systematic, fully elaborated plan
for reparations to emerge from the black freedom movement." A few scholars
have convincingly argued for the centrality of the Black Manifesto to the shift
from civil rights to black power. Angela Dillard in *Faith in the City* argued that
"the Black Manifesto, perhaps more than any other artifact of those troubled
and heady times, demonstrates how far local activists had moved from the
ethic of interracial unity, [the Reverend Martin Luther] King's 'beloved community,' and the political theology of the social gospel." In her article on the
manifesto and its call for reparations, Elaine Lechtreck noted that the manifesto "reflected a revolutionary, assertive spirit emanating from black people
during the late 1960s." James Findlay's *Church People in the Struggle* highlighted the manifesto's impact on the National Council of Churches (NCC)
and its support of civil rights/black power. But the manifesto's importance is
about more than the shift from civil rights to black power and the churches'
response to that, although that is certainly significant. Indeed, what Forman outlined in his manifesto was the growing emphasis on black economic
power, which was taking hold in many religious institutions in the United
States in the late 1960s. The manifesto transformed the War on Poverty and
the religious institutions that supported it and inextricably linked black
power, the War on Poverty, and liberal religion in America.[2]

When James Forman issued this explosive manifesto in April 1969, he had
already had a broad career in civil rights and black power activism. Forman
was one of the founding members of the Student Nonviolent Coordinating
Committee (SNCC) in 1960. A decade older than many of the other SNCC
members, he served as the organization's first executive secretary from 1961
to 1965, providing important leadership for the influential activist group.
Forman had participated in marches and demonstrations in Albany, Georgia,
and Birmingham, Alabama, and marched with Martin Luther King Jr. from

The Black Manifesto 89

Selma to Montgomery. He was instrumental in developing voter registration projects in Mississippi and elsewhere in the South. Following his tenure at SNCC, Forman attempted a partial merger of SNCC and the Black Panther Party, eventually joining the Panthers for a brief period. After ending his affiliation with the Panthers, Forman essentially served as a consultant to black power organizations.[3]

Forman initially balked at the invitation to speak at the NBEDC, which he received from the conference planning committee, since he believed that no concrete solutions to the economic problems of black people could be reached "within the framework of capitalism." He also hesitated because of IFCO's religious affiliation. He was no fan of religion. As he put it, "religion fucked up my young life." He ultimately agreed to speak, largely because he had received a separate invitation from the League of Revolutionary Black Workers in Detroit, and accepting the invitation to the NBEDC would help finance his trip. Forman decided that more than just addressing the issue of economic development, the conference should produce some definitive programs in that area for black communities. Since the conference was organized by IFCO, a religious organization, Forman determined to use the occasion to demand reparations from churches and synagogues for their roles in slavery and segregation. As he envisioned it, the Black Manifesto "would not merely involve money but would be a call for revolutionary action, a Manifesto that spoke of the human misery of black people under capitalism and imperialism, and pointed the way to ending those conditions."[4]

Forman, though, was not the only speaker at the conference. Others were black elected officials, like civil rights activist and new Georgia state representative Julian Bond; a U.S. congressman from Michigan, John Conyers; and Brother Gaidi, one of the leaders of a new black nationalist organization, the Republic of New Afrika. Bond, Conyers, and Gaidi all argued for some sort of reparations for African Americans, whether direct payment from the federal government or land reform. The conference's keynote speaker was Robert S. Browne, an economist at Fairleigh Dickinson University. Browne's talk encouraged black capitalism and individual black entrepreneurship, concepts actively encouraged by the administration of President Richard Nixon and supported by some of the convention delegates. Essentially, Browne's talk was a more modern version of what Booker T. Washington had presented seventy years earlier—a call for the creation of black jobs and black businesses.[5]

Forman's manifesto offered a very different solution. Speaking at the end of the second evening of the conference, he outlined his vision for a better economic future for black Americans. Calling African Americans like Browne, who advocated for black capitalism, "black power pimps and fraudulent leaders," Forman instead argued for reparations and black economic development. Provocatively explaining that the $500 million reparations figure was determined by calculating "fifteen dollars a nigger," Forman specified eight ways in which the $500 million would be spent. His demands included $200 million for the creation of a southern land bank to establish cooperative farms for southern black farmers, reflecting the long history of African American demands for land going back to Reconstruction; the establishment of black publishing, printing, and television businesses so that African Americans could have more control over their representation in the media; the creation of training and research skills centers for African Americans; $10 million to support the National Welfare Rights Organization in an effort to help welfare recipients organize more effectively; $20 million for the creation of the United Black Appeal, to be headed by Forman, which would establish cooperative businesses with African nations; and the creation of a black university in the South. Finally, Forman's manifesto demanded that all money raised from churches and synagogues be sent to IFCO, which would then select black community antipoverty agencies to fund.[6]

Forman ended his statement by telling the convention delegates that they would have to "declare war on the white Christian churches and synagogues" in order to win their demands. He hoped those religious institutions would see the demands in the manifesto as "modest and reasonable." Forman then issued a challenge to synagogues and white churches. If they were not willing to meet the demands outlined in the manifesto, "then we will declare war." Echoing the arguments of Malcolm X, Forman concluded: "we are prepared to fight by whatever means necessary."[7]

Other calls for reparations for African Americans had preceded Forman's manifesto. Formerly enslaved people had requested portions of their ex-masters' land as compensation in the aftermath of the Civil War. In the late nineteenth and early twentieth centuries, Callie House had created the National Ex-Slave Mutual Relief, Bounty and Pension Association as a way to fight for pensions as a form of reparations. At about the same time, Henry McNeal Turner, a bishop in the African Methodist Episcopal (AME) Church, advocated for $40 billion in reparations to former slaves. Beginning in the 1940s, the Nation of Islam called for reparations in the form of monetary compensation and the cession of southern states to African Americans. In the 1950s, Audley Moore, who had a long and influential career as a black nationalist, formed the Reparations Committee of Descendants of U.S. Slaves. Among other demands, her committee called for reparations for African Americans to be paid in 1963, the one hundredth anniversary of the Emancipation Proclamation. In the 1960s, Martin Luther King Jr., the Black

The Black Manifesto   91

Panther Party, and the Republic of New Afrika also advocated for some type of compensation for the descendants of slaves. The key difference between earlier demands for reparations and those in Forman's manifesto was that previous calls for reparations had demanded compensation from the federal government. Forman's manifesto was the first reparations demand to target churches and synagogues. And he wanted the religious institutions to make those payments to black community antipoverty agencies through IFCO. As one scholar argued, churches and synagogues were "especially vulnerable to a demand for reparations because such a demand [could] be understood perhaps best within the ancient pattern of sinfulness, contrition and penance which is inseparable from the entire historical theology of the Judeo-Christian religion[s]." In other words, reparations could be seen as white churches' and synagogues' penance for past sins.[8]

The most controversial part of Forman's manifesto, though, was not his demand for reparations or his list of the ways in which religious institutions could make those payments. It was the preamble of the manifesto, in which Forman issued a Marxist critique of capitalism and advocated for black revolution, that stirred the most debate. Indeed, Forman used the preamble in part as a direct rebuttal to Browne's support of black capitalism. In addition to calling black capitalism advocates "pimps," he referred to them as "Negroes . . . promoting all types of schemes for black capitalism." Forman argued that black power required a fight "against racism, capitalism and imperialism." That fight would create "a socialist society inside the United States." As Forman acknowledged, reparations "did not represent any kind of long-range goal . . . but an intermediate step on the path to liberation."[9]

In many ways, the Black Manifesto reflected recommendations developed in workshops held during the first two days of the conference. In those workshops, conference delegates recommended the comprehensive economic development of black communities and rejected black capitalism, which many saw as a strategy that would benefit individual black entrepreneurs but not black communities as a whole. The conference delegates overwhelmingly supported the Black Manifesto, voting to adopt it, after intense debate, by roughly a four-to-one margin.[10]

The Black Manifesto and the NBEDC had immediate and far-ranging impact. First, the founders of the NBEDC created a permanent organization, the Black Economic Development Conference (BEDC), to continue economic development planning and to publicize the Black Manifesto. All seven members of the executive board of the League of Revolutionary Black Workers joined the BEDC, which collected reparations money for the league. Scholar Michael West has called the NBEDC "a major Black Power event"

92   Chapter Four

because "it was the single most *public and collective* attempt to work out a Black-power-inspired program of *economic* action." According to West, the "most consequential outcome" of the NBEDC, the Black Manifesto, "became an instrument of political mobilization for activists on the ground." While the manifesto serves as a prime example of the shift from civil rights to black power, it also represents a fundamental connection between IFCO, religious institutions, and the long War on Poverty.[11]

The new BEDC had a steering committee that featured a number of ministers and civil rights leaders. In addition to Forman, the group included the Reverend Metz Rollins of the NCBC; the Reverend Calvin Marshall, pastor of the Varick Memorial AME Zion Church in Brooklyn; Julian Bond; Professor Browne; Cain Felder, executive director of Black Methodists for Church Renewal; Professor Vincent Harding, director of the Martin Luther King Jr. Library project at Spelman College; the Reverend Woodie White, executive secretary of the Commission on Religion and Race of the United Methodist Church; Muhammad Kenyatta, chair of the Philadelphia chapter of the BEDC; Harold Holmes, chair of the Chicago BEDC chapter; and Fannie Lou Hamer, vice chair of the Mississippi Freedom Democratic Party. These well-known, well-respected, and established leaders directed the BEDC from its beginnings, but Browne, Bond, Kenyatta, and Holmes remained the most active in the organization moving forward.[12]

In addition to the call for reparations, Forman's manifesto also called for "black people throughout the United States" to act together "by whatever means necessary" to demand those reparations from churches and synagogues. Forman recommended that black organizations call press conferences in cities throughout the United States to demand reparations. More specifically, he requested that on May 4, 1969, or a later date, blacks "commence the disruption of the racist churches and synagogues throughout the United States" to demand reparations.[13]

Of particular importance was the manifesto's and IFCO's relationship with the National Council of Churches. In response to the Black Manifesto, the NCC hastily arranged for Forman to appear at a previously scheduled meeting of its 256-member general board at the Statler Hilton in New York on Friday, May 2. Forman read the entire manifesto to the NCC board. In response, the members referred the manifesto to the executive committee of the general board for it to act on behalf of the board at its meeting on June 23.[14]

The following day, May 3, 1969, Forman met with the Reverend Ernest T. Campbell, pastor of Riverside Church in New York. Located at 490 Riverside Drive (at 120th Street) in Manhattan, Riverside Church, America's tallest church, opened in 1930, its construction financed largely by the industrialist

The Black Manifesto

FIGURE 7. James Forman presents his Black Manifesto to the general board of the National Council of Churches on May 2, 1969. Seated, left to right, Arthur Flemming, NCC president; R. H. Edwin Espy, NCC general secretary; and an unidentified gentleman. Courtesy of the United Methodist Archives, Drew University.

John D. Rockefeller. By 1969 Riverside Church had a reputation as one of the leading liberal, interdenominational Protestant churches in the country. Harry Emerson Fosdick, Riverside's first minister, was a renowned liberal clergyman who was at times denounced for his modernist theological views. The Reverend Martin Luther King Jr. had given his famous speech denouncing America's war in Vietnam just two years earlier at Riverside. Campbell, who became Riverside's pastor in 1968, had received an award for his efforts in the civil rights arena from the American Civil Liberties Union. Riverside was a liberal mainline church that had decidedly supported civil rights and the War on Poverty. It was one of America's wealthiest and most well-known churches, and it was conveniently located across the street from the headquarters of the National Council of Churches. Forman knew all of that and specifically chose Riverside for those reasons.

When Forman met with Campbell, he gave the pastor a copy of the Black Manifesto and read him the specific demands being made of Riverside Church. He then asked Campbell if he could read the manifesto to the congregation at the next day's worship service. Campbell refused because the following day was a day of communion at the church. Forman asked if he

94 Chapter Four

could read the demands on another Sunday. Campbell again refused Forman's request.[15]

On Sunday, May 4, James Forman followed through on his threat of disrupting churches when he and a handful of his associates from the BEDC strode confidently down the center aisle of Riverside Church. Forman approached Reverend Campbell, who was in the middle of his sermon, and asked to speak to the congregation. Campbell reluctantly relented. Forman addressed the shocked attendees, recounting the details of his meeting with Campbell and then issuing demands to the Riverside congregation. Forman informed the congregation that he was making these demands at Riverside Church because it was "in the heart of the Harlem community." He told the audience that he intended to circulate his memo "widely in Harlem so that the Harlem Black Community will become aware of the racist nature of the Riverside Church and its leadership." Forman then threatened the attendees: "if these demands are not met, the Harlem Community will begin to take appropriate action, for no church has a right to exist if it cannot be responsive to the needs of black people."[16]

Forman's demands to Riverside Church included rent-free office space for the BEDC at Riverside and a list of all church assets with a to-be-determined portion being donated to the BEDC. He asked that 60 percent of all of Riverside's annual income be given to the BEDC. Forman gave the church one week to meet those demands. Finally, he demanded that Riverside Church "use its influence and historic reputation to pressure all white racist Christian Churches and Jewish synagogues" to meet the $500 million demand of the Black Manifesto "due to the role of the Christian and Jewish religions in exploiting black people in this country." Forman clarified that the financial demands on Riverside Church were in addition to the $500 million demanded of all synagogues and churches. Indeed, he argued that "due to the special power and exploitative and racist role of John D. Rockefeller who endowed the Riverside Church we feel we are correct in stating that the Riverside Church must pay extra reparations to black people . . . for the money of John D. Rockefeller is still exploiting people of color all around the world." Forman also argued that because Riverside was located "directly across the street from the center of power in the Protestant religion" (NCC headquarters), it "must serve notice on 475 Riverside Drive that we are dead serious about our demands." Forman dramatically ended his speech by saying: "Time is running out. We have been slaves too long. The Church has profited from our labor. The Church is racist. We are dead serious about our demands, and we are prepared to die for their implementation. Our demands shall be met. Reparations or no Church! Victory or death."[17]

The reactions to Forman's dramatic appearance inside Riverside Church that morning varied. Some parishioners expressed anger and resentment at Forman's interruption; others expressed support for his cause. Some stared silently; others cried openly. The church organist, perhaps intentionally, perhaps coincidentally, played "May Jesus Christ Be Praised."[18] Regardless of individual reactions, it is difficult to imagine a more impassioned pronouncement or a more spectacular symbol of the importance of black power and black theology than Forman's speech at Riverside. At one of the nation's leading churches and across the street from one of the centers of American Protestant theology, Forman had accused American religious institutions of having blood on their hands. And he served notice that blacks would wait no longer for compensation for that bloodshed and those past sins.

The religious leaders and staff at 475 Riverside Drive certainly noticed. The following day, May 5, about thirty black staffers of major NCC denominations met at NCC headquarters across the street from Riverside Church to discuss the manifesto. Called by Dr. Charles S. Spivey Jr., an AME pastor and the director of the Crisis in the Nation program of the NCC, the meeting featured a wide-ranging discussion about black power, the manifesto, IFCO, reparations, and religious antipoverty activism. Lucius Walker answered the attendees' questions about IFCO and the Black Manifesto. Walker admitted that the manifesto had caught the conference by surprise. He said he was going to recommend not that the IFCO board adopt the manifesto itself, but that the programmatic demands of the manifesto be implemented. The attendees appeared to agree with Walker and formed a consensus that viewed reparations as "a challenge to the churches to give up the piece-meal approach to economic development and take one big comprehensive plan which would not only change lives but also help transfer power."[19]

The following day, Forman made his demands on another church. He walked to the headquarters of the Lutheran Church in America and dramatically attached a copy of his manifesto to the doors of the building, reminiscent of Martin Luther's nailing of his Ninety-Five Theses to the doors of a Roman Catholic church. Forman then presented his demands, including a bill for $50 million in reparations, to the Reverend Robert Marshall, president of the Lutheran Church. Marshall said he would need time to study the demands before replying to Forman.[20]

On May 7, Forman read his demands to the National Committee of Black Churchmen, many of whom, including Walker, had been present at the NBEDC. In response, the NCBC quickly adopted a statement supporting the Black Manifesto in principle. In its statement, which saluted IFCO for sponsoring the NBEDC, the NCBC argued that "the white churches and synagogues undeniably have been the moral cement of the structure of racism in this nation, and the vast majority of them continue to play that role today." The statement also called Forman "a modern-day prophet" and reminded churches of the history of support for the slave trade by Christians and of continued discriminatory practices and patterns, for which the white churches and their members needed to be accountable. In addition, the NCBC argued that the churches and synagogues were capable "out of their enormous corporate assets" of paying reparations "for their complicity in the exploitation of blacks." While acknowledging that black churches did not "stand in the same dock as the white church[es] before the bar of justice," since "black churches were the victims rather than the guardians and perpetrators of racism in America," the NCBC statement also called on black churches and caucuses to "play major roles in interpreting the justness, humanness and theological soundness of the demands of the Black Manifesto." The NCBC encouraged black churches and caucuses to accept responsibility "to share in the remuneration of the black communities" and to donate funds to IFCO for antipoverty programs in black communities since those communities had "sustained" black churches for generations.[21]

Two days later, in another dramatic episode of the Black Manifesto controversy, Forman, accompanied by the Reverend Metz Rollins of the NCBC, ventured to the Roman Catholic Archdiocese of New York to try to meet with Terence Cardinal Cooke. Cooke, though, was out of town, so Forman presented his demand for $200 million from the Catholic Church to members of the cardinal's staff. Earlier in the day, Forman had received a temporary restraining order, preventing him from again disrupting services at Riverside Church. In a pouring rain, Forman defiantly and dramatically burned the court order on the steps of the chancery office of the Archdiocese of New York as he left the building.[22]

Interestingly, Forman's presentation at Riverside Church on May 4 did not end his relationship with the church or its pastor. On Saturday, May 10, Campbell spoke on the Riverside Church's radio program and told his audience: "Reparations, restitution, redress, call it what you will; it is just and reasonable that amends be made by many institutions in society—including and perhaps especially—the church." The next day, Forman again arrived at the church, but this time he stood silently, wearing a bright African robe, through the service. Campbell delivered a sermon on Zaccheus, who determined to give half of his possessions to the poor. To drive home his point, Campbell told his congregants that "Zaccheus paid reparations." Campbell also said, "We have failed as white Christians, and we can make amends collectively. This is what reparations means to me."[23]

FIGURE 8. On the steps of the chancery office of the Roman Catholic Archdiocese of New York, James Forman burns a court order temporarily restraining him from disrupting services at Riverside Church. He had presented a demand to Catholic officials for $200 million in reparations. Courtesy of the United Methodist Archives, Drew University.

While the Riverside Church refused to donate money directly to the BEDC, Pastor Campbell issued a sermon on July 13 titled "The Case for Reparations." In it, Campbell decried Forman's call for revolution but argued that "rather than begrudge reparations, I should think that we would rejoice that our sin, in part, is reparationable." After Campbell's sermon, Riverside Church created a $450,000 grant for antipoverty projects in New York. Clearly, Forman's presentation at Riverside, for all its controversy, had been effective. He had brought attention to the church's sin of racism and convinced its members to support black antipoverty programs.[24]

In general, responses to the Black Manifesto by the Catholic Church and its affiliated organizations ranged from outright rejection to hesitant support. Two weeks after Forman's appearance at the Archdiocese of New York, the archdiocese officially rejected the manifesto's demands. At the first convention of the National Catholic Conference for Interracial Justice following the Black Manifesto, the NCCIJ elected its first black chair, Walter Hubbard. In addition, the convention passed a resolution supporting reparations to minorities and maintained that "while the language of the Black Manifesto and the political philosophy of some of its backers might be abrasive . . . Christians

98 Chapter Four

cannot hide behind the smoke screen of distasteful rhetoric to mask our criminal tolerance of racism." Lu Walker spoke at the NCCIJ conference and urged the organization to encourage Catholics to understand the importance of reparations to African Americans. Walker suggested that individual parishes raise at least $1,000 to help fund black community organizations.[25]

Months later, in the fall of 1969, the NCCIJ formed the National Catholic Committee on Reparations with the National Association of Laymen. This reparations committee, which included Father Geno Baroni, promoted the notion of reparations to Catholic parishes throughout the nation and also worked to obtain money to fund IFCO projects. The reparations committee wrote a paper, "A Catholic Position on Reparations." In the paper, which was presented to the National Conference of Catholic Bishops (NCCB), the reparations committee called the Black Manifesto a "profoundly prophetic event" that provided Catholics an opportunity not only "to correct past and continuing injustice" but also to "renew the American Church." Encouraging the Catholic Church to commit to an annual donation of about $400 million to black-controlled organizations, like IFCO, the reparations committee argued that the funds to IFCO projects would not only benefit black urban communities but would also reorient "church priorities to re-emphasize her role of concern and service for the poor and oppressed."[26]

Meanwhile, a few days following Forman's burning of the court order, in a remarkable show of support for the Black Manifesto, a coalition of seventy-five to eighty black and white students from Union Theological Seminary, which is located near Riverside Church, seized the seminary's administration building for four days and demanded that the seminary's board of trustees donate $100,000 out of the next year's budget and raise more than $1 million to support the BEDC. Following some tense negotiations, the seminary faculty voted to raise $100,000 for the BEDC, and the board of trustees voted to invest $500,000 of its endowment in black economic development and antipoverty agencies "to be determined by the black community of the seminary."[27]

A month-long flurry of activity and a series of occupations of various floors of 475 Riverside Drive followed the takeover of Union Theological Seminary. There were renewed demands for reparations and for church support of black antipoverty programs, and tense negotiations and challenges to church leadership and policy. This collection of episodic occupations forced the churches to explore their perspectives on race and poverty in America.

The actions began on Wednesday, May 14, 1969, when a group of black Presbyterians and a number of Union Theological Seminary students, many of whom had been part of the Student Interracial Ministry, a civil rights organization active in the mainline churches, occupied the offices of the United Presbyterian Church on two floors at the Interchurch Center. The sit-in was nonviolent, although office work on those two floors was discontinued for the several days of the occupation. On the first day, several of the occupiers, including some Presbyterian Church members, formed the Ad Hoc Committee for Justice from the Presbyterian Church and addressed a statement to the United Presbyterian Church General Assembly, then being held in San Antonio, Texas. The ad hoc committee's statement advocated that the general assembly support the Black Manifesto, give $80 million to IFCO for antipoverty programs, give all of its land in New Mexico to Mexican Americans, and give all of its land in the Deep South to the BEDC for the benefit of black communities. The committee signed the statement from "liberated territory" on the eleventh floor.[28]

Upon hearing of the ad hoc committee's demands, the Presbyterian General Assembly asked Forman to speak at its meeting. Forman, along with Obed Lopez, executive secretary of the Latin American Defense Organization, and Eliezer Risco of the recently formed National Council of La Raza flew to San Antonio the next day to speak to the Presbyterian General Assembly. Forman repeated the demands in the ad hoc committee statement. Risco demanded that health, education, and welfare programs and agencies maintained by the church in the United States and Latin countries, as well as their facilities, be turned over to community control and ownership. He also called for real estate holdings to be released "for the occupation and ownership of low-income families." In other words, Risco and Forman both demanded community control of the funds, land, and facilities used by poor people of color. This, indeed, would be the maximum feasible participation of the poor in action.[29]

In response to the demands from Forman and Risco, the general assembly received several recommendations from its Committee on Church and Race. The members debated those recommendations late into the night before voting to conduct a campaign to raise money "equal to or surpassing" $50 million for the poor. The assembly also voted to "find ways for people living in poverty . . . to own land and to utilize . . . lands presently owned by the Board that are not essential to operating programs of the church." More specifically, the assembly agreed to give some church-owned lands in Alabama, Georgia, South Carolina, and Mississippi to African Americans and land in New Mexico to Mexican Americans. In addition, the assembly voted to give $100,000 to IFCO for additional War on Poverty projects for black and Mexican American community-based antipoverty organizations to supplement OEO funding.[30]

FIGURE 9. *Left to right*, Obed Lopez, executive secretary of the Latin American Defense Organization; Eliezer Risco of La Raza; and James Forman appear before the General Assembly of the United Presbyterian Church. Forman asked that landholdings of the United Presbyterian Church in the Deep South be turned over to the BEDC for the benefit of poor black people and that the church give $80 million to IFCO for antipoverty projects in African American and Mexican American communities. Courtesy of the United Methodist Archives, Drew University.

The underlying mood of the assembly was supportive of the manifesto and the demands arising from it. The Committee on Church and Race issued a statement that its members were "shocked but chastened" by the demands from their "black and brown brothers," and they were "grateful" that they had "come to the church to tell us about it." Rather than approaching as supplicants, Forman and Risco had come "in a new way, to shake us, to challenge our basic attitudes, to jar us loose from our arrogance." The committee, "in penitence, some uncertainty, and gratitude," accepted "this new way of speaking ... to affirm that it may be a necessary mode of God's coming to judge and help to free us from racial attitudes that demean us."[31]

Individual members of the assembly agreed with the committee's statement. Delegate Corine Cannon argued in support of meeting Forman's and Risco's demands: "when this money comes, it's not going to Jim Forman; it's

The Black Manifesto   101

going to the black community." The Reverend Edward Machle said that he knew "no translation of the Gospel that says Jesus told the rich man to sell all he had and give it to the poor as soon as they were ready to use it responsibly. Part of stewardship is the stewardship of risk, instead of safety."[32] Despite a long and, at times, heated debate, the Presbyterian General Assembly clearly and firmly established itself as a strong supporter of many of the demands of the Black Manifesto.

One week following the general assembly meeting, its moderator, George Sweazy, wrote an open letter to all Presbyterians confirming the assembly's support of many of the Black Manifesto's demands and the reasons for that support. Sweazy wrote about "the mood of joy and accomplishment" that emanated from the meeting. While he had observed "foreboding" and "gloomy predictions" in the early parts of the assembly meeting, he noted that those feelings had been replaced by joy at the end and by actions in which "the whole Church" could "rejoice." While acknowledging that the Black Manifesto contained "much that is impossible and much to which our Church must be unalterably opposed" (a clear reference to the manifesto's call for revolution in its preamble), Sweazy argued that it was necessary to hear Forman's message and admit the church's "inheritance from old and still unrighted wrongs." He assured his readers that no church money was spent to have Forman speak at the assembly, and none of the money the assembly allocated would be given to Forman directly. But Forman had convinced the members of the assembly to support many of his demands through IFCO and other organizations. Sweazy ended his letter by noting that the assembly had concluded "in a wonderful spirit of harmony and satisfaction." He hoped that all Presbyterians would experience that same unity and joy.[33] At least initially, then, the Presbyterian Church supported the manifesto's demands for antipoverty money.

Meanwhile, the occupation of the Board of National Missions and the Commission on Ecumenical Mission and Relations offices of the United Presbyterian Church on the ninth and eleventh floors of the Interchurch Center continued until May 20. At one point during the protest, all employees on the ninth floor were asked to leave the building in support of the Black Manifesto and the demands being made on the United Presbyterian Church. Some did leave, and some remained at their desks.[34]

At the same time, Forman continued to make demands of other denominations. On May 13, he met with John Hines, presiding bishop of the Episcopal Church, and demanded $60 million and 60 percent of the church's annual profits from its assets and investments. The following day, Forman addressed a letter to the United Church of Christ with the following demands: $130 mil-

102   Chapter Four

lion for the development of a black university at Tougaloo College in Mississippi; $10 million for the United Black Appeal; and 60 percent of all the profits of the church's investments. Forman asked to meet as soon as possible with church officials and representatives of black members of the church.[35]

These church officials, however, did not respond as Forman had hoped. A week after Forman's meeting with Hines, the Episcopal Church's executive council rejected his demands but pledged to continue to support programs for the poor. Over a month after his letter to the United Church of Christ, Forman received a response from Mareta Kahlenberg, chair of the administrative committee. Kahlenberg informed Forman that while the church shared his "concern for racial and social justice," it "did not share the ideology expressed" in the introduction to the Black Manifesto. Therefore, the United Church of Christ rejected Forman's demands.[36]

Shortly after penning his letter to the United Church of Christ, on May 17 Forman flew to Seattle to attend the annual meeting of the American Baptist Convention. He demanded $60 million from the American Baptists in addition to 60 percent of the convention's income from investments. Thomas Kilgore, a black minister and president of the convention, argued that he did not think the $500 million Forman demanded from all churches and synagogues was "an unrealistic figure." While he admitted he did not agree with Forman's tactics and would not necessarily use the term "reparations," in substance he favored the idea of payments to African Americans from churches. His convention, though, disagreed. The American Baptists, like the United Church of Christ, voted not to give any money to Forman, the BEDC, or IFCO.[37]

Having had mixed results at this point—support from the Presbyterian General Assembly and rejections from the American Baptists, the Episcopal Church, and the United Church of Christ—supporters of Forman and the Black Manifesto, this time primarily Union Theological Seminary and Columbia University students along with some Interchurch Center staff members, began a sit-in on the four floors of offices of the United Methodist Church's Board of Missions at the Interchurch Center. Indeed, the staff members joined together as the Economic Liberation Committee, issued a list of demands to the United Methodist Church, and encouraged other staffers to join their protest. The Economic Liberation Committee made its demands because to that point the United Methodist Church had issued no formal response to the Black Manifesto, and the Board of Missions had taken no positive action. Instead, the Board of Missions had discussed a plan for involving black staff members in board decision making. Black staff members had proposed a model "based on the assumption of the total involvement of the

FIGURE 10. James Forman addresses the 1969 annual meeting of the American Baptist Convention in Seattle. Forman's demand for $60 million from the American Baptists was rejected by the convention delegates. Courtesy of the United Methodist Archives, Drew University.

black staff membership in the decision-making process of the Board relative to any decision involving black people, black communities or black nations." The proposed solution was the creation of a black task force to meet monthly to identify issues of import and the incorporation of task force members into the decision-making process. That proposal, though, did not include a direct response to the Black Manifesto.[38]

The Economic Liberation Committee called for the Board of Missions to publicly endorse the Black Manifesto's programmatic demands, hold a meeting of the executive committee of the Board of Missions to allocate $750,000 to the BEDC, and give that organization 60 percent of the income from the church's investments. In addition, it demanded that the Methodist Church raise more than $1 billion for black antipoverty agencies. The Economic Liberation Committee explained its involvement by telling other employees that its members had been "uncertain and confused as to what creative role" they might be able to play "in the face of recurring liberation confrontations, continuous closed door deliberations, threats and counter-threats, and the prospective intrusion of outside combatants." Members of the committee reported that their concern led them to support the NCBC and the BEDC. They encouraged fellow employees to read the information they had

FIGURE 11. James Forman speaks at the United Methodist Church Board of Missions executive committee conference with the Economic Liberation Committee at the New Yorker Hotel, May 26, 1969. Courtesy of the United Methodist Archives, Drew University.

collected related to the Black Manifesto. They listed contacts on each floor of the Interchurch Center for people who wanted further information and exhorted their colleagues to "Join us! Seek Justice! Share Light! Build Community!" The sit-in lasted just eight hours until the Board of Missions agreed to hold a special meeting of its executive committee on May 26 to consider these demands. Clearly, the Economic Liberation Committee represented a challenge to the status quo at 475 Riverside Drive.[39]

United Methodist Church officials tried to meet that challenge through its Board of Missions conference with the Economic Liberation Committee and James Forman on May 26. The Economic Liberation Committee was headed by Cain Felder, a black Methodist minister and the newly elected executive secretary of the Black Methodists for Church Renewal (BMCR). Forman again laid out the demands initially presented in his manifesto and called the BEDC "an attempt to forge unity among the black community, including the black caucuses within the denominations." Felder then eloquently explained the position of the Economic Liberation Committee and

The Black Manifesto   105

the BMCR. He called attention to what he described as the "brilliance of the Black Manifesto as a divine imperative in response to the spirit and celebration of Pentecost." Felder said that the most significant question raised by the Black Manifesto related to black economic control and black economic self-determination. He also claimed that the central issue was not money, but making people aware of the complexities of the experiences of black America. Felder ended his presentation by telling the executive committee: "We are not here to intimidate you. The word 'demand' is to communicate a deep urgency of the situation. We are presenting the 'demands' for your careful and deep consideration. We hope this sense of urgency is infused in you."[40]

Several others, including Lucius Walker, presented their understanding and support of the Black Manifesto. Walker explained the relationship between IFCO and the BEDC and chided church leaders for their fear of the Black Manifesto. He told the executive committee that it was "a sad moment that in session after session, churchmen, when deliberating over the Black Manifesto, sit in fear and gloom. This is a moment of celebration, not of apprehension." He argued that the church had an opportunity to use IFCO for the economic development of black communities. Walker saw the manifesto as "a moment in history which is a revelation of the truth. . . . this is a moment of celebration." To Walker, the Black Manifesto and the War on Poverty were inextricably linked.[41]

The discussion continued until late in the afternoon, when the executive committee issued a statement of proposed actions. The statement first noted that the executive committee had reexamined its responsibilities in light of the mandate of the 1968 Methodist conference, "The Church and the World." That conference had encouraged all Methodist groups to "listen intently" to "the black community, the Spanish speaking communities and the American Indians . . . and the poor," who experienced a lack of housing, employment, and educational opportunity. The conference had recommended the fuller incorporation of African Americans into decision-making positions throughout the church and advocated for church institutions to donate "substantial amounts of money" to antipoverty programs in minority communities. Given that mandate and the challenges made by Forman, Felder, and the Economic Liberation Committee, the executive committee recognized the need "for full involvement of disadvantaged peoples themselves in processes aimed at alleviating their conditions." In other words, the committee saw the importance of the maximum feasible participation of the poor in antipoverty programs. The executive committee also acknowledged its obligation "to re-examine and re-evaluate its policies, programs and priorities in order to address its energies and resources more directly to the pressing social ills of the United States."[42]

106   Chapter Four

Following a lengthy discussion of the action items, the meeting adjourned for the evening. In the morning, the executive committee passed a resolution committing $300,000 at the time and an additional $1 million later in the year "for the economic empowerment of black people," but the money would not be given directly to the BEDC. Forman saw that as an affront and angrily responded to the resolution: "white racism was expressed today in your action. . . . The Church is corrupt and the Church exploits. . . . It is not a question of money. It is a matter of principle. . . . We are going to continue to press our claims on the Church."[43] Felder followed Forman's tirade by telling the committee members that he would not "harangue" them, but the black representatives at the meeting found their proposal "wholly unacceptable" and rejected their resolution. Felder concluded his remarks by saying, "if you are so concerned about the people who gave the money, then give it back to them." For Forman, Felder, and the rest of the black representatives at the meeting, the board's refusal to allocate the money to the BEDC and IFCO was a rejection of its responsibilities.[44]

Lloyd C. Wicke, president of the Methodist Board of Missions, and Tracey K. Jones, general secretary of the Board of Missions, who had called the meeting of the executive committee, sent a memo to the board of managers of the Methodist Church two days later. Their memo in part summarized the meeting, noting that some of the individuals who confronted the Board of Missions were United Methodist ministers. The demands of the Black Manifesto and the Economic Liberation Committee were not outside demands, but were being made from within the church as well. Indeed, Wicke and Jones noted that "the issues raised are those that the entire United Methodist Church will be forced to face." Arguing that "repentance and obedience to God" was "the way of the Christian church when it faces crisis," Wicke and Jones encouraged the board members to pray to God that the Methodist Church could become "a New Church for a New World."[45]

Wicke and Jones followed that memo with a letter addressed to four other important groups in the Methodist Church: the Council of Bishops, the Program Council, the Council on World Service and Finance, and the Council of Secretaries. This letter encouraged an early meeting of each of the groups to discuss the demands of the Black Manifesto and the Economic Liberation Committee. Wicke and Jones asked them to consider if they saw the Economic Liberation Committee's demands, including the $750,000 to the BEDC, favorably. In a separate letter to Methodist pastors, Wicke and Jones noted that the executive committee had not considered the issue of reparations and the $500 million demanded by the Black Manifesto because "any response must be made by the authorities of the entire United Methodist

FIGURE 12. Cain Felder, executive director of Black Methodists for Church Renewal, speaks at the United Methodist Church Board of Missions executive committee conference with the Economic Liberation Committee at the New Yorker Hotel, May 26, 1969. Courtesy of the United Methodist Archives, Drew University.

Church. No one Board can, or should, speak for the whole church on these questions." Wicke and Jones concluded their letter by stressing the seriousness of the issue, telling the pastors, "whatever our position concerning the Manifesto and its demands, we dare not be insensitive to our failures in race relations. These must be redressed at a quickening pace. The Christian conscience can accept no less."[46]

The conflict at the Interchurch Center, which had led to the letters from Wicke and Jones, affected United Methodist groups elsewhere as well. At the United Methodist Conference of New and Furloughed Missionaries in Greencastle, Indiana, Theressa Hoover, associate general secretary of the Women's Division of the Board of Missions and the Methodists' highest-ranking black woman, said that Forman and the BEDC had "set the churches of the nation on edge" and had "pushed through the wall of 'pseudo-religion' and opened its window side." Hoover argued that if the churches could "react to the truths implicit in the demands of the Manifesto and not confuse the issue by over-

108   Chapter Four

reacting to the rhetoric and tactics, we may yet free ourselves, our religious institutions and our nation for the achievement of justice and dignity implicit in our own churchly rhetoric."[47]

The Economic Liberation Committee was not the last challenge from Interchurch Center employees. On June 5, notices were sent from the eighteenth floor of the Interchurch Center calling for a strike of all black and Puerto Rican workers to show support for the BEDC. On Friday, June 6, Forman and the Economic Liberation Committee occupied the NCC executive offices on the eighth floor of 475 Riverside Drive, barricading the elevator doors to prevent employees from entering. Forman communicated nine demands to Dr. Edwin Espy before ending the occupation three hours after it had begun. The demands included meeting the IFCO request of $270,000 for the BEDC, providing money for the NCBC to hold regional conferences, and requesting that the NCC encourage denominations to earmark money for the BEDC through IFCO. Espy agreed to have the task force investigate these demands. The following Monday, June 9, supporters of the BEDC and the manifesto called a strike. About half of the employees at 475 Riverside Drive did not report for work, either out of support for the strike or a reluctance to be involved.[48]

Forman and his supporters continued the demonstrations directed at provoking responses from a variety of Christian denominations. In early June, approximately thirty demonstrators occupied the offices of the Reformed Church in America, located on the eighteenth floor of the Interchurch Center, in an attempt to bring pressure on the General Synod of the Reformed Church. A few days later, Forman and his colleagues occupied the Board of World Ministries of the United Church of Christ on the sixteenth floor of the Interchurch Center for another one-day occupation, and they submitted a list of demands to that church.[49]

The ongoing conflict and the series of occupations of the Interchurch Center finally came to a head in mid-June. On Friday, June 13, the board of trustees of the Interchurch Center met with Forman and his associates and told them they would no longer have discussions on these topics as long as they continued the occupations of the building. The board of trustees also began the process of seeking an injunction against Forman to prevent further occupations. One bulletin issued by Forman's supporters named the "stooges" of the Rockefeller family as those in the process of pursuing the injunction. The statement ominously warned that "if they try to evict us with an injunction, there is going to be a bloody mess." On June 16, the Supreme Court of New York granted a restraining order against Forman and announced that a hearing on the injunction would be held a week later. The following day,

The Black Manifesto 109

Forman fought back, penning an angry open letter in which he challenged church leaders, emphatically telling them, "if the racist Christians have gotten an injunction, then let them enforce it, for I shall stay in the library of the United Church of Christ's Board of World Ministries . . . in solitude and confinement, reflecting upon the condition of my people and how the racist Christian churches have exploited our minds, enslaved our bodies, and owe us reparations."[50]

Forman's persistent demands and occupations eventually forced the NCC and its major denominations into action on the Black Manifesto. On Friday, June 20, Woodie White, executive secretary of the United Methodist Church's Commission on Religion and Race, called a meeting of top church officials. White told the attendees that Forman was more reasonable than the preamble to his manifesto might suggest. White said that Forman insisted that one did not need to accept his preamble in order to accept the demands of the manifesto and that he "was amazed at the support he has received from white churchmen." At the end of the meeting, the officials issued a statement acknowledging that the Black Manifesto had raised issues that opened church members "to new responsibilities to understand the crisis in our nation." The statement authorized a wide denominational study of the Black Manifesto, affirmed the need for "economic and community development under the leadership of black people," and recommended a review of various church agencies so that more resources could be committed to black community efforts, particularly black antipoverty and economic development organizations.[51]

Other top officials in the United Methodist Church presented their perspectives on the Black Manifesto and suggested possible responses. A. Dudley Ward penned what he called "A Possible Tentative Response to the Events of Our Time" on June 29. He said that the Black Manifesto had done the church "a great service" in calling for it to recognize "the actuality and necessity of black power as a fundamental instrument for constructive social change" and the need to support black antipoverty programs financially. Ward called for a "radical reordering of priorities" in the church toward investment in black economic development and antipoverty programs "so the scandal of poverty will be eliminated . . . and economic opportunity will be available to all." Ward particularly recommended that the United Methodist Church support IFCO and its antipoverty programs.[52]

The National Council of Churches had begun exploring ways to respond to the Black Manifesto shortly after its general board meeting on May 2. NCC leaders quickly established both a staff team and a task force. On June 4, the staff team's report acknowledged that responses to the manifesto needed to "strike out in new directions," including "the redistribution of power in our society." As a result, the staff team recommended "substantial and continuing action involving the churches" to eliminate social and economic injustice. On June 12, the task force recommended that the NCC executive committee recognize the BEDC as an agency working for economic development in the black community and that the NCC work with the BEDC where possible. The task force also recommended that the executive committee encourage member churches to use IFCO as the principal vehicle for donating funds for antipoverty and economic development agencies.[53]

A day after the task force's recommendations, Forman wrote to Espy, the executive director of the NCC, urging action. Claiming that the program demands of the Black Manifesto were "no longer in question" because "most Christians" had accepted the manifesto's demands, Forman insisted that the NCC needed to start producing funds "to demonstrate they are willing to fight racism, to divest the church of its financial holdings and to transfer [wealth] to black people." In other words, the NCC needed to move from words of support to action and financial commitment to black antipoverty programs.[54]

On June 23, the executive committee of the general board of the NCC, following a long day of deliberations, issued a general statement and specific recommendations in response to the manifesto. Acknowledging that it was "cognizant of the great injustices done to the black man . . . by white men, many of whom have been members of Christian Churches," the board declared its willingness to listen to any demand with "a readiness to make recompense." The board rejected "the ideology of the Black Manifesto" but acknowledged the BEDC "as a programmatic expression of the aspirations of black churchmen . . . directed toward the achievement of economic justice for the deprived peoples of this land." The executive committee urged the churches "to commit themselves to the raising of new money of massive proportions to be used exclusively for setting into motion the means whereby the poor and powerless . . . may assume control of their own lives in their own communities."[55] In other words, the NCC encouraged its member churches to support black community antipoverty agencies. And the executive committee further urged the churches to use IFCO as the vehicle for those antipoverty funds.

The executive committee then listed several recommendations for actions to be taken by the general board of the NCC. First, it recommended funding five regional conferences for black churchmen, reflecting its recognition of the influence of black power and black theology. Second, the committee requested that its member organizations contribute a combined total

The Black Manifesto

of $500,000 to IFCO and the NCBC in an effort to encourage the funding of black antipoverty efforts that emphasized community control and self-determination. Third, continuing the theme it had emphasized from the beginning of the War on Poverty, the NCC reminded member churches that it was their "moral responsibility" to encourage government support of antipoverty programs, and it advocated that the churches do just that. The executive committee also recommended the realignment of NCC program priorities to "meet more substantially" the objectives of programs dealing with the issues of poverty and race. This recommendation included an increasing emphasis on educational programs in the member churches "so they understand the dimensions of the present crisis, particularly the issues involved in the Manifesto," which the committee saw as "the intimate connection between poverty [and] race." Finally, the executive committee pledged "its determination to continue consultations with representatives of the Black Economic Development Conference and with other minority groups which are seeking ways by which civic and economic justice for deprived peoples can be attained."[56] To the NCC executive committee, then, the Black Manifesto and the BEDC, with their emphases on race, poverty, and community control of economic development, represented continuations of the War on Poverty. The NCC's initial response was to continue its emphasis on the moral imperatives of the War on Poverty and further shift its focus to support of black community antipoverty organizations through IFCO and the newly created BEDC.

In addition, the NCC executive committee voted to appoint a Committee of Sixteen to meet and negotiate with Forman and the BEDC and recommend program proposals to the executive committee by July 14. The Committee of Sixteen was composed of representatives of the eight major units of the NCC and eight members of black denominations in the NCC, the NCBC, and IFCO. The meeting concluded with a statement that the committee found itself "under Christian constraint to make every effort to understand these demands and by the grace of God to respond in ways consistent with the Gospel of Jesus Christ." The statement continued: "Cognizant of the great injustices done to the black man and the brown man by Christian white men throughout the entire history of our country to this very day we declare that we have no right under God to refuse to listen to any demand presented to us." The statement also said that "openness" was "not enough. There must be penitence and readiness to make recompense."[57]

Following the meeting, however, the NCBC declared the executive committee's decision unacceptable because it had not recognized the BEDC and it had not granted $270,000 to the BEDC through IFCO, as the BEDC had requested. The Reverend Metz Rollins, executive secretary of the NCBC, issued a statement expressing the NCBC's "bitter disappointment with the executive committee in its failure to act." Rollins claimed that blacks had "once more been shunted aside by white churchmen who continue to be insensitive to the blacks within their midst." Following this, the NCBC wrote to Arthur Flemming, president of the NCC, indicating it would not negotiate with the NCC until those demands had been met. The restraining order against Forman and the BEDC remained in effect until July 11, when the board of trustees of the Interchurch Center agreed to dismiss the case before the New York Supreme Court with the agreement that Forman and the BEDC would not disrupt or occupy the Interchurch Center as long as discussions and negotiations were ongoing.[58]

The NCBC was not alone in its rejection of the executive committee's statement and recommendations. The Ad Hoc Committee for Justice, which also called itself the Ad Hoc Committee of 475 Riverside Drive, also issued a statement after the executive committee meeting. The ad hoc committee expressed its support for the NCBC, arguing that "black churchmen understand the needs of the black community better than do white churchmen." The ad hoc committee called for the NCC to lift the injunction and respond positively to the demands of the NCBC. The ad hoc committee also announced that it would be holding a teach-in on June 25 about the Black Manifesto and events at 475 Riverside Drive.[59]

The NCBC met at the Interchurch Center over the two-day period of June 25–26. Following the meeting, the NCBC issued a statement adamantly opposing the NCC executive committee's action; since white churchmen had rejected the BEDC, the NCBC was "constrained to communicate to you that you have chosen to reject us [too]." The NCBC noted that this "was not a problem" for its members, as this was "inherently the norm in our racist society." The statement admonished the NCC executive committee that its decision to not recognize the BEDC was "a tragedy for the church, because we live in a day in which turmoil and tension offer opportunities never before seen, but you have failed to open the door to the opportunity to give black churchmen equal respect with yourselves." The NCBC did tell the executive committee that negotiations could be restarted by a formal recognition of the BEDC and a formal attempt to urge the denominations to support the $270,000 payment to the BEDC.[60]

At its July 14 meeting, the NCC executive committee continued to struggle with its decision regarding the Black Manifesto and the BEDC. Indeed, Edwin Espy, NCC general secretary, reported to the members of the general board a few days after the meeting that the discussion about the manifesto and the BEDC "was intense," and differences of opinion "ran so deep" that

The Black Manifesto   113

consensus among the groups was impossible. As a result, NCC president Flemming had called another executive committee meeting for August 28 so that it could make a recommendation to the general board, which was meeting in Indianapolis in September. Espy reported on the disruptions at the Interchurch Center, which had been ongoing since May. He told the general board that "in the midst of this atmosphere" the executive committee had "striven to arrive at a Christian and effectual response to all that is symbolized by the emergence" of the Black Manifesto and the BEDC. Espy said that the members of the executive committee were "distressed at their inability to reach consensus," and they hoped "under the guidance of the Holy Spirit" to be able to reach consensus on August 28. Espy assured the board members that, despite their differences of opinion, all members of the executive committee were "committed to massive response in appropriate forms to the deep needs" that confronted them "in the relations between the races."[61]

The lack of consensus in the executive committee reflected the deep divisions among the various departments and committees of the NCC. At the day-long July 14 meeting, which included several representatives of black caucus groups, the NCBC, and the BEDC, the executive committee had several documents written by various groups in the NCC for its consideration. They included a recommendation from the Division of Overseas Ministries, which declared the BEDC not "a suitable instrument for implementing" the NCC's "deep concern for racial and social justice"; a statement from the Committee on Racial Justice in the Division of Christian Life and Mission, which declared that a rejection of the BEDC would be "tantamount to a refusal to accept a concrete challenge to which the Church, in faith, must respond"; and a lengthy communication from a group of NCC staff members urging the executive committee "to reject the ideology of the Black Manifesto." In addition, Espy had received sixty-eight letters about the Black Manifesto and the BEDC, including twenty from general board and executive committee members. Of those sixty-eight letters, all but three expressed negative views concerning the manifesto. Clearly, the Black Manifesto and the BEDC had deeply divided the NCC, its various divisions and departments, and its member organizations.[62]

By this point, the Committee of Sixteen had already met twice. At its first meeting on June 30, the committee had voted to send a recommendation to the executive committee that acknowledged the BEDC "as a programmatic expression of the aspirations of Black Churchmen" without concurring with the ideology of the Black Manifesto. At the meeting on July 10, the Committee of Sixteen voted "to encourage the churches to make every effort to use the Interreligious Foundation for Community Organization as a broker in

114 Chapter Four

the utilization of funds available for work in rural and urban ghettos." The committee proposed that NCC member churches give $500,000 to IFCO "for the purpose of enabling black churchmen to organize their own immediate approach to their economic problem as they see it . . . with no strings attached." The recommendation further explained that the money would be an initial grant for "the development and strengthening of structures for self-determination and economic development." The committee further voted to "challenge the churches . . . to make inquiry concerning their moral responsibility as citizens of this land to adopt procedures which will enable their moral force to be felt in all the chambers of government" and to encourage further federal antipoverty efforts. This recommendation was considered by the executive committee at its July 14 meeting, but a decision on the matter was postponed until its meeting in August.[63]

When the Committee of Sixteen—a group that one participant saw as "rather heavily loaded with Presbyterians"—met again on July 21, it had received back from the executive committee the recommendations it had previously made. After significant deliberation, the committee essentially reaffirmed its previous recommendations with minor revisions. In addition, it approved a task force to explore the readiness of IFCO, the BEDC, and the NCBC to receive funds for antipoverty activities. And it created another task force to act as a liaison between the Committee of Sixteen and the BEDC, IFCO, and the NCBC. Finally, the committee emphasized the need to involve churches and agencies in the local communities and not just focus on the national bureaucratic response. Flemming concluded the meeting by saying, "we need dialogue at the grass roots."[64]

When the Committee of Sixteen met again in late August, it discussed and debated reports from the task forces created at the previous meeting. A good part of the discussion centered on whether the NCC's and its member churches' funds should be given to IFCO, the NCBC, or some combination of the two. Members of the NCBC felt that IFCO had more experience in the area and would be the more appropriate agency to grant funds to antipoverty and economic development agencies in black communities. NCBC members also did not want to be seen as an alternative funding agency "in opposition to IFCO." Some at the meeting questioned whether IFCO had adequate representation on its board from black churches. Espy argued that the real issue was not whether the money was given to IFCO or the NCBC, but the NCC's response to "the fundamental problems" in American society. He said that unless the NCC did something at the general board meeting in September "commensurate with the crisis," it would lose "an opportunity to serve as a catalyst." Ultimately, the Committee of Sixteen recommended that the NCC

The Black Manifesto 115

at its September general board meeting determine to give $500,000 to a combination of IFCO and the NCBC.[65]

At about the same time as the Committee of Sixteen meeting in August, Tracey K. Jones summarized the response of the United Methodist Board of Missions to the Black Manifesto. Stating that the demands made by Forman and the BEDC for "justice, economic betterment, fuller humanity and dignity for all men" were "entirely consistent with . . . the Gospel of Jesus Christ," he laid out specific developments. Jones noted that at the annual meeting of the Board of Missions in September, the board would have specific proposals for black economic development and give further consideration to the resolution of the general executive committee for an additional $1 million for black economic empowerment. In addition, the Board of Missions would review all commitments, investments, and relationships in South Africa; plan to provide aid to black colleges; and provide education to United Methodist congregations to help them understand more clearly the issues raised by the Black Manifesto and use their influence to support continued antipoverty efforts, particularly in black communities.[66]

At its general board meeting in Indianapolis in September, the NCC, on a divided vote, supported a proposal to ask its member churches to give $600,000 to the National Committee of Black Churchmen. The board also passed, again on a divided vote, a measure to establish a fund to eventually reach several million dollars for black antipoverty and economic development projects. These measures were merely suggestions to the member churches, however. No funds for either of them would come directly from the NCC itself, and none of the money in either of the proposals would go directly to the BEDC. Instead, funds would go to the NCBC, IFCO, and other black-controlled organizations.[67] Importantly, some NCC member churches, especially the Disciples of Christ, had pushed hard for the NCC to repudiate the ideology and methods of the manifesto and to place some limits on the money given to IFCO and the NCBC. A majority of the NCC board and advocates for black control of economic resources, though, opposed those moves as denigrating to African Americans. As a result, the board moved forward with funding for the NCBC and IFCO.[68]

While the NCC and the United Methodists carefully considered their responses to the manifesto through the summer, IFCO found itself in turmoil. The IFCO board had met on May 6, two days after Forman's appearance at Riverside Church and about a week after the NBEDC, at the special request of Lucius Walker. Prior to the meeting of the whole board and reflecting the influence of black power as well as the strong differences of opinion on the direction of the agency, the IFCO board met in separate caucuses for black and white members. After the caucuses, the board followed the recommendations of the black caucus and recognized the BEDC as a new organization that would function separately from IFCO but could receive IFCO funds. IFCO would serve as a conduit for funds to the BEDC, but any funds donated to IFCO would have to be specifically earmarked for the BEDC. During the meeting, Walker argued that if the BEDC "had not been relevant to the black community, it would not have been used as a basis for stating a militant viewpoint and there would have been no subsequent efforts to relate to IFCO." The board asked the churches to supply $270,000 in funds to help launch the activities of the BEDC. In addition, IFCO adamantly affirmed the programmatic aspects of the Black Manifesto without specifically endorsing the controversial preamble. Expressing his and IFCO's support for the manifesto, Walker emphatically told the board, "we swing with this and our example should be followed by the churches whose broker we are with the black community."[69]

The white IFCO caucus issued a strong rebuttal to the IFCO board's recommendations. In a statement crafted by IFCO president Marc Tanenbaum, the white members insisted that they remained committed to the original purposes of IFCO, which they saw as the creation of "a coalition of black and white leaders dedicated to overcoming racial injustices in America through collaborative development of . . . programs of economic self-determination, leadership training, and community organization on the part of the poor." The statement argued that while IFCO was receptive to proposals that addressed racial and economic injustice, the white caucus could not accept the Black Manifesto because it created "serious problems of conscience for all who are committed to social reform through the democratic process." Complaining of the "Marxist-Leninist doctrine" of the manifesto, Tanenbaum's statement said that accepting the ideological framework of the manifesto would be "an invitation to national suicide." Noting that the white caucus did not condone the disruption of services in churches and synagogues, the statement rejected what the author saw as "revolutionary ideologies [and] racist theories."[70]

The statement by Tanenbaum differed significantly from Walker's statements and demonstrated a serious chasm in perspective and ideology. Indeed, Tanenbaum admitted that his differences with Walker over the Black Manifesto posed a "serious internal crisis within IFCO." While Walker argued that the board supported the principle of the manifesto, Tanenbaum claimed that the board did not support it. Tanenbaum expressed disappointment and unhappiness at developments that made it appear that IFCO had been "publicly implicated in endorsing and support[ing] policies and programs of the

Black Manifesto." Tanenbaum acknowledged, however, that while the white board members had shown some "positive sentiment" toward his position, they had not officially voted to support his statement, which urged them to repudiate the ideology and rhetoric of the manifesto. Tanenbaum also admitted that his disagreement with Walker and the internal strife in the organization had deflected attention from IFCO's accomplishments and had "clouded IFCO's future potential," which he regretted.[71]

The statement by Tanenbaum was reflected in positions taken by Jewish religious organizations. Indeed, Jewish agencies took the strongest stand against the ideology and recommendations of the Black Manifesto of any of the major religious organizations. For example, on May 12, the Synagogue Council of America (which included the Rabbinical Council of America and the Central Conference of American Rabbis) and the National Jewish Community Relations Advisory Council (which included the American Jewish Committee, the American Jewish Congress, and B'nai B'rith) issued a joint statement on the Black Manifesto addressing both the substance of the demands and the tactics employed (i.e., the disruptions in churches and synagogues). These two Jewish organizations found both the demands and the tactics "objectionable on both moral and practical grounds." The joint statement argued that better approaches to racial injustice could be found in the Kerner Commission report, the Freedom Budget of the A. Philip Randolph Institute, and the National Urban League's Domestic Marshall Plan, all of which advocated for an expanded government presence in employment, housing, education, and welfare. The statement urged congregations to encourage more government spending on social programs. The two councils also rejected the manifesto for what they saw as the encouragement of violent actions against religious institutions.[72]

At its next meeting following the joint statement, the AJC executive committee reported that the AJC supported Tanenbaum and had urged IFCO to dissociate itself from the Black Manifesto. IFCO had refused to do so and officially had come out in support of the principle, substance, and programmatic implications of the manifesto. Bertram Gold, executive vice president of the AJC, wrote to Walker on May 7 informing him that as a result of the IFCO board's decision, "the matter of [AJC's] relationship to IFCO" was being brought to the AJC board for review. Gold concluded his letter by noting that the AJC could not "support the ideological principles and the specific tactics contained in the Black Manifesto." The AJC executive committee then voted to "instruct AJC's officers to initiate our withdrawal as an organizational member of IFCO." In addition, Tanenbaum issued his letter of resignation as president of IFCO.[73]

118 Chapter Four

The AJC executive committee adopted a resolution on the Black Manifesto, highlighting the AJC's role in the founding and initial direction of IFCO. The resolution noted that it was "with keen regret" that the AJC had viewed "the events of recent weeks which have resulted in widespread confusion regarding the present status of IFCO. The identification of IFCO in statements and actions with the Black Manifesto and its spokesmen" had become "the source of deepest concern" to the AJC because it had rejected the "substance and tactics" of the Black Manifesto "on moral and practical grounds." The resolution lamented that "despite urging IFCO has not dissociated itself from the manifesto. As a matter of conscience, therefore, regretfully, we instruct AJC's officers to initiate our withdrawal as an organizational member of IFCO." The resolution officially withdrew the AJC from IFCO, but also noted that if IFCO decided to "effect changes that would sustain and advance its original purposes and policies," the AJC would be willing to reconsider its decision to withdraw. The resolution further noted that the agency would "continue its commitment to the cause of social justice, with a renewed determination to help translate into reality the original objectives of IFCO."[74]

The day following the AJC's resolution and withdrawal from IFCO, Walker wrote a blistering letter to Gold about what he saw as the AJC's lack of support for IFCO. Walker castigated the AJC for contributing only $3,000 to IFCO over the previous two years and noted that no other Jewish agencies had made any contributions to IFCO. Walker told Gold that "to withdraw from IFCO because we pledge our meager help to people who have a case against the inhuman indifference of their fellow man would only add proof that others do not care and mitigate against IFCO's efforts to win viable change without violence." Walker's attempt to convince Gold and the AJC, however, failed.[75]

Tanenbaum clarified his own position in letters he wrote to friends and associates who had queried him about the issue. In these letters, he noted that he supported "entirely the principles of self-determination and community organization that IFCO and Lu Walker stand for, but [he] believe[d] that flamboyant calls to destroy America are counterproductive to the best interests of this important social revolution of the poor and deprived in America." He said that he continued to feel "admiration and personal friendship" toward Walker even though they did "differ on this issue."[76]

Following their joint statement on the Black Manifesto, the Synagogue Council of America and the National Jewish Community Relations Advisory Council each developed and distributed to their members guidelines for dealing with James Forman or other representatives of the BEDC who might disrupt services in synagogues. Both sets of guidelines recommended that in the event that someone interrupted a service, they should be told that they could read their demands at the end of the service. Both groups also recommended that if Forman or his representative insisted on reading demands in the middle of the service, he should be allowed to do so because "the disruptions and publicity that attend their arrest by police during services is precisely the sort of thing that Forman and his associates demand." Synagogues and Jewish community agencies should encourage Forman and his associates with the BEDC to leave, but not force them to do so. The synagogues and Jewish agencies wanted as little publicity as possible for Forman, his ideology, and his tactics.[77] Essentially, all Jewish organizations cut their ties with Forman and with IFCO.

The response of Jewish social service and community agencies reflected the internal divisions that James Forman and his Black Manifesto created, both in terms of civil rights and black power and in terms of the War on Poverty. Forman's manifesto served as a symbol of the movement toward black power and black theology and also the links between those developments and black community antipoverty agencies. Some religious organizations, like the AJC, that had supported the civil rights movement and the War on Poverty, as well as IFCO's move toward black community control of antipoverty agencies, outright rejected the manifesto and the black power antipoverty agencies that would benefit from Forman's demands. Some, like the Presbyterian Church, offered significant support, while many others, including the NCC, the Methodist Church, and the Catholic Church, offered a mixture of support and rejection.

James Forman's Black Manifesto transformed the relationship between leading religious institutions, the civil rights/black power movement, and the War on Poverty. Over time, the cracks in the ecumenical antipoverty coalition of liberal Protestant, Catholic, and Jewish support for both the War on Poverty and nascent black power organizations became giant fractures within the congregations of those religious institutions that caused irreparable damage to religion-based support for antipoverty agencies operating in black and brown communities. Those cracks also became irreparable fissures within many of those religious denominations, some of which have never healed. The Black Manifesto transformed the black power movement, the War on Poverty, and the ecumenical antipoverty coalition that had supported both.

CHAPTER FIVE

Fracturing the Antipoverty Coalition
The Aftermath of the Black Manifesto

While many religious organizations that had supported the War on Poverty and the Interreligious Foundation for Community Organization (IFCO) vigorously debated their positions on the Black Manifesto in conferences and meetings throughout the summer of 1969, denominational leaders, rabbis, ministers, pastors, and the people who sat in the pews in the churches and synagogues expressed their opinions on the matter as well. Those opinions reflected the growing division in the United States over the War on Poverty and the evolving civil rights/black power movement. As the War on Poverty became more linked to black power, in part as a result of the Black Manifesto, opposition to the War on Poverty grew. Indeed, the Johnson administration had faced increased opposition to funding the Office of Economic Opportunity (OEO) each successive year of the agency's existence. And the OEO had experienced declining support from President Lyndon Johnson himself, who had been consumed by the Vietnam War.

In 1969, there was a hostile new administration in the White House, with a president, Richard Nixon, who had advocated cuts to the OEO in his campaign. The War on Poverty had gone from one of the more popular programs of Johnson's Great Society to one of the most controversial. James Forman's Black Manifesto, which directly linked the burgeoning black power movement to the War on Poverty, both created more controversy and further divided the American public over black power and the War on Poverty. Indeed, the unpopularity of the Black Manifesto—only 2 percent of whites and 21 percent of blacks supported it—helped make the War on Poverty more unpopular as well.[1] Just as important, the responses of churches, synagogues, and their congregants to the Black Manifesto fractured the once-firm antipoverty coalition.

"Indiana has become the battleground for one of the most important conflicts facing Christianity in modern times," claimed the *Indianapolis News* in September 1969 as both the National Council of Churches (NCC) and the Episcopal Church held their general conventions in that state. Hyperbole used to sell papers, perhaps, but to many members of the Episcopal Church and the NCC, the tension was palpable. Some church officials believed that the conflict over the Black Manifesto and the churches' response to it had "ominous potential [for] a wide and permanent schism in the Christian world." The Episcopal general convention at the University of Notre Dame was particularly heated, with delegates supportive of and opposed to reparations often shouting over each other. Initially, the delegates voted in favor of granting money for reparations—but through Episcopal Church agencies, not through the Black Economic Development Conference (BEDC). After impassioned pleas from black clergy, the delegates agreed to donate $200,000 to the National Committee of Black Churchmen (NCBC) to give to the BEDC. Bishop William Marmion, who served on the committee given the task of raising the $200,000 for the NCBC, argued that the money was not "a capitulation to a threat or a payment of blackmail or a sop to our own guilty consciences, but rather . . . it is a solid investment in creative efforts to solve the problems of racism, injustice and poverty." Bishop John Craine seconded Marmion's thoughts, telling Episcopalians that the general convention "took action on behalf of our black clergy and laity in their efforts to . . . minister to the needs of their own people. . . . This is in no way connected with what many of us considered to be a false principle of reparations, nor was it in any measure a capitulation to the Black Manifesto." Rather than donate money to the BEDC, the Episcopal Church, much like the NCC, decided to give funds for antipoverty programs to the ecumenical NCBC. Many present at both conferences rightfully feared divisions within individual churches, denominations, and interdenominational groups, like the NCC. The heated arguments and debates over the manifesto and its meaning to churches spread from the conventions to local churches and individual church members.[2]

While many churches and congregants expressed opposition to the Black Manifesto and/or the churches' response to it, some churches, congregations, and religious individuals supported the manifesto and its demands. Responses

122 Chapter Five

were varied and complex. One of the earliest expressions of support for the Black Manifesto came from Stephen Rose, a leader of the Student Interracial Ministry, a seminary student–based, interracial civil rights organization. Rose, a veteran of the civil rights movement, had authored several books on interracialism and church reform, most notably *The Grass Roots Church* in 1966. In that work, he had argued for a "renewal movement" of churches that would be "radically ecumenical." According to Rose, churches that were part of the renewal movement should actively support social causes, especially those related to race and poverty. He heartily endorsed Forman's manifesto and encouraged churches to target their financing specifically toward black antipoverty and economic development projects, arguing in the pages of *Renewal*, the liberal religious magazine he created and edited, that "morally speaking, the case for reparations is clear."[3]

Rose said that his Grass Roots Manifesto and Forman's Black Manifesto were interrelated. Both, in Rose's estimation, told the truth about the hierarchy of the religious establishment and the need for change. Rose conceded that the Black Manifesto was "more realistic" about the possibilities of implementing reform than was his Grass Roots Manifesto. To him, the difference between the two was that the Grass Roots Manifesto advocated structural renewal and the Black Manifesto articulated a revolutionary commitment. Rose agreed that the structural renewal he called for required a complete investment on the part of the churches to reparations and to support of black antipoverty and economic development programs.[4]

Another expression of support for the manifesto came from the Second United Methodist Conference of New and Furloughed Missionaries. Writing to Lloyd Wicke, Tracey Jones, and the United Methodist Board of Missions in June 1969, as the Board of Missions was deliberating its position on the Black Manifesto, the members of this conference of missionaries said that the manifesto expressed "the anguish and bold determination of the black community." The Black Manifesto reminded the letter writers of "long ages of injustice against black people . . . in which [the church and its] overwhelmingly white structures are still involved." These former missionaries affirmed their support of the Board of Missions and urged it "to reconsider the means by which funds will be channeled and used under the complete control of black leadership for black economic development and self-determination." The former missionaries supported both the Black Manifesto and the designation of Methodist funds to IFCO and black antipoverty organizations.[5]

The executive committee of the Division of Christian Social Concern of the American Baptist Convention expressed similar sentiments. In a pastoral letter to American Baptist churches, the leaders of the Division of Christian

Social Concern recognized that the manifesto had "occasioned a great deal of dismay and controversy" among American Baptists. While disavowing the ideology of the manifesto, the committee argued that its denomination could not "afford the luxury of believing that the grave ills which beset our nation can be confronted and healed without the abrasive conflict which these angry and desperate voices represent." The committee viewed Forman's demand for reparations "as a gift of God's mercy and grace, a unique opportunity to begin the process of cleansing our churches of the sickness of racism." To the committee, repentance meant "the redressing of past inequities." In order to repent of the sins of slavery and racism, the committee recommended that American Baptist churches donate to IFCO and its antipoverty programs. The American Baptist Division of Christian Social Concern, then, gave the Black Manifesto and IFCO its full-throated support.[6]

Other Protestant religious bodies had very different perspectives on the Black Manifesto. The executive committee of the Division of Overseas Ministries of the NCC saw the manifesto as calling for the overthrow of the social, political, and economic system in the United States through violence to establish "control by the black minority of the population." As a result, the Division of Overseas Ministries completely rejected Forman, the manifesto, the BEDC, and the demands being made to the NCC.[7]

Church parishioners began sending letters and telegrams to church officials in the immediate aftermath of Forman's manifesto and his interruption of services at Riverside Church. The mail regarding the manifesto inundated the offices of Jones and Wicke of the United Methodist Church to the point that staffers tallied it. Between mid-May and mid-August 1969, Jones's and Wicke's offices received more than 350 letters addressing the Black Manifesto and the executive committee's response. United Methodist staff compiled statistics about the region where the letter writer lived, information about the individual letter writer, and, most important, the nature of the writer's reaction to the Black Manifesto and the executive committee's action. Assessing the data, United Methodist staff determined that only 47 of the letters supported the manifesto and the United Methodist support of it; another 73 expressed no opinion, but asked questions about it; and an overwhelming majority of 234 of 354 letter writers opposed the Black Manifesto and/or the executive committee's support of it (101 of those—the largest number by far—were from the Southeast region). Many of the writers, as described by Methodist staff, "launch[ed] off into a discourse reflecting extreme conservatism or racial prejudice." This analysis demonstrated that there was strong opposition to the Black Manifesto and its support of IFCO and black antipoverty programs.[8]

124   Chapter Five

Four themes dominated the disapproving letters. First, many argued that the Board of Missions had "capitulated to coercion" by granting funds to IFCO and other groups. Most of those letters included a disclaimer that the writer was not against supporting the poor and had supported civil rights in the past. A second theme was that the Methodist Church, which had for so long supported civil rights and integration, was now advocating for racial separatism with its support of the Black Manifesto. Third, some letter writers argued that allocating $300,000 for IFCO and antipoverty programs would endanger support for other church social programs. Finally, a sizable minority of the letters expressed blatant racism or antipathy toward blacks. An examination of some of these letters is important in determining how ordinary whites in the church pews responded to the Black Manifesto and their church's support of it.[9] Their renouncing of the manifesto seemed to fuel their opposition to the War on Poverty. And some of the churches, once among the strongest supporters of the War on Poverty, in response to the Black Manifesto, distanced themselves from it.

One prime example of the letters written to the Board of Missions addresses at least three of the themes identified above. Written by Mrs. Paul Rundle of Ellicott City, Maryland, the seven-page letter reflects the reaction of many white churchgoers to the Black Manifesto. Rundle opened her letter by noting that she had seen something on the news the previous night "that really made me sick." What caused that reaction was the decision by the Board of Missions to give $300,000 to "the militant black leader." Rundle wanted the board to know that she was no racist: "before you file this letter in the wastebasket let me tell you that I have and do support the decisions of the Board of Missions . . . to help those who suffer in our society." She named specifically her support of the Delta Ministry and the Fund for Reconciliation. Rundle emphasized her lack of prejudice: "I believe and work for equality and justice for all Americans regardless of race or color. I work with and have many friends who are of other races and I agree that there have been injustices."[10]

Rundle's first objection to Methodist support of the manifesto's demands was that Forman's manifesto amounted to coercion, and the United Methodist Church "should not bow to the militants." As she saw it, giving in to Forman's demands would "*undermine* the work of many black ministers and workers who are trying to bring about reconciliation between the races . . . and the work and effectiveness of white liberals who try to raise the money for the Board of Missions in the local churches." For Rundle, the lesson from the board's actions was that "there can be no reconciliation—only black power and more militants and worse tactics." She then added dramatically that if the church continued to cave in to the demands of militants like Forman, "historians will be writing on the rise and fall of the USA."[11]

Rundle's second objection was that reparations could not work. Asking "once you capitulate on their terms where do you stop," Rundle noted that other nonwhite groups in the United States, particularly "American Indians," had legitimate claims of mistreatment as well. Giving in to Forman's demands would simply lead to more demands from other groups. She also believed that reparations would not work because they would not "get to the people they are intended to help." In her vision, Forman would pocket most of the money, leaving little for people in need.[12]

Rundle then essentially questioned the faith of the members of the Board of Missions. She wondered if the board had "reached this decision with prayer and with the guidance of the Holy Spirit. From here it does not look like the kind of decision Our Lord would have reached." Noting that the United Church of Christ "decided to make *no* contribution," Rundle told the board that "God couldn't have been leading *all* of you." She ended her letter with some questions, including whom the $300,000 would go to and how it would be managed. But the two central questions she posed were these: "How do we explain this action to those who are less liberal than we?" and "Do you really feel this is God's will?" Clearly, Rundle did not believe that giving $300,000 to IFCO was God's will. The actions of the Board of Missions had her questioning her church and the faith of its leaders.[13]

Other letters to church officials raised fewer questions and instead leveled racist harangues at Forman and church leaders. On May 7, just a few days after Forman interrupted the services at Riverside Church, Mrs. Mary Dollger of New York wrote to the Reverend Jon Regier of the NCC blasting Forman and the NCC. In her letter, Dollger made no pretense of being a liberal on issues of race. She told Regier, "what that Negro James Forman did and what he demands are outrageous. His acts are typical of bold, brazen, violent, white-hater Negroes and to cater to that man will denote *weakness*. Remember—'Give a Negro a bone and he wants the carcass.'" Reflecting on her grandparents, who lived in poverty during the Civil War, Dollger argued: "I do not agree that there is any guilt on the part of whites. There is no Negro today who lives in the poverty my grandparents lived in. . . . Negroes today enjoy relief money and have the time to riot—not to work. My folks were worse than slaves, Rev. Regier—slaves were guaranteed food—I repeat. I owe Negroes *nothing* and *neither does any white*."[14]

Dollger then urged Regier to not give in to Forman's demands and chided him for considering it: "Imagine him threatening to kill us if his demands are not met! Will you bow to that? For shame!" She then asked, "Have you and all

126   Chapter Five

the rest of the clergymen had the Hell scared out of you? I say again, 'Shame on you if you give one bit of attention or one dollar to that Forman who plans with his people to take over our country.' Forman *must be squelched.*" Dollger then left no doubt about the racist underpinnings of her diatribe. She concluded her letter by telling Regier, "that guy Forman should take all of his people to Africa where they can live as their tribes do. . . . This is a *white* country. . . . Forman should be thrown into jail or kicked out to Africa."[15]

Some fundamentalist church leaders expressed similar opinions as Dollger. The Reverend Carl McIntire, a conservative fundamentalist radio preacher and president of the International Council of Christian Churches, posted a "Christian Manifesto" on the door of Riverside Church in September 1969. McIntire's manifesto called Forman's document the "voice of hell" and demanded $3 billion in reparations from "liberal churches" for their apostasy and for stealing the truth from fundamentalists.[16]

Most expressions of opposition to the manifesto were not posted on church doors. In addition to letters written to church leaders, many mainline Protestant churchgoers voiced their opinions on the Black Manifesto and the War on Poverty in the pages of church newsletters. The September 1969 issue of the *Christian Advocate*, a United Methodist Church magazine, for instance, contained a number of letters by Methodist parishioners addressing the Black Manifesto and the article about it in the previous issue of the *Christian Advocate*. Letters to the editors in this issue tended to reflect some of the same objections to the manifesto raised by Rundle, rather than the blatant racism expressed by Dollger. For instance, a letter from Paul Beck of Ambler, Pennsylvania, noted that he felt "great disappointment and a sense of being sold out" after reading the magazine's piece on the manifesto. Beck concluded his letter by saying: "I support justice for all, especially for the oppressed persons in our land, but I do not support any part of the Black Manifesto and its philosophy."[17]

Other letter writers were more expansive in explaining their opposition to the manifesto. Hugh Fouke of Indianapolis said that the manifesto was "a caustic, smart-aleck appraisal of the desire of a few Negroes to get a very large donation for their reparations. . . . I do not think that their appraisal of the church of Jesus Christ and some supposed need for millions or billions of dollars should be any basis for a Christian response." Fouke claimed that churches had spent millions over the years supporting black churches and colleges, an effort that he believed had been lost on Forman. Fouke concluded by arguing that Methodists should not "be browbeaten into offering untrained, uneducated, and inexperienced Negroes millions of dollars which they know nothing about administering."[18]

Letter writer Hugh Barber of Trussville, Alabama, also said that the concept of reparations was misguided. Calling Forman "an opportunist and a blackmailer" and reparations "unintelligent and impractical," Barber argued that "no sum of money can ever make reparations for the injustice of slavery as practiced in this nation." He found reparations absurd in part because "no black man living in America today was ever a slave in the United States." Like other letter writers, Barber emphasized the social programs and other efforts of the Methodist Church and its affiliates toward the poor. He warned that if the Methodist Church continued to give money and support to Forman, it would "cost the United Methodist Church millions of dollars, the departure of thousands of sincere and devoted Christians from its fellowship, and . . . do irreparable hurt to every missionary program of Methodism." Further, "many wonderful leaders of United Methodism . . . will be forced into silence or into untenable positions of restricted activity."[19]

In addition to letters from church members, Jones and Wicke received mail from Methodist ministers from across the country who expressed their own and their parishioners' objections to United Methodist support of the Black Manifesto and IFCO. N. C. McPherson, the senior minister at Grace United Methodist Church in Dayton, Ohio, wrote a letter to Jones that provides a prime example of these communications. McPherson told Jones that he was "greatly surprised, as were millions of Methodists," when he learned of the Board of Missions vote to appropriate $300,000 to IFCO in response to Forman's demands. McPherson noted that he and his congregation had direct experience with the manifesto, as Charles Tate, a representative of the BEDC, had interrupted their services on May 18 to read it. McPherson said that his church "has black members who are greatly disturbed by this illegal invasion of our worship service and the foolish demands of this small group of blacks; certainly, our white members are distressed also."[20]

McPherson outlined four objections to the Board of Missions decision. He reminded Jones that the United Methodist Church was winding up a campaign to raise $20 million for the Fund for Reconciliation, which, according to McPherson, would provide a large percentage of its funds "to aid the black people of our country." Implicit in this argument was that one organization providing funds for black people was enough. Second, McPherson claimed that the Board of Missions had caved in to Forman's demands, which amounted to extortion. His third objection centered on the question of integration versus racial separatism. As McPherson saw it, the United Methodists had been "working for a long time to overcome segregation in the church. . . . We are an integrated church and many of our local congregations are integrated or fast becoming integrated." Given that move toward

128   Chapter Five

integration, McPherson questioned why the Board of Missions would create a committee composed solely of black churchmen to administer the funds to IFCO. Reflecting the difficulty many whites had in understanding black power, McPherson argued, "this is segregation, no matter what you may want to call it!" Finally, McPherson noted that it would be very difficult to sell this to people in his church. He told Jones that he would do everything in his power "to prevent a 'laymen's rebellion,' but it is not going to be easy." McPherson concluded by saying that he prayed the Methodists would not do anything "under the pressure of threats" from Forman and his allies. He questioned the wisdom of continuing the funding of IFCO, "unless they set their own house in order and decide whether they are to be an arm of the churches or the Black Manifesto group."[21] To McPherson and many other Methodists, IFCO's affiliation with Forman and the Black Manifesto made it highly suspect and likely unworthy of continued financial support from the churches and their congregants.

Representatives of other Methodist groups also warned of the fracturing of the church that could be caused by the Black Manifesto. Bishop J. Gordon Howard, head of the United Methodist Churches of the Philadelphia Area, reported to his constituents on the Black Manifesto and on the church's deliberations and debates about it. He emphasized that divisions and disagreements should not "sour the relations between black and white United Methodists." Howard adamantly encouraged the members of Philadelphia Methodist churches, regardless of their perspective on the Black Manifesto and the BEDC, to continue to support official United Methodist agencies that supported black antipoverty and economic development programs, such as the Fund for Reconciliation.[22]

Bishop Roy Short, president of the Southeastern Jurisdictional Council of the United Methodist Church, expounded on the responses of his council. According to Short, the immediate reaction to the Black Manifesto by many in the church was shock at both the language and the call for violence. The second result of the manifesto, as Short saw it, was division within the leadership of the churches. Noting that the resulting cleavage had "sometimes been sharp and deep," he said that denominational responses had varied, but most had responded with some sort of support for antipoverty projects aimed at black communities. Short further noted that the Methodist response included allocating $160,000 to the Black Methodists for Church Renewal (BMCR) and that the BMCR was planning on requesting funding of $3 million from the general conference in 1970. Of that $3 million, $1 million would go directly to the BMCR, $1 million to the BEDC, and $1 million to IFCO and its antipoverty programs.[23] Short's response reflected the ongoing

Fracturing the Antipoverty Coalition 129

debates in the United Methodist Church over the Black Manifesto and the funding of antipoverty programs.

Bishop W. Ralph Ward of Syracuse, New York, in a speech delivered to the Western New York Annual Conference of the United Methodist Church, acknowledged the realities of the black experience: the Black Manifesto came out of "the ghetto, the poverty, the discrimination black persons in this otherwise affluent society daily endure." But Ward said he could not "in conscience accept or support" the ideological framework of the manifesto. He acknowledged, however, that the churches had the resources to fulfill Forman's requests and that the Methodist Church needed to create new priorities, such as including more African Americans in decision-making positions, to address some of the issues Forman's manifesto raised, whether the church decided to meet his funding demands or not.[24]

Other prominent Methodist leaders also expressed strong concerns about the Black Manifesto. In August 1969, Reuben Mueller, who as president of the NCC from 1963 to 1966 had actively campaigned for civil rights legislation and testified in support of the War on Poverty, issued a blistering attack against the manifesto in the pages of *Together*, the United Methodist denominational magazine. While acknowledging the significance of slavery and racism to the American past and present, Mueller called Forman's demands for reparations "preposterous," and he blamed a black power "minority" who had "rejected integration." He noted the angry responses from many white churchgoers in letters sent to him. According to Mueller, the letter writers "vehemently" opposed granting any church money to Forman or the BEDC. As a result, Mueller recommended rejecting the Black Manifesto, but encouraged Methodists to continue to support the Fund for Reconciliation and other Methodist antipoverty and black economic development programs.[25]

The United Methodist Church Women's Division (now United Methodist Women), which was actively involved in the War on Poverty, debated and considered the Black Manifesto and its meaning to the church. In an article in *Response*, the magazine of the Women's Division, Carolyn Wilhelm, the secretary for racial justice in the Women's Division, presented an extensive analysis of the manifesto and possible responses to it. Arguing that the crisis presented by the Black Manifesto could "mean danger or new opportunity," Wilhelm noted that the choices made would "make a difference for the way we will live in 1990." She linked Forman's demands to poverty in America and antipoverty efforts, particularly the Poor People's Campaign. Wilhelm said that together the Black Manifesto and the Poor People's Campaign highlighted "the inadequacy of [the churches'] action in fulfilling the American commitment for equality and justice for all." She encouraged her readers to "search out the meaning and the possibility of 'reparations'" and to consider how churchwomen would attempt to meet the needs raised by the manifesto and the Poor People's Campaign. Wilhelm clearly saw a direct link between antipoverty efforts and the Black Manifesto.[26]

Meanwhile, United Methodist leaders gave the manifesto and the church's response to it long and thoughtful consideration. In general, the church leadership was able to agree that the manifesto had challenged "the conscience of the church by activating nascent values of restitution" and had "shaken the structure of the church to rethink its priorities." Church leaders saw the manifesto as an opportunity for the church to address issues of structural racism. In discussions throughout the summer, church leaders agreed that one possible approach would be to work with black religious organizations, like the NCBC and the BMCR, as well as with IFCO. Working with those organizations would help redirect the energies and resources of the church toward addressing issues of racism and poverty. This summer-long process of developing a response to the Black Manifesto influenced the United Methodist Board of Missions annual meeting in the fall.[27]

The Board of Missions of the United Methodists held its annual meeting in Boston in October. The board again rejected giving any funds to the BEDC, now seen as much too controversial to support. Instead, the board voted to spend $1.3 million for a variety of educational and antipoverty projects. More than $500,000 would go to support black United Methodist colleges. The remainder was designated for antipoverty programs "expressing self-determination . . . of black or brown communities." The antipoverty agency receiving the largest donation—$300,000—was IFCO. In addition, $50,000 was earmarked for the NCBC for programs focused on economic development and $25,000 went to the BMCR, an amount that group saw as inadequate. Although James Forman and the Black Manifesto had not been successful in convincing the United Methodist Board of Missions to give money to the BEDC, they had convinced a significant majority of the board members to contribute more to antipoverty and economic development projects, particularly those targeting black and brown communities.[28]

Of course, other Protestant denominations wrestled with the meaning of the Black Manifesto as well and arrived at their own interpretations and responses. Some Protestant denominations contributed to black church organizations. The response of the general board of the Disciples of Christ (also known as the Christian Church), a denominational member of the NCC, reflected the thoughtfulness with which many of the NCC members approached the manifesto. The official view of the Disciples of Christ was that the manifesto did not allow for an "easy yes or no." Arguing that the manifesto contained "an ideology we cannot accept, a methodology we cannot approve, and a language which we feel is excessive and inflammatory," the general board of the Christian Church also noted that the manifesto had raised issues central to American life, which required "a radical change in attitude and commitment." On the whole, though, the official position of the Disciples of Christ was to reject much of the language and ideology of the manifesto. In a detailed exposition, church leaders rejected what they saw as the racism, call to violence, black separatism, extortion, revenge, and "blanket denunciation" of the church in the manifesto. They encouraged the NCC to repudiate the ideology and methods of the manifesto and to attach some strings for any money given to IFCO and the NCBC, namely that any money given to them not go to the BEDC.[29]

The general board of the Disciples of Christ also recommended a series of actions in response to the Black Manifesto. Importantly, the item at the top of its list was an expansion of the War on Poverty. Calling for church members to support legislation and actions that would "materially change the plight of the poor, many of whom are minority persons," Disciples of Christ leaders stated that the War on Poverty had been a "limited effort" to that point and required significant expansion. The Disciples of Christ called on its member churches to donate 5–10 percent of their funds to antipoverty programs and programs that addressed the "urban crisis." The board recommended that church units invest 15 percent of their funds in institutions that loaned money to the poor and racial minorities and encouraged the development of multiracial staff in all church organizations. The general board brought those recommendations to the general assembly of the church, which met in Seattle in August 1969.[30]

In July 1969, the Reverend George Beazley Jr., a Disciples of Christ minister, authored a column in the newsletter of the Council on Christian Unity, explaining the Black Manifesto and the response of the Disciples of Christ. The Council on Christian Unity was created in 1910 by the Disciples of Christ to emphasize the church's ecumenical vision and its focus on the need for unity among all Christians. In his column, Beazley claimed that the Black Manifesto sought the overthrow of the government, promoted black racism, and sought reparations through threats of violence. To Beazley, the clergy who supported the manifesto were confused and ill-informed. Beazley criticized the president of the NCC, who had "violated the rules of procedure" in his support of the manifesto. Despite his criticism of the manifesto and the NCC's support of it, Beazley urged member churches to continue their support of the NCC and their representatives to the organization.[31]

Others added their concerns about the manifesto. Following the conventions of the NCC and the Episcopal Church in September 1969, *Interchurch,*

132 Chapter Five

the magazine of the NCC, published an article clarifying the Black Manifesto and the decisions by both bodies of religious leaders. The author, Robert Gildea, a United Methodist minister, argued that with his manifesto, James Forman "may have unwittingly applied a hatchet to one of the black man's most concerned friends"—the church. According to Gildea, "the impetus for the bulk of federal civil rights legislation in the last decade came mostly from church groups."[32]

Gildeas wrote that "no issue in the last quarter century has shaken the foundations of American churches, nor so divided church people, as has the radical threats and Marxist rhetoric of Forman's Black Manifesto." In particular, he highlighted divisions among parishioners. According to Gildea, laymen "were up in arms, . . . confusion abounded, and harried pastors" suffered frayed nerves as a result of the manifesto. Clergy were upset largely because many people in the pews were canceling their support of the churches in reaction to the NCC's encouraging financial support of IFCO and the NCBC. Gildea noted that one large congregation in Indianapolis had lost more than $5,000 in pledges in a ten-day period. He further argued that "if the division of opinion manifest in the Episcopal and Disciples conventions is any criterion, the issue threatens to . . . drive a wedge through the NCC and render it impotent."[33]

Despite his critique of the Black Manifesto and the division it had created in mainline Christian churches, Gildea did give credit to Forman. Gildea found it hard to imagine that "any church body would be responding as boldly to the plight of blacks had not Forman spoken in such revolutionary tones." In other words, if Forman had appealed to the NCC and its member churches through normal channels, he likely would not have been successful. It was the brashness and radicalism of both his methods and approach that pushed the NCC and the Episcopalians into action.[34]

Gildea, though, reminded his readers that the battle over NCC funding in response to the Black Manifesto was not over. The general board's decision needed approval from the NCC General Assembly in December 1969. While the eight-hundred-member assembly generally approved the board's recommendations, Gildea thought the assembly would examine this action much more closely, since the manifesto and the NCC board's decision were so controversial. He noted that "delegates to the assembly tend to be closer to the grassroots than the general board, and the darts they have felt because of the board's Indianapolis action may make them gun-shy." And even if the assembly approved the board's decision, Gildea reminded his readers, "the guy in the pew" would make the final decision by writing—or not writing—checks to support IFCO and/or the NCBC.[35]

Fracturing the Antipoverty Coalition 133

One of the more intriguing denominational responses to the Black Manifesto came from the largely white Mennonite Church. The Mennonites are one of a number of Swiss Anabaptist sects—including the Amish, the Hutterites, the Brethren, and the Apostolic Christians—who fled to America in the nineteenth century to escape religious persecution. Anabaptists' core beliefs center on adult baptism, the separation of church and state, separatism from or nonconformity with the world, and nonviolence. The Mennonites might seem like an unlikely religious group to engage with the Black Manifesto, but they did. According to historians Tobin Miller Shearer and Felipe Hinojosa, the Black Manifesto led to intense discussions about race in the Mennonite Church. Shearer has written, "The topic of reparations and black power galvanized the church," and "more than any document at the end of the 1960s, James Forman's Black Manifesto changed the way leaders of the Mennonite church . . . approached racial issues."[36]

The Mennonite Church had begun to address racial issues in 1968, one year prior to Forman's manifesto, by creating the Urban Racial Council. After the Black Manifesto, black Mennonites challenged their church to contribute $500,000 to a black-controlled "compassion fund," as John Powell, the leader of the Urban Racial Council said, "for the purpose of developing and expanding ways of serving the urban poor and minorities in new and more meaningful ways." In addition, leaders of the Urban Racial Council held discussions with Latino/a Mennonite leaders about forming an interethnic organization of black and brown Mennonites. Those meetings resulted in the creation of the Minority Ministries Council, which "emerged from the Urban Racial Council as the preeminent Mennonite voice for racial justice." The initial Mennonite response to the manifesto was to call for increased giving to denominational mission programs. Eventually, the Minority Ministries Council distributed funds to denominational service programs. But according to both Shearer and Hinojosa, the manifesto did more than lead Mennonites to create more service programs and donate funds to church-run antipoverty agencies. It led white Mennonites to talk about racism with African American and Latino/a religious leaders and communities. These conversations "exposed racial inequities, challenged urban missions, and birthed fresh programs." Shearer convincingly argues that "instead of encouraging churchly strife, the radical document invited careful conversation and measured change." So, rather than leading to a separation of the races, the Black Manifesto, in the case of Mennonites, brought whites, African Americans, and Latino/as together through the Minority Ministries Council and encouraged additional support of black- and brown-led antipoverty programs.[37]

134   Chapter Five

While in the Mennonite Church the Black Manifesto brought blacks and whites together, the manifesto highlighted racial divisions within mainline Protestant denominations. For instance, a heated confrontation over race and the church developed between two Episcopal churches—one white and one black—in the Detroit area. On June 1, 1969, nineteen members of the Detroit chapter of the BEDC visited Christ Church Cranbrook after receiving permission from church staff. Cranbrook, a predominantly, although not exclusively, white church, sits in the high-income suburb of Bloomfield Hills about twenty miles north of Detroit. At the time, Bloomfield Hills was home to the presidents and board members of all of the major American automobile companies; many of the residences were designed by well-known architects Frank Lloyd Wright, Albert Kahn, and Minoru Yamasaki. The BEDC visit to the Cranbrook church included a reading of the Black Manifesto and a demand for $100,000 from the church. As the historian Keith Dye has explained, Christ Church Cranbrook had a history of supporting black community antipoverty programs. Indeed, Dye argued that the church's "social consciousness," money, and prestige were the primary reasons the BEDC made its demands at Cranbrook. But the Black Manifesto and the BEDC's appearance at Cranbrook created a crisis for the Reverend Gerald O'Grady Jr., the rector of Christ Church, and his parishioners: "pay reparations or face the possibility of more widespread social upheaval."[38]

Reverend O'Grady handled the BEDC demands by encouraging parishioners to send him their views and by holding three "feedback sessions." Both written and oral responses demonstrated that the congregation of Christ Church was fundamentally divided over the Black Manifesto and the BEDC's demands. Some congregants, like Frederick C. Matthai, encouraged the church to support the manifesto and offered to donate money to the cause. Others, like Frank Storey, called the manifesto "extortion" and implored O'Grady to reject its demands. The controversy at Christ Church drew a response from Bishop Richard Emrich of the Michigan Diocese of the Episcopal Church. Emrich penned a column on June 15, 1969, for the *Detroit News* titled "Not a Dime for Forman," which openly opposed the manifesto. In response to Emrich's column, Robert Morrison, the minister of Saint Joseph's Episcopal Church, a predominantly black church in Detroit, excoriated the ministers of Christ Church. Arguing that the bishop, the staff, and the membership of Christ Church had "no understanding as to the plight of non-white people . . . or to the pervasiveness of the racism which oppresses them" and noting that the bishop's column had identified them "as racists," the minister of Saint Joseph's decided to "have no further relationship whatever with the staff or governing body of Christ Church Cranbrook." Morrison encouraged all members of Christ Church who were "truly seeking a humane and just society to leave that church immediately." Unlike the case of the Mennonite Church, responses to the Black Manifesto at Cranbrook divided black and white congregants instead of bringing them together.[39]

The Black Manifesto received complicated responses from black religious organizations as well. For example, the Black Methodists for Church Renewal in Ohio, while expressing its shared concerns with the Black Manifesto about the past treatment by white churches of African Americans, argued that it did not want its denomination "to continue its abuse of its black Methodist churches by allocating OUR FUNDS TO AN OUTSIDE GROUP. WE FEEL THAT THE UNITED METHODIST CHURCH SHOULD CARE FOR MEMBERS OF THE FAMILY FIRST." Concerned that the United Methodist decision to give money to IFCO and the BEDC would mean a lack of support for black Methodist churches, the BMCR in Ohio requested $600,000 per year from white Methodist churches in Ohio to help with black church community programs, ecumenical programs with other black denominations, the renovation of black churches, the training and hiring of black ministers, and welfare rights programs. In other words, the BMCR in Ohio, reflecting the core principles of black power—self-definition and community control—agreed with the basic arguments presented in the Black Manifesto but wanted resources that it could use to address problems it saw locally and regionally, rather than have to apply for money from IFCO or the BEDC.[40]

Black religious leaders in Dallas had a similar response to the manifesto. Black clergy in Dallas emphatically rejected "the content of the Black Manifesto, the methods with which it is being presented, and the goals which it clearly desires." At the same time, they admitted that the manifesto had accurately highlighted the poverty and racism that defined the lives of too many African Americans in the Dallas area. They further admitted, somewhat grudgingly, that the manifesto had brought black and white clergy together. The ministers asked: "Could it be that God has raised up James Forman to cause us to unite our efforts to overcome the racism . . . which has invaded and indeed does now pervade the church?" The ministers' response was yes, and they intended to take advantage of the willingness of white clergy to listen to them by advocating for white churches to support black institutional antipoverty programs. The ministers expressed a wariness of IFCO, in part because of concerns about the local control of resources, but mostly because they saw Lucius Walker as a black person set up by major white denominations "to perform the mission of the church." The black clergy of Dallas argued that "persons who reject the black community by joining 'white' churches have real difficulty relating to that black community."[41]

136   Chapter Five

Undoubtedly, the clearest and most thorough response to the Black Manifesto by a black clergyman was written by Gayraud Wilmore, the chair of the Division of Church and Race of the Board of National Missions for the Presbyterian Church. In his June 1969 essay, "The Church's Response to the Black Manifesto," Wilmore noted that the purpose of his analysis was "to dispel some of the fear and hysteria" that characterized some of the reactions of white Christians to the Black Manifesto. In his essay, Wilmore expounded on both the history and the theological meaning of the manifesto and what the manifesto meant for churches. He argued that, rather than precipitating a crisis, the manifesto revealed a crisis in the churches related to a lack of "theological clarity" and enthusiasm toward the black power movement and what he called "battle fatigue" over civil rights. Wilmore stated that the focus on racial integration by white churches led them to denigrate black racial identity and black religion. According to Wilmore, white Christians had never come to the realization that integration was no longer a goal of most black people, who instead had moved to black pride and self-determination. He argued that "the theological defense of integration never took account of the painful deracination and dehumanization which black people were called upon to suffer as the price of a powerless and humiliating assimilation into an essentially racist white Christian Church and culture."[42]

Wilmore further noted that there were examples in history of reparations toward other oppressed groups, and reparations made sense based on the principle of penance in Christian theology. He argued that "if reparations are truly an acceptable form of the concrete expression of repentance, then the white churches of the nation have a religious duty to demonstrate the seriousness and sincerity of the Christian conscience by repaying to oppressed minorities whatever reasonable portion can be calculated from the benefits which have accrued to them through slavery and black subjugation." To Wilmore, the concept of reparations was "a creative and . . . practical way to concretize the theological doctrine of repentance." In response to criticisms of the tactics used by Forman and others, Wilmore compared those actions to Jesus Christ's cleansing of the temple, Martin Luther's nailing of the Ninety-Five Theses to the church door in Wittenberg, the Boston Tea Party, and other disruptive acts that led to revolutionary change. Wilmore concluded his essay by arguing that the $500 million in reparations demanded by Forman was well within the means of the churches and that black and white Christians should support "enthusiastically the demands of the Black Manifesto."[43]

One of the leading black preachers and civil rights leaders of the period gave his perspective on the debate over the Black Manifesto. Ralph Abernathy, a friend and confidant of Martin Luther King Jr. and president of the Southern Christian Leadership Conference, wrote an article in the *Christian Century* addressing the message and controversy of the Black Manifesto. Abernathy acknowledged that his first reaction to the manifesto was mixed at best, and he wondered if James Forman had gone too far in both his methods and his message. After giving it more consideration, however, Abernathy began to see Forman as "a prophet" who had pulled "the covers off the economic life of the churches" that had failed to give their riches to the poor. Abernathy provocatively concluded his article with a question directed at his fellow Christians: "Will we ignore the divine message which is coming to the church through the Black Manifesto?"[44]

Not all Christian leaders saw the Black Manifesto as a divine message. Indeed, one of the significant consequences of the manifesto was the development of a power struggle between blacks and whites in mainline Protestant denominations. African Americans comprised about a quarter of the constituents in the member churches of the NCC in 1969. Yet they held few leadership positions outside of all-black churches. Through organizations like the NCBC and the BMCR, African American clergy used the Black Manifesto to demand more influence in denominational decision making. Charles Spivey Jr., director of the Department of Social Justice of the NCC, argued that discussions about money "were missing the real point." Instead, Spivey maintained, "the overriding issue is now redistribution of power."[45]

The manifesto challenged assumptions held by white parishioners and led to the funding of black-controlled antipoverty and economic development programs. While white churches consistently rejected the idea of reparations and had a negative reaction to the revolutionary ideology of the Black Manifesto, many whites admitted that it had raised issues that would have gone unnoticed otherwise. The Reverend Harry Fifield, pastor of Fifth Presbyterian Church in Atlanta, noted that his parishioners told him that the manifesto had "sensitized them to the needs of the Negro." Many mainline Protestant denominations initiated new black economic development programs, while circumventing any direct involvement with Forman and the BEDC. The Reverend J. Edward Carothers, head of national missions for the United Methodist Church, said that the manifesto and the related demonstrations had made it possible for his organization "to shift priorities away from traditional projects like elementary schools and concentrate on community organization" and antipoverty programs.[46]

Some Christian clergy and publications suggested that the Black Manifesto had not gone far enough in its demands. The editors of *Christian Century* suggested as much: the manifesto had demanded "far too little." In

138   Chapter Five

addition, the editorial argued that the manifesto fell short because it placed the churches "in their traditional philanthropic and charitable approach to poverty instead of insisting that they become wholeheartedly involved in the more risky politics of [the] American economy." The editorial further chastised the churches' traditional approach of "a combination of moralistic rhetoric and conventional charity" and urged them to engage more actively in issues related to poverty and social injustice.[47]

As part of their discussion of the Black Manifesto, some church organizations made a point of defending IFCO. In its newsletter, *Mission Memo*, the United Methodist Board of Missions noted that IFCO was one of the ways in which the board supported "the dispossessed and oppressed peoples" in the country and that the board's philosophy was to help "disadvantaged people . . . form their own organizations to obtain solutions to their poverty-stricken conditions." The article concluded that an ecumenical antipoverty organization like IFCO was necessary in order for churches and church organizations to engage effectively in efforts to address poverty in communities.[48]

The issue of funding antipoverty organizations was raised by the Black Manifesto in a period when the funding emphasis in churches was undergoing a fundamental change. In 1968–1969, for the first time since the Great Depression, national programs of the mainline Protestant churches faced a cutback in finances. This was the result not of fewer donations, but of a shift in priorities with local denominations keeping more of their members' donations for local programs rather than funneling the money to the national organizations. Some Protestant leaders welcomed the growing tendency of individual churches keeping more money for local social justice and antipoverty programs. Others argued that this development would hurt the national organizations, which had donated millions to civil rights and community groups, and that it would benefit wealthy congregations, which would keep the money for programs in their own areas rather than sending some of it to benefit church organizations in areas with high percentages of poverty. As some congregations reacted negatively to the Black Manifesto, church leaders worried that keeping more money in the local congregations in the end would mean less money for IFCO and other antipoverty organizations located in black and brown communities.[49]

IFCO itself was worried about that possibility. Lu Walker spent much of the summer of 1969 trying to minimize the fallout from IFCO's affiliation with the Black Manifesto and the BEDC. He wrote a number of letters to church leaders explaining IFCO's position and encouraging their continued support. For example, in July Walker wrote to Robert Hoppe of the Ohio Synod of the United Presbyterian Church. Walker argued that IFCO had

Fracturing the Antipoverty Coalition 139

been "an influence for reason and the orderly expression by aggrieved minority and poor citizens." According to him, sometimes that expression included hostility and rage, as in the Black Manifesto. The result of the manifesto, as far as Walker was concerned, was that IFCO was caught in the middle of the churches and the black power activists and, as a result, was vulnerable to attack. Walker implored Hoppe that the Ohio Synod continue its support of IFCO because the organization needed that help more than ever and because "the demise of IFCO would . . . deprive the churches of its most viable link with the angry indigenous community."[50]

The IFCO board had attempted to address some of the concerns expressed by churches about the agency's relationship with the BEDC at its June 1969 meeting. Walker told the board that it needed to "accept the [BEDC] as an autonomous entity and must deal with it on its own terms." He emphasized that the BEDC and IFCO had separate agendas, and IFCO's was funding community antipoverty organizations. While it had a relationship with the BEDC, the two organizations were not linked together. Walker made his statement at the meeting in part to address concerns raised by board members that the Methodist Church was hesitating to give money to IFCO, and the American Church Union had decided to review its membership in IFCO because its member denominations did not know where IFCO stood in relation to the BEDC and the Black Manifesto. Walker spent much of his summer distancing IFCO from the BEDC and the manifesto and clarifying IFCO's programs and purpose.[51]

IFCO's relationship with the BEDC and the manifesto continued to cause confusion and hurt its fundraising abilities in the following months. Indeed, it was enough of a concern that Walker and IFCO hired a public relations and fundraising consultant, Harold Oram, Inc., to conduct a study to determine ways in which IFCO could increase its financial support. The study concluded that since IFCO did not "directly initiate its own programs" and served "primarily as a conduit for the churches in support of these programs . . . it seemed evident that IFCO had to strengthen its own image and bring it into sharper focus before it could elicit substantial support from the larger philanthropic community." The report noted that, in particular, as a result of IFCO's connection to the Black Manifesto and the BEDC, "foundations were uncertain of IFCO's role as a mover and a shaker in helping those who have neither voice nor power in determining their lives." To counter this "fuzzy" identity, the report recommended that IFCO could continue along its original lines of serving as a conduit, providing church funds to black and brown antipoverty organizations, or, if it wanted "to break out of this pattern" and "increase its fund-raising potential," it could "set forth its own

140   Chapter Five

objectives, with its own programs, and obtain undesignated funds from the highest church levels." Despite the consultant's recommendations, IFCO maintained its relationship with the BEDC, making a grant of $80,000 to the BEDC in February 1970 to support some of its efforts toward organizing poor black communities.[52]

Eventually, though, the differences between the two organizations and the continued controversies surrounding the BEDC led IFCO to end their relationship. In January 1971, Walker wrote to the Reverend Calvin Marshall, executive director of the BEDC, explaining that IFCO had "reached a difficult decision" based on "the advice of [its] attorney" to terminate all grant relationships with the BEDC; IFCO would no longer be responsible "for the administration of funds designated for the Black Economic Development Conference." Walker explained the reason for IFCO's decision as the BEDC's "repeated failure to cooperate with the administrative procedures IFCO follows in all grant relationships."[53]

Walker followed his letter to Marshall with a letter to those who had contributed money to IFCO for the BEDC. He told the BEDC contributors that IFCO had "defended and supported BEDC against strong opposition and criticism because we believed in the programs BEDC proposed to do and accepted BEDC's word that it would abide by IFCO's regular reporting procedures." Walker informed the contributors that the BEDC had failed to comply with those procedures, thus placing IFCO in potential legal jeopardy. As a result, IFCO was terminating its relationship with the BEDC.[54]

While the BEDC's failure to comply with IFCO's reporting procedures undoubtedly was one reason for IFCO's ending their relationship, the BEDC's reputation and perceived militant stance also seem to have influenced Walker and IFCO. On the one-year anniversary of the Black Manifesto, the BEDC had issued *A Call to Be* written by Calvin Marshall. In addition to Marshall's advocating continued provocative challenges to systemic racism, the back cover of the publication included a photo of urban violence with the quote "A response to be?"—insinuating that violence by black people would be one response to the failure by the white power structure to meet the demands of the BEDC. Members of the IFCO board had responded negatively to that publication, and it seemed to impact their deliberations about their relationship with the BEDC. Indeed, Walker later suggested that its support of the BEDC was one of IFCO's few failures.[55]

While IFCO distanced itself from the BEDC (which stopped operations in 1973), it aligned more closely with another prominent black nationalist organization, the Black Economic Research Center (BERC). Founded on October 1, 1969, in the aftermath of the controversy over the Black Manifesto and during a renewed focus on black antipoverty programs, BERC was a privately funded, nonprofit research development organization that focused on what its founders described as "the economic aspects of the Black condition with a view toward discovering more effective ways to win for the Black man the full measure of dignity, security, power and economic well-being to which he is entitled." IFCO was one of the first organizations to fund BERC, awarding a grant for $60,000 in 1969 to support its study of a land bank in the South and to help publish its journal, the *Review of Black Political Economy*. BERC also received money from the OEO, and its representatives met several times with OEO officials, including the director at the time, Donald Rumsfeld, to discuss the land bank and rural black poverty. In other words, BERC linked the War on Poverty with the emphasis on self-definition and community control emanating from the black power movement.[56]

IFCO's relationship with BERC developed over the years. In 1972, IFCO granted BERC $37,500 for a number of projects geared toward studying and ameliorating black poverty. Those projects included preparing research and analyzing data on black communities and their relations to economic systems; providing financial and technical support to black community antipoverty projects; and providing a library focused on materials related to black economic development. IFCO expanded its relationship with BERC in part due to the advice and suggestions of its sponsors, including Julian Bond, Shirley Chisholm, Charles V. Hamilton, and Andrew Young. Chisholm, for example, had been involved in black antipoverty and economic development efforts in the Bedford-Stuyvesant community in New York for years. Her experience there led to her political career and her encouragement of other projects, like BERC, that focused on issues related to black economic development. Chisholm, like IFCO, continued to fight the long War on Poverty.[57]

IFCO's relationship with BERC highlighted the fact that in the 1970s IFCO was the largest nonwhite-controlled foundation in the United States. Indeed, IFCO's board was majority nonwhite: thirty-five African Americans, three Mexican Americans, two Native Americans, and twelve whites. It was also the largest interreligious foundation in the country, continuing as a conduit between largely white affluent denominations and largely black and brown communities. In the constitution of its board and in the recipients of its grants, IFCO and the coalition it created were both interfaith and interracial, representing both religious and racial ecumenism. As one IFCO report noted, the agency served as "a bridge between church and society, between a number of denominations concerned with social change, between blacks and whites, between the people who have resources to give and the people who best know how to use those resources effectively." While the ecumenical

142   Chapter Five

antipoverty coalition IFCO represented had been fractured in the aftermath of the Black Manifesto, it remained active, though more fragile than it previously was.[58]

While IFCO's efforts focused on black power antipoverty programs, it also spent much of its time and funding on antipoverty and economic development projects in Latino/a, Asian, and Native American communities. In the early to mid-1970s, for instance, IFCO funded black nationalist organizations, like the Africa Information Service, which compiled and distributed information on liberation movements and struggles for economic independence in Africa, along with the African Heritage Studies Association, the African Liberation Support Committee, the Black Appalachian Commission, the Committee for a Unified Newark, and the National Conference of Black Lawyers. In addition, it supported the Alaska Federation of Natives, American Indians United, the American Indian Movement Center, Los Padres, and the El Barrio Communications Project in Los Angeles. In other words, IFCO actively encouraged a wide range of projects related to empowering black, brown, indigenous, and Asian poor people.[59]

IFCO continued to fund antipoverty and economic development projects in the 1970s. But it did so without the direct leadership of Lu Walker. In 1973, Walker left to become head of the Division of Church and Society and associate general secretary for the NCC, reflecting the continued close relationship between IFCO and the NCC. Ann Douglas, previously associate director and grants administrator for IFCO, replaced Walker. At the same time that Walker moved from IFCO to the NCC, he and Douglas decided to close IFCO's branch offices as a budget-cutting move. The economic recession of the 1970s, related in part to rising oil prices, had impacted church members and denominations and led to reduced contributions to IFCO.[60]

Despite this budget crunch, IFCO continued to fund the National Welfare Rights Organization, the American Indian Movement, and other groups. And it developed some programs of its own. Most prominent among these was the National Black United Fund, which raised seed money and gave administrative aid to black economic development agencies in eight American cities. Essentially, the National Black United Fund served as a national network of black philanthropic, economic development, and antipoverty agencies. Another significant program that IFCO developed during this period was the Cabral Institute, which opened in September 1972 and provided training for community organizers working at the National Black United Fund and other antipoverty and economic development projects. The Cabral Institute particularly emphasized community development and self-determination for African Americans, Mexican Americans, and Native Americans. IFCO's continued close relationship with the NCC was reflected in the fact that Cabral Institute trainings took place at the Interchurch Center in New York. In his new position at the NCC, Walker helped to facilitate that relationship.[61]

At the time that Walker moved to the NCC, IFCO applied to become a "related movement" of the NCC and its Division of Church and Society, which Walker would head. In its application to the NCC, IFCO stated that its purpose for seeking the new affiliation was "to implement common programs and strategy among religious groups for the development of community organizations among the poor and others as a part of the urban mission, ministry and program of such religious groups, [and] to conduct research and [create] educational materials in connection with the building of such programs and strategy." While programmatic alignment and cohesiveness were significant, a closer affiliation with the NCC also allowed Walker to remain actively involved with IFCO's activities. In many ways, Walker continued to lead IFCO from his position within the NCC. And the new affiliation allowed IFCO to shift some costs to the NCC and reduce some of its ever-present budget concerns.[62]

As a related movement of the NCC, IFCO continued its focus on funding antipoverty, economic development, and community organizing projects in black, Latino/a, Asian, and Native American communities. In a 1976 report to the NCC, IFCO explained what made the organization both significant and unique. The report acknowledged that in the 1960s, as a result of the War on Poverty, "some Protestant mission boards began to be heavy supporters of community organization as a mission style." What made IFCO different was that early in its history it had shifted to include black and brown people's control of both its board and staff, "a unique arrangement for any church agency or foundation." The report argued that "for once, the churches were setting the pace by supporting indigenous leadership and control of an institution affecting the lives of the poor. Money for development of organizations and institutions controlled by Blacks, by Indians, by Mexican-Americans was being done by church persons. Analysis and evaluation of these projects were being done by minority peoples themselves—an obvious improvement over the style of sending white analysts into ghetto neighborhoods." In other words, IFCO was part of an ecumenical War on Poverty controlled by the people in the communities.[63]

Despite this unique place in the world of antipoverty and community organizations, IFCO moved to an even closer affiliation with the NCC. In October 1976, IFCO and the NCC agreed that "the general activities which had been performed by IFCO will hereafter be performed by the IFCO Program Committee as an integral part of the National Council of Churches." IFCO

144   Chapter Five

staffers would become part of the NCC staff, "while the IFCO program will remain a separately identifiable program under the general supervision of the National Council of Churches." Douglas and Walker wrote a memo to the IFCO executive committee explaining their reasons for recommending the evolution to direct NCC supervision of IFCO and its programs. According to Walker and Douglas, a move to more direct supervision would help IFCO deal with further budget cuts, would help offset some of the decline in IFCO revenue, and would result in a more efficient use of funds contributed to IFCO by eliminating administrative duplication. Walker and Douglas wrote that such a move reflected "a new reality in ecumenism. The founders of IFCO dreamed of these possibilities but could not enter the promised land. By entering these agreements, NCC and IFCO will have taken possession of the land." Of course, the new arrangement also meant the close and continued supervision of IFCO by Walker in his position in the NCC.[64]

Although IFCO had evolved as an organization, it remained committed to working with churches to fund and develop community antipoverty organizations. To many, it was fulfilling its mission well. In 1978, two United Presbyterian Church representatives to the IFCO board reported on the changes and accomplishments at IFCO since its inception in 1967. The authors of the report noted that IFCO had been in existence for eleven years at that point because it had "met real needs, both in communities it [had] served, and in the denominations for which it [had] been an agent, sounding board, and an avenue of communication with an important segment of America's poor and minority populations." IFCO had "been of real service to the church and the world."[65]

But the direct affiliation IFCO had established with the NCC lasted a relatively short period. In November 1978, the NCC dismissed Walker from his position as head of the Division of Church and Society because during the previous two years his division had created a budget deficit of more than $200,000. Of course, Walker had spent much of that money on IFCO and related projects. When the NCC terminated Walker, it also ended its direct supervision of and relationship with IFCO, although IFCO would continue its affiliation with some denominations. As a symbol of this terminated association, IFCO moved its headquarters out of the Interchurch Center to a new home in Harlem. The move included Walker, who in January 1979 become the head of a newly independent IFCO, replacing Douglas, who had ended her time leading the organization the previous year.[66]

Walker's return to IFCO coincided with some new directions in the group's policies and programs. By 1978, every mainline Protestant denomination and many Catholic organizations had created grants programs targeting poverty and economic inequality. These antipoverty and economic development programs included the Catholic Campaign for Human Development, the United Presbyterian Church Fund for Self-Development of Peoples, and the American Baptist Convention's Minority Development Campaign. This evolution reduced IFCO's usefulness to the churches as a grant-making body. In addition, IFCO had begun to emphasize and fund efforts at addressing poverty and economic justice internationally. In particular, two IFCO programs, the Material Assistance Support System and Relief for Africans in Need in the Sahel focused on aid to nations in southern and western Africa. Since most churches related to IFCO through their national ministries divisions, IFCO's growing focus on global poverty made it difficult for those church divisions to justify support for IFCO. At about the same time, the Internal Revenue Service classified IFCO as a 509(a) public charity, which led private foundations to begin to use IFCO as their fiscal agent in providing funds to community antipoverty organizations. Even as IFCO's relationship with churches and religious organizations diminished, it continued to be involved directly in funding and developing community economic development and antipoverty organizations, particularly in black and brown communities.[67]

As IFCO evolved in the 1980s, its emphasis on racial and economic justice both domestically and internationally continued and expanded. In the 1980s, IFCO helped found and fund the National Anti-Klan Network (which later became the Center for Democratic Renewal) in response to a revival of the Klan during the administration of President Ronald Reagan. IFCO's growing international efforts focused on funding aid efforts in Central America, particularly in Nicaragua, Honduras, and Guatemala, which had been devastated by American policies for decades. But domestic community organizing remained "the top priority" on its agenda. Providing training and technical assistance, serving as a fiscal agent, and facilitating funding and networking for black and brown community antipoverty and economic development organizations remained "critical components of IFCO's mission and identity." IFCO continued not just to fund but also "to nurture and support the organizations that it helped get started, networking them into a larger arena and watching them flourish."[68]

The criteria for selecting worthy projects remained similar to those from twenty years earlier. The primary requirement to receive IFCO funding continued to be the capability of the project's staff to organize their community effectively. Other criteria included community need, project leadership development, and indigenous participation and control. Twenty years after its founding, IFCO's guidelines demonstrated its continued link to the ideals of both the War on Poverty and black power.[69]

146 Chapter Five

At its Twentieth Anniversary Conference, IFCO honored organizations that had "established an exemplary record of community organization and advocacy for social change." The honorees in 1987 included the Funding Exchange, a community-based antipoverty and social movement funding network; the Farm Labor Organizing Committee, an independent union of migrant farm workers in the Midwest; and the Campaign for Human Development, which by that time was the largest church-based agency funding community organization in poor communities of color in the United States. As it celebrated its twentieth anniversary, IFCO had evolved, but remained focused on its initial mission of working with churches and church organizations to fund antipoverty and economic development projects in poor communities, particularly African American and Latino/a communities.[70] Indeed, IFCO has continued to fight the War on Poverty as an ecumenical antipoverty agency into the twenty-first century.

However, IFCO's accomplishments since the late 1970s have been without the support of some of the religious denominations and organizations that backed it initially. The Black Manifesto damaged IFCO in the eyes of some supporters. Additionally, and more significantly, the Black Manifesto irreparably affected some religious support of the War on Poverty. After the manifesto, the War on Poverty was increasingly seen by some members of white churches as a radical program that appeased black revolutionaries. Financial support for IFCO declined, and so did political and institutional support from many mainline churches, synagogues, and other religious institutions, many of which had previously been strong advocates of the War on Poverty. Thus, when the administrations of Richard Nixon, Gerald Ford, and Ronald Reagan targeted War on Poverty programs for elimination or significant reduction, some early fans of the War on Poverty remained silent. While the link between religion and antipoverty programs was not completely severed, after the Black Manifesto it was greatly damaged. The ecumenical antipoverty coalition that formed in support of the War on Poverty and IFCO had been permanently fractured. But a reshaped ecumenical coalition of antipoverty programs continued, in somewhat different form, into the twenty-first century.

CONCLUSION

"To Become as Radical as Christ"
Faith-Based Activism and the Long War on Poverty in the Twenty-First Century

The ecumenical antipoverty coalition represented by the Interreligious Foundation for Community Organization (IFCO)—key to the War on Poverty—has continued in evolved form into the twenty-first century. That has been the case, in part, because of the decline of a federally based War on Poverty. Attacks on the federal War on Poverty took root during the administration of President Richard Nixon. In 1971, Nixon vetoed amendments to the Economic Opportunity Act in an effort to defund the Office of Economic Opportunity (OEO). Congress, though, overrode Nixon's veto, and the OEO continued. In his 1974 budget message to Congress, Nixon requested no further funding for the OEO, but once again a Democratic Congress continued funding the agency. Nixon did, though, successfully transfer Volunteers in Service to America (VISTA) and thirteen other programs out of the OEO. As historian Emma Folwell has shown, Nixon's New Federalism and the removal of antipoverty programs from the OEO allowed opponents of community action, like the state Republican Party in Mississippi, to "reinforce white control over antipoverty programs and undermine African American delegate agencies" and reestablish white supremacy in that state. President Gerald Ford succeeded where Nixon had failed, abolishing the OEO on January 4, 1975, through the Head Start, Economic Opportunity and Community Partnership Act and replacing the OEO with the Community Services Administration (CSA).[1]

148   Conclusion

These developments, though, did not mean the end of the War on Poverty. When Jimmy Carter became president in 1977, he appointed Graciela Olivarez as director of the CSA. Olivarez, the first Latina to head a federal agency, was a civil rights and War on Poverty veteran and, like Sargent Shriver, a devout Catholic. Indeed, Olivarez saw the CSA as continuing the War on Poverty and infused the agency with an energy and enthusiasm for antipoverty efforts that it had not experienced since Shriver left in 1968. But, despite her efforts, the CSA faced continued challenges from both within and without the Carter administration. Olivarez left the agency in 1980, and the Reagan administration abolished the CSA in 1981, ending the presence of an official, centralized federal antipoverty agency.[2]

The War on Poverty, though, still did not end. The federal government continued to fund antipoverty agencies through community service block grants, and community action agencies continued to use those funds as well as money from private foundations and state and local governments to fight poverty in communities across the country. Many of the antipoverty agencies that exist today are faith-based and receive funding from religious organizations, like the Catholic Campaign for Human Development (CHD), or ecumenical agencies, like IFCO.

In the fifty years since its inception, the CHD has provided more than $300 million in community organizing and economic development grants to community- and faith-based antipoverty organizations, and it has trained numerous priests, nuns, and laypeople to organize communities against poverty. The CHD provides 15–20 percent of the operating funds of faith-based organizations and has been "a key sponsor of faith-based community organizing . . . for several decades."[3] Of course, the CHD had its origins in the civil rights and antipoverty activism of individuals like Fathers John Egan and Geno Baroni.

Many of the organizations CHD has funded over the years are "heirs to the legacy of Saul Alinsky." They are community- or faith-based groups that have organized around issues of housing, jobs, education, and health. CHD-funded groups have challenged redlining practices in real estate, brought attention to the low rates of child support enforcement, helped clean up toxic waste dumps in poor neighborhoods, and advocated for increased health care accessibility for poor people. In 1971, one of the first groups the CHD funded was the Contract Buyers League (originally called the Contract Buyers of Lawndale), the anti–housing discrimination organization formed by Jack Egan and others in Chicago. Eventually, the CBL evolved into the Gamaliel Foundation, a major faith-based antipoverty organization with affiliates across the United States. The faith-based organization that one scholar calls

Faith-Based Activism

"the most influential project" to receive CHD money, Communities Organized for Public Service (COPS), incorporates "intensive theological reflection into its training," as do many other CHD recipients. The CHD and the groups it funds emphasize empowerment; the CHD calls the organizations it supports "poor empowerment groups," and its literature over the years has advocated offering "a hand up, not a handout," the same slogan used by the Office of Economic Opportunity when the federal government's War on Poverty began in 1964. Indeed, the CHD and many of the organizations it funds, including COPS and the Gamaliel Foundation, incorporate the language and the community organization ideals of the War on Poverty.[4]

COPS, founded in the mid-1970s in San Antonio, built on the notion of faith-based community organizing and antipoverty efforts established by the CHD. COPS used Saul Alinsky's model of community organizing but linked "it much more intimately with the religious congregations and faith commitments of participants. As a result of this innovative work, COPS generated far greater political participation among poor residents than had existed previously." Over the years, COPS established itself as one of "the stronger versions of faith-based community organizing."[5]

COPS is not an isolated example. Scholars have identified four major faith-based community organization networks. COPS is a member of one of those networks, the Industrial Areas Foundation (IAF); Monsignor John Egan was a member of its board of trustees for years. The other prominent faith-based networks are the Pacific Institute for Community Organization based in Oakland, the Gamaliel Foundation (Chicago), and the Direct Action and Research Training Center (Miami). These four networks coordinate, advise, and direct more than 150 faith-based organizations in the United States. These religious agencies actively engage in issues related to poverty, like housing (often building low-cost homes), education, economic development, job training, and health care. Faith-based organizations as a whole impact the lives of more than two million Americans. And they demonstrate direct links between themselves, church-based antipoverty organizations, and the ecumenical antipoverty coalition created in the 1960s.[6]

Importantly, a significant number of faith-based antipoverty organizations are run by African Americans or Latino/as. In the year 2000, 56 percent of all faith-based antipoverty organizations had predominantly Latino/a or black staffs. While that is the case, "the internal culture of organizing tends to implicitly suppress identity-based political claims, due to its commitment to cross-racial organizing and coalition-formation." Many of the leaders and organizers of these faith-based agencies are women. In particular, Puerto Rican and African American Pentecostal women have been active in community antipoverty work, blending "a passion for transformative social action with an urgency to win souls for the Kingdom."[7]

One of the groups of religious Latinas most actively involved in antipoverty efforts since the 1970s is Las Hermanas. Organized in 1971 in Houston by fifty Chicana nuns and women religious influenced by Vatican II, liberation theology, the Chicano/a movement, and feminism and initially led by Gregoria Ortega, a Victory Noll sister, and Gloria Gallardo, a sister of the Holy Ghost, Las Hermanas fights for social justice for Latino/as. Using the motto "unidas en accíon y oración/united in action and prayer," Las Hermanas advocates for a number of causes important to Latinas, including antipoverty community organizing. Las Hermanas serves as an example of ethnically distinct Chicano/a antipoverty activism by religious organizations.[8]

Las Hermanas also was inspired by Católicos por La Raza, a Chicano/a activist organization formed in November 1969 in Los Angeles. A joint effort of Chicano/a law school students at Loyola Marymount University, students at Los Angeles City College, and the newspaper *La Raza*, Católicos launched a movement to challenge the Catholic Church in Los Angeles. Inspired by James Forman's Black Manifesto and his challenge to churches and synagogues, the members of Católicos por La Raza directly confronted Cardinal Frances McIntyre, one of the most outspoken conservatives in the Catholic hierarchy. McIntyre had either opposed or stayed silent on many civil rights issues over the years. For example, in 1964, the National Catholic Conference for Interracial Justice (NCCIJ) held a vigil outside the Los Angeles Archdiocese to protest McIntyre's refusal to support civil rights legislation. That protest included Martin Luther King Jr. as the featured speaker and a reading of a poem (written by television writer and director Rod Serling) by the actor Dick Van Dyke. The Católicos picketed McIntyre's residence in the fall of 1969 and held a prayer vigil in front of Saint Basil's Church in Los Angeles on Thanksgiving Day, demanding that McIntyre pay attention to poverty in the community. In early December, the Católicos issued a press release urging Catholics to work toward the day "when no members of the Catholic clergy are wealthier than the poorest Mexican-American." Cardinal McIntyre refused to meet with representatives of the Católicos, reportedly saying, "I was here before there were Mexicans. I came to Los Angeles twenty-one years ago." On Christmas Eve, members of the Católicos, intentionally following Forman's example, confronted parishioners at Saint Basil's Church, demanding that Catholics support antipoverty efforts in the Chicano/a community.[9]

The members of Católicos por La Raza focused on the connection of the church to the poor and "called attention to the contradictions within the church concerning the poverty of the people and the wealth of the church."

Faith-Based Activism

They believed that they and the church needed to identify with the poor as Christ did. Richard Cruz, one of the founders of the Católicos, at a press conference announcing the formation of the group noted that the members had committed themselves to "the return of the Catholic Church to the oppressed Chicano community." Cruz said that the organization wanted the church "to become as radical as Christ." An article in *La Raza* in 1970 explained the beliefs of the Católicos regarding their faith and poverty: "because of our Catholic training we know that Christ, the founder of Catholicism was a genuinely poor man. . . . We know that He . . . did all in His power to feed and educate the poor." The Católicos believed that their duty as faithful Catholics was "to not only love the poor but to be as Christlike as possible." Much like Fathers Baroni and Egan and Sargent Shriver, these young Chicano/as saw a direct relationship between their faith and their antipoverty activism.[10]

The link between Católicos por La Raza and Forman and his Black Manifesto is clear. Dolores del Grito in an article titled "Jesus Christ as a Revolutionist" (1970) asked, "Why are the Blacks DEMANDING reparation from the Church? Why have the Young Lords in Harlem taken over a church for a community center? Why did Raza in Los Angeles enter a church on Christmas Eve?"[11] The answer to del Grito and many others was the connection between religion, racial identity, and antipoverty activism.

The twenty-first-century efforts by blacks and Latino/as on issues related to poverty are not surprising. They are the descendants of the black and Latino/a antipoverty organizations created in the 1960s and 1970s that, inspired by black power, feminism, and Chicano/a activism, reshaped the War on Poverty. Some scholars have noted that the religious antipoverty activism of Las Hermanas and Los Padres can be seen as "an ecclesiastical variation on the Latino movements that were generated by the War on Poverty and the radicalism of the late 1960s." Others have observed the connection between the movements of the late 1960s and the faith-based antipoverty organizations active today. Indeed, "the Chicano, civil rights, feminist, and liberation theology movements helped birth many grassroots religious organizations, associations, and faith-based groups that . . . have provided the long-term capacity to carry on" antipoverty activism in Latino/a communities since the 1970s. Some faith-based antipoverty organizations, like the Center for Third World Organizing, intentionally root themselves in the cultural and racial identities of neighborhoods. Activist organizations, like the Center for Third World Organizing, COPS, Las Hermanas, the Latino Pastoral Action Center, and others, continue to fight a Latino/a War on Poverty in the twenty-first century.[12]

The Catholic Church remains one of the key sponsors of faith-based antipoverty community organizing in the United States, particularly through

152   Conclusion

the CHD. The continued presence of the CHD and the programs it sponsors demonstrates that the War on Poverty did not end in the 1970s. It continues today largely through community- and faith-based antipoverty organizations, some of which are funded and whose community organizers are trained by the CHD and other religious groups. America's War on Poverty has not been solely government-based, although many of the groups receiving funds from the CHD have received funds from a combination of federal, state, and local governments.

As scholars Axel R. Schäfer, Alison Collis Greene, and others have shown, this mixed public-private state developed in the second half of the twentieth century. Indeed, since World War II, both secular and religious charities and nonprofit organizations have received federal money to carry out their missions. The term "Cold War subsidiarity" is used by some scholars to describe this postwar relationship, which featured the federal government funding and regulating the activities of private and nonprofit organizations. This fueled the growth of nonprofits from a total of fifty thousand in 1950 to 1.4 million in 1992. Many of these were not nominally religious organizations, but organizations with deep religious commitments. The crucial involvement of churches, synagogues, and other religious organizations in the War on Poverty was part of that trend. For example, religious colleges and universities embraced the Upward Bound program, which enabled the recruitment of low-income students. In addition, the OEO "helped finance congregation-based child care, church-based antipoverty programs, job-creation schemes, migrant worker support, and mental health centers." Often, it was the OEO that approached churches and religious agencies. For example, OEO officials contacted the administrators of an Episcopal Church–funded halfway house and encouraged them to apply for agency antipoverty funds. In a 1966 interview in the *Catholic Standard*, Shriver noted the central relationship between religious organizations and the War on Poverty: "Three or four years ago it was impossible for a federal agency to give a direct grant to a religious group. Today we are giving hundreds of grants without violating the principle of separation of church and state." The War on Poverty money given to faith-based community organizations, like IFCO, is a central example of that relationship. In other words, America's long War on Poverty has reflected and enhanced the development of the nation's evolving public-private state.[13]

A twenty-first-century example of this public-private state and its connection to religious antipoverty organizations was President Barack Obama's Office of Faith-Based and Neighborhood Partnerships (OFBNP), an expansion and redefinition of the Office of Faith-Based and Community Initiatives (OFBCI), which was created by one of the first executive orders signed by President George W. Bush in January 2001. The Bush administration's program, which one scholar called "the culmination of a process of postwar state building that has seen religious organizations receive public funds while retaining their autonomy and asserting their distinctive spiritual dimension," was possible in part because of the inclusion of "charitable choice," a provision in the Personal Responsibility and Work Opportunity Reconciliation Act signed by President Bill Clinton in 1996. That provision required that religious agencies, most of which were coalitions of religious organizations rather than individual churches or synagogues, receive equal consideration for federal money. But faith-based agencies could not discriminate against recipients based on religion and could not require that they participate in religious practices in order to receive program benefits. These elements of charitable choice evolved directly from mainline churches and ecumenical religious organizations' role in implementing antipoverty programs in the 1960s. In addition, the growing influence and rhetoric of the religious right in the 1970s and 1980s led to more interest and activism from conservative religious organizations in antipoverty programs. Indeed, the National Association of Evangelicals provided early support for charitable choice, and conservative politicians became more supportive of the involvement of religious organizations in antipoverty programs. President Bush's initiative built on charitable choice and served as an example of his "compassionate conservatism," which "constituted a promise to empower private religious and community organizations and thereby expand their role in the provision of social services." In many ways, the OFBCI continued and expanded on the pattern established by the OEO of creating partnerships between the federal government and religious organizations in antipoverty efforts. The Bush administration's initiative, though, differed from the philosophy and approach of organizations like COPS, which "work through religious institutions to reshape government policy via the exercise of democratic power." The Bush program emphasized changing individuals and their morals, and it provided significant funding to conservative evangelical and fundamentalist relief organizations, like evangelist Franklin Graham's Samaritan's Purse. In addition, Bush's initiative gave federal funds directly to churches, not just to religious charities and relief agencies.[14]

President Obama's OFBNP, though, connected more directly to the perspective of COPS and other faith-based antipoverty organizations. Obama, a former community organizer who had worked for a faith-based antipoverty organization (the Developing Communities Project of the Calumet Community Religious Conference, whose slogan is "Christ organizing in the midst of community") in Chicago, noted that its top priority would be "making

154   Conclusion

community groups an integral part of our economic recovery and poverty a burden fewer have to bear." Further reflecting this coalescing of church and state, Obama appointed Joshua DuBois, a twenty-six-year-old Pentecostal minister who had served as a campaign advisor, to lead the new office, much to the chagrin of skeptics of government funding of religious organizations and charities, who had hoped for the elimination of the office. The Obama administration promised more transparency with OFBNP programs and that it would incorporate a broader range of religious organizations, not just conservative and evangelical ones. Indeed, the Obama program highlighted the fact that faith-based agencies were as likely to be on the left as on the right. In 2013, the Obama administration replaced DuBois with Melissa Rogers, an attorney and director of the Center for Religion and Public Affairs at the Wake Forest University Divinity School. The administration viewed Rogers as an expert who could provide advice on thorny church-state separation issues, like same-sex marriage. When she was appointed, a White House spokesperson noted that Rogers would "work to advance the President's vision by promoting partnerships that serve the common good in ways that respect church-state separation and religious freedom." Obama's White House office exemplified the continued development of the public-private antipoverty effort that formed during the War on Poverty in the 1960s and has continued in the twenty-first century, largely through faith-based organizations.[15]

This reliance on faith-based organizations to provide community antipoverty programs, though, has limitations. A number of studies have shown that churches, synagogues, and faith-based organizations do not have the resources to address poverty and income inequality in the United States adequately. The bankruptcy or dissolution of many religious charitable organizations during the Great Depression is a prime example of the inability of faith-based organizations to meet the economic demands of the poor. The federal government is the only entity that possesses the capacity to address fully the issues of poverty and income inequality. The privatization of antipoverty programs often means the retrenchment of federal government efforts and conservative attacks on poor people. That does not mean that faith-based organizations and their efforts should be dismissed or treated as insignificant. Indeed, as this book has shown, faith-based community antipoverty organizations that originated during the War on Poverty and continue to fight poverty in the twenty-first century have had a substantial impact on poor and unemployed people in communities throughout America. While ideally the federal government should lead the efforts to reduce or end poverty—and those efforts must include a federally led redistribution of wealth in the United States—in a political climate that makes the expansion of government antipoverty efforts and wealth redistribution difficult at best, religious and faith-based organizations remain significant. As I have demonstrated in this book, many churches, synagogues, priests, nuns, ministers, and rabbis have been deeply and theologically committed to helping the poor, and they often provide spaces in communities for antipoverty programs to operate.[16]

Fathers John Egan and Geno Baroni and the organizations and programs they developed and supported are prime examples of those people and places. In 1983, after thirteen years at the University of Notre Dame, Egan returned to Chicago. There, he continued his involvement in a number of antipoverty organizations, including what became Interfaith Worker Justice. In 1999, Egan began campaigning against the payday loan industry, which charges astronomical interest rates to low-wage, often black and Latino/a workers. After his death at age eighty-four in 2001, the group was renamed the Monsignor John Egan Campaign for Payday Loan Reform. In 2005, the Illinois General Assembly passed the Egan Payday Loan Reform Act, creating significant regulations for the payday loan industry. Baroni founded the National Center for Urban Ethnic Affairs (NCUEA) in 1970 as a response to the Kerner Commission's conclusion that white ethnic racism had played an important role in urban violence in the late 1960s. The NCUEA, reflecting the influence of the War on Poverty and black power, emphasized self-determination and community control, and it trained community organizers to develop local leadership in white ethnic urban areas to challenge various government agencies on issues related to poverty, jobs, income, and education. Father Baroni served as assistant secretary for the Department of Housing and Urban Development, the highest federal office ever held by a Catholic priest, during the administration of President Jimmy Carter and then returned to the NCUEA in the early 1980s before dying of abdominal cancer in 1984 at the age of fifty-three. Monsignor George Higgins, former director of the National Catholic Welfare Conference, eulogized Baroni as "one of the most innovative and most effective Catholic social actionists of his generation." In addition to their individual efforts, the organizations that Egan, Baroni, and others helped develop in the 1960s and 1970s, including the NCCIJ, CCUM, IFCO, and, particularly, the CHD, have continued fighting racism and poverty in the twenty-first century and demonstrate the continuity of the long War on Poverty. These organizations and their antipoverty efforts also demonstrate that the War on Poverty and the ecumenical antipoverty coalition have not been static. They have evolved over the fifty-plus years of their existence, and they have influenced and shaped each other.[17]

156   Conclusion

While direct links exist between the War on Poverty, the Black Manifesto, and continued antipoverty activism by religious and faith-based organizations, a connection also exists with contemporary reparations efforts. Clearly, James Forman's Black Manifesto, despite the controversy over it, forced many churches and religious organizations to admit their guilt in the collective sins of slavery, segregation, and racial violence. While they might have disagreed with the rhetoric and radical politics of the manifesto, many churches and religious organizations increased their contributions to faith-based antipoverty agencies, like IFCO. For the most part, they did not contribute as much as Forman demanded, but they admitted their guilt and gave to antipoverty programs. They clearly saw themselves as paying a form of reparations. Forman's manifesto has served as an example for those since who have argued for reparations for African Americans. The work of scholars Martha Biondi, Elaine Lechtreck, and V. P. Franklin highlights the significance of Forman's manifesto to the movement for reparations. The Black Manifesto clearly influenced groups like the National Coalition of Blacks for Reparations in America, formed in 1987, and the Millions for Reparations rally in Washington, D.C., in 2002.[18]

Several examples of the federal government and the states paying reparations to injured groups exist. The most notable federal example was the 1988 apology and compensation given to Japanese Americans who were imprisoned in detention camps during World War II and their descendants. On the state level, Florida in 1994 agreed to pay compensation to the survivors of the Rosewood massacre. Other nations have compensated victims of genocide and ethnic cleansing. Most notably, Germany paid billions in reparations to survivors of the Holocaust and to the state of Israel. Reparations are not an unusual occurrence.[19]

If the United States were to undertake reparations, what would that look like? Franklin has called for the creation of a "Reparations Superfund," which would fund a host of health care, education, antidrug, antiviolence, and antipoverty programs directed toward African Americans. Some have called for direct payments to African Americans, while others have advocated for expansive job training and public works programs. The journalist Ta-Nehisi Coates, in his brilliant 2014 article, "The Case for Reparations" in the *Atlantic*, argued that any reparations would need to address the wealth gap—really more of a chasm—that separates whites and blacks in America. But Coates argued for more than an economic repayment or, as he stated, "more than recompense for past injustices." Instead, Coates contended that what America needs "is a national reckoning that would lead to spiritual renewal. . . . Reparations would mean a revolution of the American consciousness, a reconciling of our self-image as the great democratizer with the facts of our history."[20] Sargent Shriver, Geno Baroni, John Egan, and antipoverty leaders in the NCC gave a similar call for spiritual renewal to Americans of faith in the 1960s.

The drive for reparations has gained some momentum in recent years with the arrival and influence of the Black Lives Matter movement. With the grassroots protests that appeared initially following the killing of Trayvon Martin in Florida and that grew significantly with the killing of Michael Brown in Missouri, challenges to systemic and institutional racism have been on the rise. Some of the similarities between Black Lives Matter and the arguments by Coates and others for reparations are their scathing critiques of the prevalence and perniciousness of institutional racism in the United States in law enforcement, housing, and political parties.

The election of Donald Trump in 2016 and the Republican control of all three branches of government suggested just how entrenched that institutional racism remains in America, and there may be further attacks on the remnants of government War on Poverty programs. The Trump administration's first proposed budget included cuts to many antipoverty programs—VISTA, AmeriCorps, Upward Bound—as well as other Great Society programs. Clearly, the Trump years will not be kind to government antipoverty efforts. It seems likely that, at least for the foreseeable future, antipoverty efforts will remain some sort of church-state hybrid, with religious organizations continuing to play a central role in the delivery of programs. While this is not ideal, given the amount of resources needed to address the overwhelming poverty in America, it seems as though a church-state hybrid or an ecumenical antipoverty coalition may be the only way in the near future that the War on Poverty will continue to be fought. Those efforts, though limited in scope, have made a difference in the lives of millions of Americans over the past fifty years.

In the long term, what is needed in America is a true War on Poverty, one that would link broad universal economic and redistributive reforms with race-specific policies involving some form of reparations for African Americans. Evident from the fallout over Forman's Black Manifesto—the racial divisions it exposed in American society and the failure of some religious organizations to see those divisions and support reparations—was that many Americans in 1969 failed to deal squarely with their nation's racial past. Unfortunately, that remains true today. Several aspects of the 2016 presidential election demonstrated that. As Ta-Nehisi Coates noted in another seminal essay, "My President Was Black," the research of political scientist Philip Klinkner (based on the American National Election Study) demonstrated that the most predictive poll question asked of likely voters in the 2016 election was not about either Hillary Clinton or Donald Trump. It was, "Is Barack Obama a Muslim?"[21] Of course, white nationalists' unabashed support of Donald Trump; his appointment of Steve Bannon to his administration, though short-lived; Trump's failure to condemn the white nationalists in Charlottesville, Virginia, in 2017; and the related controversy over Confederate statues that celebrate former slaveholders all speak to the clear desire of many white Americans to continue to deny America's racist past and present. Our failure as a nation to engage with that past fully and embrace reparations in 1969 damaged antipoverty efforts then. Our failure to do so now continues to thwart a true War on Poverty, one that would involve the national reckoning and spiritual renewal that Coates suggests and that Sargent Shriver called for in 1965. In the words of Richard Cruz of Católicos por La Raza, a full-scale attempt to tackle poverty in America would require us to be "as radical as Christ." The ecumenical antipoverty coalition that formed around the War on Poverty in the 1960s is an example of that radicalism in action.

MANUSCRIPT REPOSITORIES AND COLLECTIONS

ACUA   American Catholic History Research Center and University Archives, Catholic University of America, Washington, D.C.

AJC   American Jewish Committee Records Online, ajcarchives.org

FJEP   Father John Egan Papers, UNDA

GCBP   Father Geno C. Baroni Papers, UNDA

JFKL   John F. Kennedy Presidential Library, Boston, Massachusetts

MUA   Marquette University Archives, Milwaukee, Wisconsin

NARW   National Assembly of Religious Women Records, UNDA

PHS   Presbyterian Historical Society, Philadelphia, Pennsylvania

SCRBC   Schomburg Center for Research in Black Culture, New York

UMA   United Methodist Archives, Drew University, Madison, New Jersey

UNDA   University of Notre Dame Archives, Notre Dame, Indiana

NOTES

Introduction

1. Address by Sargent Shriver before the General Assembly of the United Presbyterian Church in the USA, May 25, 1965, Shriver Papers, box 47, John F. Kennedy Presidential Library (JFKL).

2. White House Council of Economic Advisers, *War on Poverty 50 Years Later*; and U.S. House of Representatives Budget Committee, *War on Poverty*. For an extended analysis of the Moynihan Report and its legacy, see Geary, *Beyond Civil Rights*.

3. Kiffmeyer, "To Judge Harshly."

4. Hall, "Long Civil Rights Movement." For key examples of this recent scholarship, see R. Williams, *Politics of Public Housing*; Kiffmeyer, *Reformers to Radicals*; Bauman, *Race and the War on Poverty*; Korstad and Leloudis, *To Right These Wrongs*; Sanders, *Chance for Change*; Folwell, "From Massive Resistance"; and Orleck and Hazirjian, *War on Poverty*.

5. Moynihan, *Maximum Feasible Misunderstanding*; Murray, *Losing Ground*; Matusow, *Unraveling of America*; Orleck, *Storming Caesars Palace*; Clayson, *Freedom Is Not Enough*; Rodriguez, *Tejano Diaspora*; Sanders, *Chance for Change*; Folwell, "From Massive Resistance"; Bauman, *Race and the War on Poverty*; Hanhardt, *Safe Space*; Carroll, *Mobilizing New York*; and Cobb, *Native Activism*.

6. Findlay, *Church People*; D. Chappell, *Stone of Hope*; George, *One Mississippi, Two Mississippi*; Collier-Thomas, *Jesus, Jobs, and Justice*; Adams, *Black Women's Christian Activism*; Robertson, *Christian Sisterhood*; and Weisenfeld, *African American Women*.

7. McGreevy, *Parish Boundaries*; and McGreevy, *Catholicism and American Freedom*.

8. Sugrue, "Catholic Encounter," 67.

9. Heineman, "Model City"; Ashmore, "More than a Head Start"; Ashmore, *Carry It On*; Meeker, "Queerly Disadvantaged"; and Phelps, *People's War on Poverty*.

10. M. Chappell, *War on Welfare*; C. Murray, *Losing Ground*.

11. For an excellent summary of the origins of the War on Poverty, see Brauer, "Kennedy, Johnson and the War on Poverty." For an insightful discussion of the intellectual origins of the War on Poverty, see O'Connor, *Poverty Knowledge*, 50–53, 126–28. See

162 Notes to Introduction and Chapter One

also Orleck, "Introduction," in Orleck and Hazirjian, *War on Poverty*, 5–11; Bauman, "Race, Class and Political Power," 15–70; Cloward and Ohlin, *Delinquency and Opportunity*; Harrington, *Other America*; MacDonald, "Our Invisible Poor."

12. Bauman, "Race, Class and Political Power," esp. chapter 1.

13. For more on community-based antipoverty organizations in Los Angeles, see Bauman, *Race and the War on Poverty*. On the OEO's practice of targeting CAAs outside of traditional bureaucracies, see Schäfer, *Piety and Public Funding*, 199.

14. For the best works on evangelicalism in the twentieth century, see Sutton, *American Apocalypse*; and Dochuk, *From Bible Belt to Sunbelt*.

Chapter 1. "Kind of a Secular Sacrament"

1. John Kifner, "Poverty Pickets Get Paper-Bag Dousing on Madison Avenue," *New York Times*, May 28, 1966; "A Little Kiss, Part I," *Mad Men*, March 25, 2012.

2. Stossel, *Sarge*, 10, 11. The Bill Moyers quote is from his foreword to Stossel's book, xvi.

3. R. Joseph, "Sargent Shriver's Spiritual Weapons," 57.

4. Sargent Shriver, speech to the Ohio Catholic Education Association, Cleveland, Ohio, September 23, 1965, Shriver Papers, box 48, John F. Kennedy Presidential Library (JFKL).

5. Engel, "Influence of Saul Alinsky," 646.

6. Zielinski, "Working for Interracial Justice," 234–50; Stossel, *Sarge*, 121–29; McGreevy, *Parish Boundaries*, 86, 148; Southern, *John LaFarge*, xiii–xix.

7. Stossel, *Sarge*, 234–50; and Southern, *John LaFarge*, 328.

8. Zielinski, "Working for Interracial Justice," 234, 250. See also O'Connor, *Poverty Knowledge*, 50–53, 126–28; NCCIJ Press Release, n.d., Geno C. Baroni Papers (GCBP), 6/01, University of Notre Dame Archives (UNDA); "History of NCCIJ," 1978, National Assembly of Religious Women (U.S.) Records (NARW), 11/01, UNDA; Paul Murray, "From the Sidelines to the Front Lines"; and Ahmann to NCCIJ Board Members, November 10, 1959, NCCIJ Records, Board of Directors Files, ser. 2, box 1, Marquette University Archives (MUA).

9. Ahmann, "Preface," in Ahmann, *Race*, x. On Heschel, see Raboteau, *American Prophets*, esp. chapter 1.

10. Martin Luther King Jr., "A Challenge to the Churches and Synagogues," in Ahmann, *Race*, 155–69. For the best and most comprehensive analysis of the centrality of economic justice to King's ideology, see Jackson, *From Civil Rights to Human Rights*.

11. Schultz, *Tri-Faith America*, 180–81; McGreevy, "Racial Justice," 221; Hoy, "Lives on the Color Line"; Paul Murray, "54 Miles to Freedom"; and Southern, *John LaFarge*, 346.

12. NCCIJ Board of Directors meeting minutes, July 27–28, 1963, NCCIJ Records, ser. 2, box 1, MUA.

13. Phil Casey, "Social Issues Held Moral Issues," *Washington Post*, September 10, 1966.

Notes to Chapter One

163

14. O'Rourke, *Geno*, 7–42.

15. Ibid.; MacGregor, *Steadfast in the Faith*, 304–34; MacGregor, *Parish for the Federal City*, 341–43.

16. Baroni, "Church and the War on Poverty," 185; Engel, "Influence of Saul Alinsky," 640; Father Geno Baroni, Testimony to the House Subcommittee on Appropriations for the District of Columbia—Hearings on Appropriations for the District of Columbia's Public Welfare Department, 1965, Father Geno C. Baroni Papers (GCBP), 3/05, UNDA; Brown and McKeown, *The Poor Belong to Us*, 9; and Southern, *John LaFarge*, 371. On the importance of Vatican II to Catholic civil rights activism, see McGreevy, "Racial Justice."

17. Baroni, "Church and the War on Poverty," 184.

18. Ibid., 186–90.

19. Ibid., 192–93. As an inner-city priest, Baroni clearly saw the War on Poverty and community action as geared toward primarily African American urban dwellers. He never mentioned the possibility that rural parishes might be able to use community action as well. This thinking also reflected his view that the War on Poverty was an extension of the civil rights movement.

20. Baroni, "The Church and the Inner City," n.d., GCBP, 3/5, UNDA.

21. Baroni, "Church and the War on Poverty," 191.

22. Baroni, "Inner City Initiatives," *Community*, September 1966, 8.

23. Baroni, "Church and the War on Poverty," 187–88; Baroni, "A Little War on Poverty," *Christianity Today*, June 19, 1964.

24. Engel, "Influence of Saul Alinsky," 646. See also Frisbie, *Alley in Chicago*, 75–80; O'Connor, *Poverty Knowledge*, 53, 134; Orleck, "Introduction," in Orleck and Hazirjian, *War on Poverty*, 12; and Satter, *Family Properties*, 120. On Hillenbrand, see Koeth, "Mental Grandchildren," 104. On Dorothy Day, see Raboteau, *American Prophets*, chapter 3.

25. Quote is from Engel, "Influence of Saul Alinsky," 646. For a detailed discussion of Cardinal Cody's battles with Father Egan and other activist priests in Chicago, see Dahm, *Power and Authority*. For more on the CBL and segregated housing in Chicago, see Coates, "Case for Reparations," 57–58. See also Frisbie, *Alley in Chicago*, 80–110, 179–81, 209–10; Satter, *Family Properties*, 123–46, 233–44, 316–17; and Unsworth, "Chicago's Jack Egan."

26. Baroni to O'Boyle, February 10, 1966, GCBP, 16/04, UNDA.

27. Egan, "Responsibility of Church and Synagogue," 93.

28. Ibid., 96–98.

29. Frisbie, *Alley in Chicago*, 235–36.

30. NCCIJ Board of Directors meeting minutes, February 23 and November 17, 1963, NCCIJ Records, ser. 2, box 1, MUA.

31. NCCIJ Report of the Executive Director, August 1, 1963, NCCIJ Records, ser. 2, box 1; Kennedy telegram to Hilliard, November 14, 1963, NCCIJ Records, ser. 6, National Conventions, box 4, both MUA. See also "Resolutions Adopted by Council Delegates in Convention," November 17, 1963, NCCIJ Records, ser. 6, box 4, MUA.

164 Notes to Chapter One

32. NCCIJ Report of the Executive Director, August 1, 1964, NCCIJ Records, ser. 2, box 1, MUA; "The Human Face of Poverty: A Challenge to Interracial Action—Resolutions Adopted by the Delegates to the Convention of the NCCIJ," August 1965, GCBP, 6/01, UNDA. See also NCCIJ *Commitment* newsletter, September–October 1963, Monsignor Reynold Hillenbrand Papers, 29/29, UNDA. For more on multiracialism and the War on Poverty, see Bauman, *Race and the War on Poverty.*

33. "Human Face of Poverty"; and NCCIJ Report of the Executive Director, August 1965, NCCIJ Records, ser. 2, box 1, MUA.

34. NCCIJ Staff Report, October 21–November 21, 1967, NCCIJ Records, ser. 1, box 2, MUA.

35. A detailed discussion of IFCO and its significance is in chapter 3.

36. Minutes of the meeting of the Board of Directors of NCCIJ, August 20, 1967, GCBP, 29/01, UNDA; Report of Inter-Religious Foundation for Community Organization, March 16, 1967, GCBP, 27/02, UNDA; Steven W. Roberts, "Religious Groups Join to Help Poor," *New York Times*, May 11, 1967.

37. NCCIJ Board Resolution—August 18, 1967, GCBP, 29/01, UNDA.

38. "NCCIJ Report of the Executive Director—February 1968," GCBP, 35/08, UNDA. For more on IFCO, black power, and churches' efforts in the War on Poverty, see chapters 3 and 4.

39. Jones, "Not a Color, but an Attitude"; Jones, *Selma of the North*, 142–43, 254; and Heineman, "Model City," 878–83. On the significance and various types of black power organizations, see P. Joseph, "Rethinking the Black Power Era."

40. Davis, *History of Black Catholics*, 258; "A Statement of the Black Catholic Clergy Caucus, April 18, 1968," in Wilmore and Cone, *Black Theology*, 322; "Brief History of the National Black Sisters Conference," August 1977, NARW, 15/11, UNDA; and Sister M. Martin de Porres Grey, "Black Religious Women as Part of the Answer," National Black Sisters Conference Proceedings, July 1971, IFCO Records, box 3, folder 11, Schomburg Center for Research in Black Culture (SCRBC). See also Davis, "God of Our Weary Years"; Sharps, "Black Catholics in the United States"; and Nickels, *Black Catholic Protest*, 313–14. For more on the evolution of black power and its impact on religious organizations and the War on Poverty, see chapters 3 and 4.

41. Southern, *John LaFarge*, 377.

42. Ahmann to NCCIJ Board of Directors, July 16, 1968; and Rawson L. Wood to NCCIJ Board of Directors, November 8, 1968, both NCCIJ Records, ser. 2, box 4, MUA.

43. Harris to NCCIJ Board of Directors, July 26, 1969; Report of the NCCIJ Executive Director, August 1969, both NCCIJ Records, ser. 2, box 4; and Report of the NCCIJ Executive Director, April 1971, NCCIJ Records, ser. 2, box 6, all MUA.

44. "Possible Program Directions in the 1970s," December 3, 1971, NCCIJ Records, ser. 2, box 6, MUA.

45. Ahmann to Traxler, June 1972, NCCIJ Records, ser. 2, box 6; and minutes of the NCCIJ Board of Directors meeting, February 2, 1975, NCCIJ Records, ser. 2, box 8, both MUA.

Notes to Chapters One and Two 165

46. NCCIJ Press Release, August 20, 1967, NCCIJ Records, ser. 15, Urban Services Department, box 1, MUA; Egan to Baroni, July 13, 1967, GCBP, 27/02, UNDA; and Egan to Seliga, October 6, 1967, NCCIJ Records, ser. 15, box 1, MUA. See also Frisbie, *Alley in Chicago*, 236–38, 241–44.

47. Ahmann to Seliga, n.d., NCCIJ Records, ser. 15, box 1, MUA.

48. Frisbie, *Alley in Chicago*, ix–x, 230–31, 265–66.

49. Engel, "Influence of Saul Alinsky," 648; and Frisbie, *Alley in Chicago*, 243. See also "Catholic Committee on Urban Ministry," flyer, n.d., NARW, 11/02, UNDA; Msgr. John Egan to Father Geno Baroni, April 28, 1967, and minutes of Community Organization meeting, April 25, 1967, both GCBP, 27/02, UNDA; Egan to CCUM Executive Committee, May 11, 1972, NCCIJ Records, ser. 2, box 7, MUA; and Egan, Roach, and Murnion, "Catholic Committee on Urban Ministry," 279–81.

50. Egan to Raskob Foundation for Catholic Activities, October 31, 1973, IFCO Records, box 47, folder 34, SCRBC; Egan to CCUM Members, July 17, 1972, NCCIJ Records, ser. 2, box 7, MUA; and Satter, *Family Properties*, 380.

51. James Forman's Black Manifesto is the focus of chapter 4.

52. "Resolution on the Crusade against Poverty," National Center for Urban Ethnic Affairs Records (NCUEA), 13/64, UNDA; Engel, "Influence of Saul Alinsky," 649–53.

53. Minutes of the Seventh General Meeting of the National Conference of Catholic Bishops, November 10–14, 1969; and "Resolution on the Crusade against Poverty," both NCUEA, 13/64, UNDA. See also Engel, "Influence of Saul Alinsky," 657.

54. Memo from USCC Task Force to Bishop Bernardin, March 7, 1970, GCBP, 13/64, UNDA.

55. Monsignor Jack Egan to Bishop Joseph Bernardin, November 12, 1970, Urban Task Force Papers, National Conference of Catholic Bishops Archives, American Catholic History Research Center and University Archives, Catholic University of America (ACUA); and Engel, "Influence of Saul Alinsky," 660–61.

Chapter 2. The Conscience of the Church

1. Address by Sargent Shriver before the General Assembly of the United Presbyterian Church in the USA, May 25, 1965, Shriver Papers, box 47, John F. Kennedy Presidential Library (JFKL).

2. Findlay, *Church People*, 3–19; and Sullivan, *Party Faithful*, 21.

3. Findlay, *Church People*, 37; Espy to President Johnson, November 22, 1965, National Council of Churches Records (NCC), RG 4, ser. III, box 33, folder 15, Presbyterian Historical Society (PHS).

4. Shirley E. Greene to Dr. George Mace and others, July 6, 1955, NCC, RG 4, ser. IV—Committee on Church and Economic Life, 1948–1970, box 43, folder 9, PHS.

5. "The Churches and Persistent Pockets of Poverty," *NCC Information Service*, October 13, 1962, NCC, RG 4, ser. IV, box 43, folder 9, PHS.

6. Ibid.; Brauer, "Kennedy, Johnson and the War on Poverty," 102–3.

166 Notes to Chapter Two

7. "Prospectus of a Plan to Enable Churches to Discharge Their Responsibility in Relation to Juvenile Delinquency," April 12, 1960, NCC, RG 14, ser. I, box 2, folder 6, PHS; and "The Case for NCC Participation in a Tri-Faith National Community Service Corporation to Combat Poverty," 1965, NCC, RG 6, ser. I, box 7, folder 16, PHS. For more on juvenile delinquency and its relationship to the War on Poverty, see Bauman, *Race and the War on Poverty*, 17–20.

8. "Meeting of the Poverty Film Production Committee," March 7, 1963, NCC, RG 4, ser. IV, box 43, folder 9, PHS. For more on the theory of the culture of poverty and some criticisms of it, see Lewis, *Five Families*; Lewis, *Children of Sanchez*; Wilson, *Truly Disadvantaged*; and Wilson, *Declining Significance of Race*.

9. National Council of the Churches of Christ in the United States of America, "Resolution on Elimination of Poverty," February 26, 1964, NCC, RG 6, ser. IV, box 41, folder 35, PHS.

10. "Action Objectives for the Program of the Churches toward the Elimination of Poverty in the U.S.A.," 1964, NCC, RG 6, ser. IV, box 41, folder 2, PHS.

11. Reverend Shirley E. Greene, "The Elimination of Poverty (a War to Be Waged on Several Fronts)," April 1, 1964, NCC, RG 14, ser. I, box 13, folder 16, PHS. See also Cameron P. Hall, Chairman, Staff Anti-Poverty Committee, "The National Council of Churches' Program on the Church and the Elimination of Poverty," September 8, 1964, NCC, RG 11, ser. I, box 1, folder 23; and "JOIN the National Council's Anti-Poverty Task Force," pamphlet, NCC, RG 9, ser. III, box 45, folder 23, both PHS.

12. *Anti-Poverty Bulletin*, September 1964, January 1965, and March 1965, NCC, RG 6, ser. IV, box 43, folder 26, PHS.

13. *Anti-Poverty Bulletin*, March 1965, ibid.

14. Watt, *Farm Workers and the Churches*, 5, 39–44; and Lowell, *Great Church-State Fraud*, 178–79.

15. Mueller served as president of the NCC from 1963 to 1966. He played a central role in uniting the Evangelical United Brethren Church with the Methodist Church to create the United Methodist Church in 1968.

16. Reuben H. Mueller, Statement on Issues Related to the Elimination of Poverty, House Committee on Education and Labor, April 14, 1964, NCC, RG 6, ser. IV, box 41, folder 36, PHS, emphases in original.

17. Minutes of Staff Anti-Poverty Committee, October 23, 1964, NCC, RG 6, ser. IV, box 41, folder 35, PHS.

18. Cameron P. Hall to Dr. R. H. Edwin Espy, November 6, 1964, NCC, RG 5, ser. IV, box 16, folder 30, PHS.

19. "Poverty Action Targets for the Churches," May 1964, NCC, RG 11, ser. I, box 1, folder 23; Report of the Director of Community Action, September 15, 1964, NCC, RG 6, ser. I, box 6, folder 14, both PHS.

20. Manis, "City Mothers," 132; Commission on Religion and Race meeting minutes, November 5, 1964, NCC, RG 6, ser. I, box 6, folder 14, PHS; and minutes of the Staff Anti-Poverty Committee, January 5, 1965, NCC, RG 10, ser. V, box 22, folder 6, PHS.

Notes to Chapter Two

21. Cameron P. Hall, "Report on the Anti-Poverty Committee," December 1964, NCC, RG 6, ser. I, box 41, folder 35, PHS.

22. Clark, *Christian Case against Poverty*, 103, 109, 117, 124.

23. Greenwood, *One-Fifth of a Nation*, 3, 6, 47.

24. Greenwood, *How Churches Fight Poverty*.

25. "Neighborhood Organization Study—Westminster Neighborhood Association," n.d., Los Angeles Area Federation of Settlements and Neighborhood Centers Records, box 2, California Social Welfare Archives, University of Southern California. For more on the relationship between violence in Watts and the War on Poverty, see Bauman, *Race and the War on Poverty*, esp. chapter 2.

26. Shirley Greene, "Unified Field Program of the Churches against Poverty," 1965, NCC, RG 6, ser. VII, box 61, folder 5; Shirley Greene, "Report of the Staff Anti-Poverty Coordinator," October 1, 1965, NCC, RG 6, ser. VII, box 61, folder 6, both PHS; "Case for NCC Participation."

27. "The Church and the Economic Opportunity Act," 1964, NCC, RG 6, box 61, folder 6, PHS.

28. "The Church and Office of Economic Opportunity Programs," and "Poverty," statement adopted by the Lutheran Church in America, June 1966, both Board of Social Ministry, Lutheran Church in America, Division of Human Relations and Economic Affairs of the General Board of Church and Society, United Methodist Church, box 1441-5-8:03, United Methodist Archives (UMA), Drew University.

29. "The Church and Office of Economic Opportunity Programs," 3, 11.

30. Shirley Greene, Memo No. 5 to Field Staff, November 15, 1965; and Greene, Memo No. 8 to Field Staff, February 21, 1966, both NCC, RG 6, ser. IV, box 41, folder 2, PHS. See also Bauman, "Race, Class and Political Power," 76–79, 82–83.

31. Larold K. Schulz to Anti-Poverty Task Force, January 6, 1967, NCC, RG 6, ser. VII, box 61, folder 5; and Anti-Poverty Task Force to Congress, October 1967, NCC, RG 6, ser. IV, box 41, folder 2, both PHS.

32. Carothers is quoted in Greenwood, *How Churches Fight Poverty*, 7. See also Greene, "Unified Field Program of the Churches against Poverty."

33. Larold K. Schulz to Morris I. Leibman, National Advisory Council on Economic Opportunity, August 17, 1967, NCC, RG 4, ser. III, box 33, folder 37, PHS.

34. "The Church and the Anti-Poverty Program," statement adopted by the General Board of the National Council of Churches of Christ in the USA, December 3, 1966, NCC, RG 6, ser. I, box 7, folder 16; Division of Christian Life and Mission, "A Resolution on Involvement of the Poor," January 5, 1966, NCC, RG 6, ser. IV, box 43, folder 26, both PHS.

35. "Statement by Poor People to General Board of the National Council of Churches," February 1966, NCC, RG 6, ser. IV, box 41, folder 2, PHS.

36. Shirley Greene, "Report of the Staff Anti-Poverty Coordinator," October 1, 1965, NCC, RG 6, ser. VII, box 61, folder 6, PHS.

37. Carothers to Regier, November 29, 1966, NCC, RG 4, ser. III, box 33, folder 37, PHS.

168   Notes to Chapter Two

38. Carothers to Edwin Espy, February 8, 1967, ibid.

39. Carothers to Espy, June 22, 1967, ibid.

40. For the most comprehensive work on the CDGM, see Sanders, *Chance for Change*. See chapter 5 for additional information on NCC support of the CDGM.

41. Espy to Carothers, June 27, 1967, NCC, RG 4, ser. III, box 33, folder 37, PHS.

42. Carothers to Espy, January 25, 1968; and McDaniel to Department of Social Justice, January 17, 1968, both NCC, RG 4, ser. III, box 34, folder 13, PHS.

43. Schaller, *Churches' War on Poverty*, 39–43.

44. Ibid., 43–44.

45. "Memorandum regarding the Formation of the Interreligious Committee against Poverty," July 1965, National Conference of Catholic Charities Records (NCCC), box 178, American Catholic History Research Center and University Archives, Catholic University of America (ACUA). For more on ecumenical efforts on other issues in the 1950s and 1960s, see Kruse, *One Nation under God*.

46. Memo to Executive Committee, Division of Christian Life and Mission, from NCC Anti-Poverty Task Force, April 19, 1965, NCC, RG 6, ser. I, box 7, folder 16, PHS; and Bishop Raymond Gallagher to Mathew Ahmann, July 22, 1965, NCCC, box 178, ACUA.

47. "Memorandum regarding the Formation of the Interreligious Committee against Poverty"; "Case for NCC Participation."

48. "Memorandum regarding the Formation of the Interreligious Committee against Poverty"; Anti-Poverty Task Force meeting minutes, April 13, 1965, and "Special Conditions Applicable to the Use of OEO Grant Funds in Church-Related Schools or School Systems," December 11, 1964, all NCC, RG 6, ser. III, box 41, folder 2, PHS; and Lowell, *Great Church-State Fraud*, 176–77.

49. Schaller, *Churches' War on Poverty*, 79–82; Netting, "Secular and Religious Funding," 591–92.

50. Kelley's interreligious committee's opposition to a constitutional amendment on prayer in schools served as an example for the creation of an interreligious anti-poverty agency. Dean M. Kelley, "The Church and the Poverty Program," *Christian Century*, June 8, 1966, 741–44. See also Schaller, *Churches' War on Poverty*, 83–85; and Kruse, *One Nation under God*, 213–24.

51. "Memorandum regarding the Formation of the Interreligious Committee against Poverty."

52. Ibid.; *Anti-Poverty Bulletin*, June 1965, NCC, RG 6, ser. IV, box 43, folder 26, PHS.

53. "A Prospectus for an Inter-Religious Committee against Poverty," June 1965, ibid.

54. "WICS: Women in Community Service" pamphlet, United Church Women Records, box 1227-3-2:05, UMA, Drew University; Weiner, *Story of WICS*, 20–22; Collier-Thomas, *Jesus, Jobs, and Justice*, 450–53; and Greenwood, *How Churches Fight Poverty*, 135.

55. WICS pamphlet; and *Anti-Poverty Bulletin*, May 1966, NCC, RG 6, ser. IV, box 43, folder 26, PHS.

56. Minutes of the organizational meeting of the Interreligious Committee against Poverty, January 18, 1966, NCC, RG 4, ser. III, box 33, folder 28, PHS.

Notes to Chapter Two

57. Ibid.

58. "Statement Submitted to the Sub-Committee on Employment, Manpower and Poverty of the Senate Committee on Labor and Public Welfare by the Interreligious Committee against Poverty," July 14, 1966, NCC, RG 95, box 22, folder 16, PHS.

59. "A Statement on Poverty: Position Paper by ICAP," September 12, 1966, NCC, RG 4, ser. III, box 33, folder 28, PHS.

60. Davies, *From Opportunity to Entitlement*, 196. See also Bauman, "Race, Class and Political Power," 87–96.

61. Interreligious Committee against Poverty, Testimony on the Economic Opportunity Act Amendments of 1967, July 28, 1967, NCCC, box 178, ACUA; Shriver to Thomas Hinton, June 21, 1967, NCC, RG 4, ser. III, box 33, folder 37, PHS.

62. "Ministry to the Job Corps," October 3, 1966, NCC, RG 6, ser. IV, box 43, folder 12, PHS; Rufus Cornelsen to Dr. R. Edwin Espy, September 26, 1966, NCC, RG 4, ser. III, box 33, folder 28, PHS; Thomas Hinton to Members of the National Catholic Coordinating Committee on Economic Opportunity, April 28, 1967; and "OEO Signs Contract for Job Placement," OEO Press Release, April 25, 1967, both NCCC, box 178, ACUA.

63. Minutes of the Interreligious Committee against Poverty, November 9, 1967, NCCC, box 178, ACUA.

64. Thomas Hinton to ICAP Staff Committee, October 17, 1968; and minutes of the Interreligious Committee against Poverty, October 16, 1968, both NCCC, box 178, ACUA.

65. Thomas Hinton, "Memo on Activities in Which the NCCS Has Been Involved with the National Council of Churches and the Synagogue Council of America," December 1968, NCC, RG 5, ser. IV, box 18, folder 27, PHS; and Schaller, *Churches' War on Poverty*, 31.

66. *The Church and Poverty—A One Hour Special*, transcript, CBS News, March 27, 1966, Producer— Dale Chalmers, Writer—Jonathan Donald, Correspondent—Stuart Novins, NCC, RG 16, ser. II, box 6, folder 9, PHS.

67. Ibid.

68. Ibid.

69. Ibid.

70. Miller, "Billy Graham, Civil Rights," 173–84, quote on 173. See also Miller, *Billy Graham*, 107.

71. Schäfer, *Piety and Public Funding*, 171–72.

72. *The Church and Poverty*.

73. Ibid.

74. Shriver to Rodney Shaw, April 21, 1965, Administrative Records of the Division of Human Relations and Economic Affairs of the General Board of Church and Society, box 1441-5-8:04, UMA.

75. Statement of R. Sargent Shriver, House Subcommittee on the War on Poverty Program, 89th Cong., 1st sess., April 12, 1965, quoted in R. Joseph, "Sargent Shriver's Spiritual Weapons," 67.

170 Notes to Chapters Two and Three

76. Walker Knight, "Shriver Interview: The Church and the Poverty War," *Home Missions*, June 1967, NCCC, box 178, ACUA.

77. Shriver to President Johnson, May 23, 1967; and Shriver to Joseph Califano, May 19, 1967, both Sargent Shriver Papers, OEO Correspondence, box 38, JFKL.

78. Address by Sargent Shriver to United Church Women, New York, February 28, 1966, Shriver Papers, box 50, JFKL.

79. Shriver, "America, Race and the World," 143–44.

80. Speech by Sargent Shriver to Methodist Board of Missions Annual Meeting, Denver, Colorado, January 12, 1968, Shriver Papers, box 57, JFKL.

Chapter 3. Creating an Ecumenical Antipoverty Coalition

1. Findlay, *Church People*, 188–89; Lechtreck, "We Are Demanding $500 Million," 65–66n7; Dave Campbell, "The History and Program of the Interreligious Foundation for Community Organization," Women's Division, United Methodist Church, box 2593-7-4:03, United Methodist Archives (UMA), Drew University; IFCO Status Report, December 1968, National Council of Churches Records (NCC), RG 5, ser. IV, box 18, folder 30, Presbyterian Historical Society (PHS); "The Rev. Lucius Walker Jr. Biographical Information," IFCO Records, box 3, folder 6, Schomburg Center for Research in Black Culture (SCRBC).

2. "The Board of National Missions and the Interreligious Foundation for Community Organization," August 1969, NCC, RG 4, ser. III, box 34, folder 21. See also Campbell, "History and Program"; Memo to Leroy Brininger, November 13, 1967, NCC, RG 6, ser. IV, box 49, folder 1, PHS; IFCO Status Report, December 1968; IFCO Report, May 26, 1969, United Methodist Church, Women's Division, box 2593-7-4:05, UMA; "Background to Foreground," Father John Egan Papers (FJEP), box 82, folder 1, University of Notre Dame Archives (UNDA).

3. Campbell, "History and Program"; IFCO Status Report, December 1968; IFCO Report; IFCO By-Laws, 1966, FJEP, box 164, box 2B, UNDA.

4. Minutes of ICAP staff meeting, February 28, 1968, NCCC, box 178, ACUA.

5. AJC Executive Committee meeting minutes, October 1947, quoted in Sanua, *Let Us Prove Strong*, 33; Cohen, *Not Free to Desist*, 383–407.

6. A. M. Sonnabend, "The Sanctity of the Human Being," *AJC Committee Reporter* 21, no. 1 (1964): 12; AJC annual meeting transcript, April 29–May 3, 1964, 24–26 (Hoffman), quoted in Sanua, *Let Us Prove Strong*, 159. See also Cohen, *Not Free to Desist*, 383–407; and Sanua, *Let Us Prove Strong*, 158–64.

7. The American Jewish Committee, "Statement of Poverty," Fifty-Seventh Annual Meeting, April 29, 1964; and "Guidelines on the Role and Responsibility of AJC in the Anti-Poverty Program," American Jewish Committee Fifty-Eighth Annual Meeting, May 22, 1965, both Poverty File, AJC Resolutions and Statements Collections, American Jewish Committee Records Online (AJC). See also Cohen, *Not Free to Desist*, 383–407; and Sanua, *Let Us Prove Strong*, 166–67.

Notes to Chapter Three 171

8. Hirsch to Shriver, December 2, 1964, Shriver Papers, box 46, John F. Kennedy Presidential Library (JFKL).

9. Tanenbaum, "Role of the Church and Synagogue," 189; Sanua, *Let Us Prove Strong*, 462–64.

10. Rabbi Marc Tanenbaum to Rabbi Bernard Mandelbaum, November 26, 1968, AJC Interreligious Affairs Department, Black-Jewish Relations File, AJC; Tanenbaum quoted in Campbell, "History and Program."

11. Campbell, "History and Program"; IFCO Status Report, December 1968; Notes on Structure and Function of IFCO Black Caucus, IFCO Records, box 2, folder 1, SCRBC; "The Board of National Missions and the Interreligious Foundation for Community Organization." For more on Reverend Cleage, see Dillard, "Religion and Radicalism"; and Dillard, *Faith in the City*. Interracial battles over limited antipoverty funds were not unique to IFCO. For examples of this occurring in Los Angeles, see Bauman, *Race and the War on Poverty*, esp. chapters 3 and 5; and Bauman, "Neighborhood Adult Participation Project."

12. IFCO Status Report, December 1968; "Fact Sheet on National Committee of Black Churchmen," September 17, 1969, NCC, RG 5, ser. IV, box 19, folder 19, PHS; Findlay, *Church People*, 189. See also Shattuck, *Episcopalians and Race*, 166; and Dillard, *Faith in the City*, 293.

13. "Findings of Black Methodists for Church Renewal," 1968, box 2574-6-4:07, UMA. See also Shattuck, *Episcopalians and Race*, 166–69, 181; Swartz, *Moral Minority*, 189–90; Dupont, *Mississippi Praying*, 233; and Alvis, *Religion and Race*, 128–30.

14. IFCO Status Report, December 1968.

15. For more on the WLCAC, TELACU, CSAC, and other culturally nationalist antipoverty agencies, see Bauman, *Race and the War on Poverty*; and Bauman, "Black Power and Chicano Movements."

16. Most of the best works on black power are by Peniel Joseph. See his edited collection, *The Black Power Movement*; "Rethinking the Black Power Era"; and *Waiting 'til the Midnight Hour*. For an excellent recent work, see R. Williams, *Concrete Demands*. On Marcus Garvey's religious thinking, see Hough, *Black Power and White Protestants*, 31.

17. West, "Whose Black Power?," 279–80.

18. David R. Hunter to Committee of 16, July 17, 1969, NCC, RG 5, ser. IV, box 13, folder 21, PHS; Cone, *Speaking the Truth*, 38; Cone, *Black Theology of Liberation*, 14.

19. Cleage, *Black Christian Nationalism*, 42–43, xii, 44; Dillard, *Faith in the City*, 293.

20. Cone, *Black Theology of Liberation*, v.

21. IFCO Board of Directors minutes, December 11, 1968, IFCO Records, box 1, folder 1, SCRBC; "The Board of National Missions and the Interreligious Foundation for Community Organization."

22. Kay Longcope, "IFCO in Action: City Projects Funded by Interreligious Unit," *Approach: The Mission/Education Weekly*, April 29, 1968, NCC, RG 5, ser. IV, box 14, folder 26, PHS; IFCO-Funded Projects, September 1967–May 1969, IFCO Records,

172 Notes to Chapter Three

box 19, folder 2, SCRBC; "Projects Funded by the Interreligious Foundation for Community Organization (IFCO)," September 1967–April 1969, NCC, RG 5, ser. IV, box 18, folder 30, PHS; "The Board of National Missions and the Interreligious Foundation for Community Organization."

23. Longcope, "IFCO in Action"; IFCO-Funded Projects; "Projects Funded by the Interreligious Foundation for Community Organization (IFCO)"; Progress Report of the Los Angeles Black Congress, 1968, IFCO Records, box 30, folder 25, SCRBC. For more on Karenga, the Los Angeles Black Congress, and the US organization, see Brown, *Fighting for US*.

24. "Projects Funded by IFCO," September 1967–April 1970, IFCO Records, box 19, folder 2, SCRBC. For more on the connections between the War on Poverty and empowerment movements, see Bauman, *Race and the War on Poverty*; and Bauman, "Black Power and Chicano Movements."

25. Longcope, "IFCO in Action"; IFCO Status Report, June 1968, IFCO Records, box 19, folder 2, SCRBC; IFCO Criteria for Funding Community Organizations, June 13, 1967, IFCO Records, box 19, folder 2, SCRBC.

26. IFCO Status Report, December 1968. See also Campbell, "History and Program"; Alvin Duskin, Institute for Urban Affairs, to Lucius Walker, November 3, 1967, Geno C. Baroni Papers (GCBP), 27/02, UNDA.

27. Walker to Trevor Austin Hoy, July 16, 1968, IFCO Records, box 3, folder 2, SCRBC.

28. Walker to Walter Bremond, July 18, 1968, IFCO Records, box 30, folder 25, SCRBC.

29. "IFCO to Train Organizers of Blacks in Watts," *Approach*, May 27, 1968; "Briefings from the Department of Social Justice," January 1968, NCC, RG 6, ser. IV, Committee on Church and Economic Life, box 49, PHS; IFCO Status Report, December 1968; Brown, *Fighting for US*, 82–84.

30. Campbell, "History and Program"; Louis Gothard, Union Theological Seminary Speech, May 1969, IFCO Records, SCRBC.

31. "Who Is IFCO?," brochure, 1968, NCC, RG 5, ser. IV, box 14, folder 29, PHS.

32. Dan Jardin, "U.S. Probes Religious Groups on Financing L.A. Militants," *National Catholic Reporter*, May 7, 1969; Ronald Koziol, "Police Find Churches Aid Militants," *Chicago Tribune*, May 11, 1969; "Tax-Exempt Group Tied to Dissidents," *New York Times*, May 13, 1969. For more on the Black Panthers' relationship with police, see P. Joseph, *Waiting 'til the Midnight Hour*.

33. "Tax-Exempt Group Tied to Dissidents"; "Response by IFCO," *National Catholic Reporter*, May 16, 1969. On FBI surveillance of the US organization, the Black Panthers, and the Black Congress, see Brown, *Fighting for US*.

34. FBI Agent Report, May 8, 1969, box 8, folder 5, IFCO Records, SCRBC.

35. Detroit FBI Office Report to FBI Director, August 7, 1968; and New York FBI Office Report to the FBI Director, August 12, 1968, both Federal Bureau of Investigation, COINTELPRO Files, https://vault.fbi.gov/cointel-pro (accessed February 2, 2016). See also FBI Agent Report, May 8, 1969, and FBI Agent Report, May 15, 1969, both box 8, folder 5, IFCO Records, SCRBC.

Notes to Chapters Three and Four

36. Confidential FBI Source Report, June 6, 1969, and Confidential FBI Source Report, July 8, 1969, box 8, folder 5; Urgent Message from FBI Agent to Director, June 13, 1969, box 8, folder 6, all IFCO Records, SCRBC; IFCO 20th Anniversary Conference Program, 1987, Father John Egan Papers (FJEP), box 164, UNDA.

37. Detroit FBI Office to FBI Director, October 1, 1969, Federal Bureau of Investigation, COINTELPRO Files, https://vault.fbi.gov/cointel-pro (accessed February 2, 2016). For more on the League of Revolutionary Black Workers, see Geschwender, *Class, Race, and Worker Insurgency*.

38. IFCO 20th Anniversary Conference Program.

39. Board of Christian Social Concerns of the United Methodist Church, statement, May 20, 1969; Board of Christian Social Concerns of the United Methodist Church, letter, May 22, 1969, both box 1444-5-1:10, UMA.

40. Statement of Dr. J. Edward Carothers, May 12, 1969, Records of the National Division of the General Board of Ministries, box 2539-3-5:4, UMA.

41. "The Board of National Missions and the Interreligious Foundation for Community Organization."

42. David R. Hunter to Mr. James E. Kinnear, May 16, 1969, NCC, RG 4, ser. III, box 34, folder 15, PHS.

43. IFCO Board of Directors minutes, September 9–10, 1968, box 1, folder 1, IFCO Records, SCRBC. For more on CDCs and their relationship to the War on Poverty, see Ferguson, *Top Down*; Hill and Rabig, *Business of Black Power*; Bauman, *Race and the War on Poverty*, chapters 4 and 5; and Bauman, "Black Power and Chicano Movements."

44. Walker to Right Reverend Paul Moore, Diocese of Washington, July 15, 1968, box 14, folder 5, IFCO Records, SCRBC; "A Report of IFCO," April 1970, NCC, RG 5, ser. IV, box 14, folder 30, PHS.

45. IFCO to Economic Development Council of Greater Detroit, January 9, 1969, box 14, folder 6, IFCO Records, SCRBC; "The Board of National Missions and the Interreligious Foundation for Community Organization."

46. IFCO, National Black Economic Development Conference brochure, 1969, NCC, RG 6, ser. III, box 35, folder 14, PHS.

47. National Black Economic Development Conference Press Release, April 22, 1969, box 15, folder 2, IFCO Records, SCRBC. On the dearth of discussions on the NBEDC in historical scholarship on black power, see West, "Whose Black Power?," 278–79.

48. Black Economic Development Conference, Press Release, September 10, 1969, box 15, folder 2, IFCO Records, SCRBC; "A Report of IFCO"; "IFCO: The Interreligious Foundation for Community Organization," United Methodist Church, Women's Division, box 2593-7-4:05, UMA; West, "Whose Black Power?," 280.

49. See Bauman, *Race and the War on Poverty*, esp. chapters 4 and 5.

Chapter 4. The Black Manifesto

1. "Black Manifesto: To the White Christian Churches and the Jewish Synagogues in the United States of America and All Other Racist Institutions," National Black

174 Notes to Chapter Four

Economic Development Conference, April 26, 1969, National Council of Churches Records (NCC), RG 4, ser. III, box 34, folder 15, Presbyterian Historical Society (PHS).

2. P. Joseph, *Waiting 'til the Midnight Hour*; R. D. G. Kelley, *Freedom Dreams*, 120; R. Williams, *Concrete Demands*; West, "Whose Black Power?"; Dillard, *Faith in the City*, 296–97; Lechtreck, "We Are Demanding $500 Million," 40; Findlay, *Church People*.

3. The best source for Forman's activist career is Forman, *Making of Black Revolutionaries*. See also Lechtreck, "We Are Demanding $500 Million," 39–40.

4. Forman, *Making of Black Revolutionaries*, 543–545. See also R. Williams, *Concrete Demands*, 183.

5. R. Williams, *Concrete Demands*, 183; West, "Whose Black Power?," 280; Lechtreck, "We Are Demanding $500 Million," 43–44; "A Report of IFCO," April 1970, NCC, RG 5, ser. IV, box 14, folder 30, PHS.

6. "Black Manifesto," 1, 2. See also L. Williams, "Christianity and Reparations," 40; R. Williams, *Concrete Demands*, 184; and West, "Whose Black Power?," 281–82. Robin Kelley notes that $500 million was "a paltry sum" given that it amounted only to $15 per African American at the time. Kelley, *Freedom Dreams*, 121–22. Forman's demand for a land bank reflected a growing emphasis on agrarianism in black nationalist thought. See Rickford, "We Can't Grow Food."

7. "Black Manifesto," 3.

8. Bedau, "Compensatory Justice," 136. See also R. Williams, *Concrete Demands*, 65, 185; West, "Whose Black Power?," 280; Biondi, "Rise of the Reparations Movement," 7; and Berry, *My Face Is Black Is True*. Some of the key recent scholarship that has addressed reparations efforts includes Berry, *My Face Is Black Is True*; Biondi, "Rise of the Reparations Movement"; Robinson, *The Debt*; Roy E. Finkenbine, "Historians and Reparations," *OAH Newsletter*, February 2006, 3; and a special issue of the *Journal of African American History* in 2012. See Franklin, "Introduction."

9. "Black Manifesto," 1, 2; and Forman, *Making of Black Revolutionaries*, 545. See also West, "Whose Black Power?," 282; and Findlay, *Church People*, 201.

10. IFCO Press Release, May 5, 1969, RG 5, ser. IV, box 18, folder 30; "The Board of National Missions and the Interreligious Foundation for Community Organization," August 1969, RG 4, ser. III, box 34, folder 21, both NCC, PHS; "A Report of IFCO"; and "IFCO: The Interreligious Foundation for Community Organization," May 26, 1969, box 2593-7-4:05, Women's Division, United Methodist Archives (UMA), Drew University.

11. West, "Whose Black Power?," 282–83, emphases in original; Dillard, *Faith in the City*, 296; and Geschwender, *Class, Race, and Worker Insurgency*, 144.

12. David R. Hunter to Committee of 16, July 17, 1969, NCC, RG 5, ser. IV, box 13, folder 21, PHS. See also Lechtreck, "We Are Demanding $500 Million," 66–67n29.

13. "Black Manifesto," 13.

14. "Response of the Executive Committee of the National Council of Churches to the Black Manifesto," May 2, 1969, NCC, RG 4, ser. III, box 34, folder 15, PHS.

15. James Forman to the Board of Deacons and the Membership of Riverside Church, May 4, 1969, NCC, RG 4, ser. III, box 34, folder 18, PHS.

Notes to Chapter Four 175

16. Ibid.

17. Ibid. See also McGraw, "Down by the Riverside."

18. McGraw, "Down by the Riverside."

19. Earnest A. Smith, "Meeting of Black Staff of Major Denominations," May 6, 1969, box 2593-7-4:02, UMA.

20. *Religious Newsweekly*, May 27, 1969, NCC, RG 9, ser. I, box 1, folder 9, PHS.

21. "Statement of the Board of Directors, NCBC," May 7, 1969, box 1444-5-1:10, UMA. See also "A Chronicle of the Black Manifesto Debate in National Religious Bodies as of August 21, 1969," box 1440-4-3:12, UMA.

22. "Chronicle of the Black Manifesto Debate"; *Religious Newsweekly*.

23. Campbell's radio message is quoted in Arnold Lubasch, "Pastor at Riverside Pledges a Fund for the Poor," *New York Times*, May 11, 1969. Campbell's Zaccheus sermon is quoted in Lechtreck, "We Are Demanding $500 Million," 49.

24. Campbell is quoted in Edward B. Fiske, "Forman Stirs Church Power Struggle," *New York Times*, July 27, 1969. Campbell's sermon led to his book *The Christian Manifesto* (1970), in which he advocated for Christians' involvement in antipoverty efforts and other social issues. See also Lechtreck, "We Are Demanding $500 Million," 50; and Cline, *From Reconciliation to Revolution*, 189.

25. NCCIJ *Commitment* newsletter, September–October 1969, Monsignor Reynold Hillenbrand Papers, 136/09, UNDA. In addition to Walker's talk, the NCCIJ program featured presentations by Jesse Jackson of Operation Breadbasket, Cesar Chavez of the United Farm Workers, and Arthur Fletcher, assistant secretary of labor for the Nixon administration and one of the key architects of affirmative action. See also NCCIJ Press Release, August 8, 1969; and NCCIJ 1969 National Convention program, both George Gilmary Higgins Papers, box 162, folder 8, American Catholic History Research Center and University Archives, Catholic University of America (ACUA); and Lechtreck, "We Are Demanding $500 Million," 48.

26. James T. Harris Jr., Executive Director, NCCIJ, to Councils and Commissions, November 7, 1969, Higgins Papers, box 162, folder 8, ACUA. See also Cline, *From Reconciliation to Revolution*, 189.

27. Handy, *History of Union Theological Seminary*, 281–82. See also "Chronicle of the Black Manifesto Debate"; and Cline, *From Reconciliation to Revolution*, 188.

28. Statement of Ad Hoc Committee for Justice from the Presbyterian Church to the United Presbyterian Church, USA, May 14, 1969, box 1440-4-5:10; and Tracey K. Jones memo to Council of Secretaries, regarding Events at 475, July 14, 1969, box 2593-7-4:05, both UMA; and "Chronicle of the Black Manifesto Debate." See also Findlay, *Church People*, 204; Cline, *From Reconciliation to Revolution*, 187; Lechtreck, "We Are Demanding $500 Million," 56.

29. Risco quoted in Brackenridge and García-Treto, *Iglesia Presbiteriana*, 213; Mantler, *Power to the Poor*, 56–59. See also "Chronicle of the Black Manifesto Debate."

30. "Response of United Presbyterian Church, USA, to Demands of NBEDC," May 19, 1969, NCC, RG 11, ser. I, box 2, folder 3, PHS.

31. Ibid.

176   Notes to Chapter Four

32. Ibid.

33. George Sweazy to Fellow Presbyterians, May 21, 1969, box 2593-7-4:01, UMA.

34. Ad Hoc Committee report, June 23, 1969, box 2593-7-4:02, UMA; and Jones memo to Council of Secretaries.

35. Lechtreck, "We Are Demanding $500 Million," 52; James Forman to Dr. Ben Herbster, President, and Dr. Howard Spragg, Executive Vice President, United Church of Christ, May 14, 1969, box 1440-4-5:10, UMA.

36. Lechtreck, "We Are Demanding $500 Million," 52; Mareta Kahlenberg to Forman, June 18, 1969, box 1440-4-5:10, UMA.

37. "Chronicle of the Black Manifesto Debate."

38. "A Model for Involving Black Staff Members in Board of Missions Decisions," box 2593-7-4:01; and "The Economic Liberation Committee Demands," box 1444-5-1:10, both UMA.

39. "Economic Liberation Committee Demands"; and "Chronicle of the Black Manifesto Debate."

40. See Board of Missions of the United Methodist Church, General Executive Committee meeting minutes, May 26–27, 1969, box 2593-7-4:04; *United Methodist Information*, June 2, 1969, box 1444-5-1:10, both UMA; and Economic Liberation Committee Demands. After serving as director of the United Methodist Black Caucus, Cain Felder served as pastor of Grace United Methodist Church from 1972 to 1975, taught in the Department of Biblical Studies at Princeton University, and has been a professor at the Howard University School of Divinity since 1981.

41. Board of Missions, General Executive Committee meeting minutes.

42. Board of Missions, General Executive Committee, "Proposed Action," May 26, 1969, box 2593-7-4:01, UMA.

43. Board of Missions, General Executive Committee meeting minutes. See also Economic Liberation Committee Demands; *United Methodist Information*, June 2, 1969; and "Chronicle of the Black Manifesto Debate."

44. Board of Missions, General Executive Committee meeting minutes.

45. Lloyd C. Wicke and Tracey K. Jones to Members of the Board of Managers, May 29, 1969, box 2574-6-4:08, UMA.

46. *United Methodist Information*, June 17, 1969, box 2593-7-4:06, UMA.

47. Quoted in Betty Thompson, "A View from 475," *Engage*, July 15, 1969, 14, box 1350-3-1:41, UMA.

48. "NBEDC Liberates NCC Offices," *Crisis in the Nation*, June 6, 1969, RG 9, box 1, folder 10, UMA; Jones memo to Council of Secretaries; John Biersdorf, Executive Director, National Council of Churches, Department of Ministry memo, July 1, 1969, RG 9, ser. I, box 1, folder 11; and Jon Regier to Dr. Dudley Ward, June 12, 1969, RG 6, ser. I, box 7, folder 18, both NCC, PHS.

49. Jones memo to Council of Secretaries.

50. Forman's June 13 statement is quoted in Thompson, "View from 475," 12. Forman's open letter, June 17, 1969, IFCO Records, box 17, folder 6, SCRBC; and Jones memo to Council of Secretaries.

Notes to Chapter Four

51. Jones memo to Council of Secretaries; John A. Lovelace, "The Black Manifesto" and "Questions and Answers," both *Christian Advocate*, July 10, 1969, NCC, RG 9, ser. I, box 1, folder 11, PHS.

52. A. Dudley Ward, "A Possible Tentative Response to the Events of Our Time," June 29, 1969, box 2587-6-2:02, UMA.

53. "Report from Staff Team on Black Manifesto," June 4, 1969, RG 11, ser. I, box 2, folder 4; and Jon Regier to Dr. Dudley Ward, June 12, 1969, RG 6, ser. I, box 7, folder 18, both NCC, PHS.

54. Forman to Espy, June 13, 1969, box 1440-4-5:10, UMA.

55. "Statement on the Black Manifesto," June 23, 1969, NCC, RG 4, ser. III, box 34, folder 15, PHS.

56. Ibid.

57. Ibid. See also Thompson, "View from 475"; Jones memo to Council of Secretaries; and "Chronicle of the Black Manifesto Debate."

58. Rollins quoted in Thompson, "View from 475," 11. See also Jones memo to Council of Secretaries; and "Chronicle of the Black Manifesto Debate."

59. Statement of Ad Hoc Committee of 475 Riverside Drive, June 23, 1969, box 1440-4-5:10, UMA.

60. Thompson, "View from 475," 11.

61. R. H. Edwin Espy to Members of the General Board, July 17, 1969, NCC, RG 9, ser. I, box 1, folder 11, PHS.

62. Executive Committee of the General Board meeting minutes, July 14, 1969, NCC, RG 4, ser. III, box 34, folder 15, PHS.

63. Ibid.; Committee of Sixteen meeting minutes, June 30, 1969, and July 10, 1969, both NCC, RG 4, ser. III, box 34, folder 21, PHS.

64. Quoted in Hubert C. Noble to Dr. Gerald Knoff, July 22, 1969, NCC, RG 9, ser. I, box 1, folder 11, PHS. See also Committee of Sixteen meeting minutes, July 21, 1969, NCC, RG 4, ser. III, box 34, folder 21, PHS.

65. Committee of Sixteen meeting minutes, August 28, 1969, NCC, RG 5, ser. IV, box 13, folder 21, PHS.

66. Tracey K. Jones, "Patterns of Response of the Board of Missions to the Black Manifesto," August 29, 1969, box 2793-7-4:05, UMA.

67. *United Methodist Information*, November 20, 1969, box 1444-5-1:10, UMA; David Rohn, "Response to Manifesto Is Told by Clergy," *Indianapolis News*, September 24, 1969.

68. Robert L. Gildea, "Black Manifesto Clarified," *Interchurch*, October 1969, NCC, RG 5, ser. IV, box 13, folder 18, PHS.

69. IFCO Press Release. See also "The Board of National Missions and the Interreligious Foundation for Community Organization"; "A Report of IFCO"; and Findlay, *Church People*, 211.

70. Statement Issued by Member Groups of IFCO, read by Marc H. Tanenbaum, IFCO president, to white caucus of IFCO, May 6, 1969, NCC, RG 5, ser. IV, box 13, folder 17, PHS.

178   Notes to Chapters Four and Five

71. "IFCO President, Executive Differ on Stand: Rabbi Hits Manifesto's Ideology, Rhetoric," *Religious News Service*, May 12, 1969, NCC, RG 5, ser. IV, box 13, folder 17, PHS.

72. "The Black Manifesto of the Black Economic Development Conference," a policy statement issued by the Synagogue Council of America and the National Jewish Community Relations Advisory Council, May 12, 1969; and Synagogue Council of America and National Jewish Community Relations Advisory Council Press Release, May 12, 1969, both Bertram Gold Executive Papers, Black Manifesto File, American Jewish Committee Records Online (AJC). President Johnson appointed the Kerner Commission in 1967 in response to continued racial unrest in American cities. The commission report, issued in 1968, highlighted continued segregation and a lack of economic opportunities for African Americans in major cities.

73. Bertram H. Gold to Lucius Walker, May 7, 1969, box 16, folder 3, SCRBC; American Jewish Committee Executive Committee meeting minutes, May 15, 1969, AJC.

74. American Jewish Committee Resolution on IFCO, May 15, 1969, AJC.

75. Walker to Gold, May 16, 1969, box 16, folder 3, SCRBC.

76. Rabbi Marc H. Tanenbaum to Reverend Glenn Hatfield, June 6, 1969, AJC Interreligious Affairs Department, AJC.

77. Arnold Aronson to Member Agencies, May 28, 1969, AJC.

Chapter 5. Fracturing the Antipoverty Coalition

1. These figures are from a Gallup poll conducted in June 1969 and are noted in both Shearer, *Daily Demonstrators*, 190; and M. Newman, *Getting Right with God*, 188.

2. David Rohn, "Response to Manifesto Is Told by Clergy," *Indianapolis News*, September 24, 1969 (includes Craine quote); and "Diocese Pledges Funds to Black Group," *Washington Post*, September 14, 1969 (Marmion). See also Robert L. Gildea, "Black Manifesto Clarified," *Interchurch*, October 1969, National Council of Churches Records (NCC), RG 5, ser. IV, box 13, folder 18, Presbyterian Historical Society (PHS); Lechtreck, "We Are Demanding $500 Million," 52–53.

3. Rose, *The Grass Roots Church*, 5, 6; Rose, "Reparations Now!," 14. See also Rose, "Putting It to the Churches"; and Cline, *From Reconciliation to Revolution*, 189.

4. Rose, "Reparations Now!"

5. Second United Methodist Conference of New and Furloughed Missionaries to Wicke, Jones and the Board of Missions of the United Methodist Church, June 20, 1969, box 1440-4-3:24, United Methodist Archives (UMA), Drew University.

6. Executive Committee of the Division of Christian Social Concern, American Baptist Convention, "A Pastoral Letter to the Churches on the Black Manifesto and American Racism," box 1440-4-3:03, UMA.

7. NCC Division of Overseas Ministries Executive Committee meeting minutes, June 17, 1969, box 1440-4-3:05, UMA.

8. "Analysis of Mail Received by Dr. Tracey K. Jones, Jr., and Bishop Lloyd C. Wicke," August 21, 1969, box 1440-4-3:12, UMA.

9. Ibid.

Notes to Chapter Five   179

10. Mrs. Paul Rundle to Mrs. J. Boyd Tyrrell, United Methodist Church Board of Missions, May 28, 1969, UMA.

11. Ibid., emphasis in original.

12. Ibid.

13. Ibid., emphases in original.

14. Mrs. Mary Dollger to Reverend Jon Regier, May 7, 1969, NCC, RG 6, ser. I, box 7, folder 18, PHS, emphases in original.

15. Ibid., emphases in original.

16. Ruotsila, *Fighting Fundamentalist*, 1; "Church Reparations Demanded for Fundamentalists," *New York Times*, September 15, 1969; Lechtreck, "We Are Demanding $500 Million," 63.

17. G. Paul Beck Jr. to Editors of the *Christian Advocate*, September 4, 1969, 6.

18. Hugh Fouke to Editors of the *Christian Advocate*, September 4, 1969, 5.

19. W. Hugh Barber to Editors of the *Christian Advocate*, September 4, 1969, 5–6.

20. N. C. McPherson Jr. to Dr. Tracey K. Jones, May 29, 1969, box 2593-7-4:01, UMA.

21. Ibid.

22. Bishop J. Gordon Howard to the United Methodist Churches of the Philadelphia Area, June 11, 1969, box 2593-7-4:02, UMA.

23. Bishop Roy Short, speech at the meeting of the Southeastern Jurisdictional Council of the United Methodist Church, November 17, 1969, published in *United Methodist Information*, November 20, 1969, box 1444-5-1:10, UMA.

24. W. Ralph Ward, "Situation Changes, Church No Longer Left Untouched," *Mission Memo*, September 1969, UMA.

25. Reuben H. Mueller, "Churches Reject Black Manifesto Plan," *Together*, August 1969.

26. Carolyn Wilhelm, "Where the Action Is . . . or—What's with the Black Manifesto?," *Response*, July–August 1969, 21–25.

27. "Church Policy and the Black Manifesto," box 1440-4-4:12, UMA.

28. Lloyd C. Wicke and Tracey K. Jones to United Methodist Church Pastors and Leaders, October 30, 1969, box 2593-7-4:06, UMA.

29. Gildea, "Black Manifesto Clarified"; "Response of the Christian Church (Disciples of Christ) to the Black Manifesto," May 27, 1969, box 1440-4-3:03, UMA.

30. "Response of the Christian Church."

31. "Beazley Buzz," *News on Christian Unity*, July 22, 1969, box 1440-4-3:03, UMA.

32. Gildea, "Black Manifesto Clarified," 7.

33. Ibid., 7, 8.

34. Ibid., 7.

35. Ibid., 8.

36. Shearer, *Daily Demonstrators*, 192, 199. See also Hinojosa, *Latino Mennonites*, 80–82.

37. Powell quoted in Hinojosa, *Latino Mennonites*, 82. Shearer, *Daily Demonstrators*, 214. Both Hinojosa and Shearer made this argument, although Hinojosa also pointed out resistance by some white Mennonites, particularly as the War on Poverty became more controversial.

180 Notes to Chapter Five

38. Dye, "Lessons in Hearing," 78. The community of Bloomfield Hills is the wealthiest in the state of Michigan based on average income, while Detroit is one of the poorest cities in the United States.

39. Letters quoted in Dye, "Lessons in Hearing," 82. See also Reverend Robert E. Morrison to the Rector, Wardens and Vestry of Christ Church Cranbrook, June 18, 1969, box 1440-4-3:01, UMA. Importantly, Dye argued that the manifesto led to greater social activism at Cranbrook.

40. "Proposals by the Black Methodists for Church Renewal of Ohio of the United Methodist Church to Our White Brothers and Sisters of the United Methodist Church," June 10, 1969, box 1440-4-5:05, UMA, emphasis in original.

41. Clifton Kirkpatrick, Greater Dallas Council of Churches, "The Black Manifesto: A Cause for Concern," box 1440-4-3:01, UMA.

42. Gayraud S. Wilmore Jr., "The Church's Response to the Black Manifesto," June 23, 1969, NCC, RG 5, ser. IV, box 13, folder 17, 7, 18, PHS.

43. Ibid., 6, 7, 18.

44. Ralph Abernathy, "A Black Preacher Looks at the Black Manifesto," *Christian Century*, August 13, 1969, 1064–65.

45. Quoted in Edward B. Fiske, "Forman Stirs Church Power Struggle," *New York Times*, July 27, 1969.

46. Ibid.

47. "The Issue Is Economic Justice," *Christian Century*, June 25, 1969, 2.

48. "The National Division and IFCO," *Mission Memo*, September 1969, 11.

49. "Protestants Give on a Local Basis," *New York Times*, August 10, 1969.

50. Lu Walker to Robert A. Hoppe, Synod of Ohio, United Presbyterian Church, July 30, 1969, IFCO Records, box 16, folder 3, SCRBC.

51. IFCO Board of Directors meeting minutes, June 11, 1969, IFCO Records, box 1, folder 1, SCRBC.

52. Harold Oram, Inc., Public Relations and Fund Raising to Walker, February 16, 1970, box 1, folder 1; and IFCO Press Release, February 12, 1970, box 1, folder 3, both IFCO Records, SCRBC.

53. Lu Walker to Reverend Calvin Marshall, January 29, 1971, IFCO Records, box 18, folder 3, SCRBC.

54. Lu Walker to Contributors to BEDC, January 29, 1971, IFCO Records, box 18, folder 3, SCRBC.

55. Calvin Marshall, *A Call to Be*, IFCO Records, box 18, folder 3, SCRBC; "IFCO: Black-Controlled Philanthropy," *Non-Profit Report*, June 1971, FJEP, box 82, folder 1, UNDA.

56. "IFCO Project Evaluation & Recommendation: Black Economic Research Center," 1969, box 29, folder 5; and Albert Abrahams, Assistant Director of OEO, to Robert Browne, June 23, 1970, box 40, folder 5, both BERC Records, SCRBC.

57. "IFCO Project Evaluation & Recommendation"; and BERC Annual Report, 1972, BERC Records, box 2, folder 1, SCRBC. For more on Chisholm and antipoverty and economic development efforts in Bedford-Stuyvesant, see Woodsworth, *Battle for Bed-Stuy*.

Notes to Chapter Five and Conclusion 181

58. "IFCO: How Firm a Foundation?," March 15, 1972, FJEP, box 81, folder 4, UNDA. See also "IFCO: Black-Controlled Philanthropy."

59. "Projects Funded by IFCO, 1970," box 19, folder 2; and "A Summary of 1973 Funded Projects Provided by the Interreligious Foundation for Community Organization," box 21, folder 6, both IFCO Records, SCRBC. See also IFCO 20th Anniversary Conference Program, 1987, FJEP, box 164, folder 2A, UNDA.

60. Tracy Early, "A Tough Assignment for IFCO's New Director," 1974, FJEP, box 80, folder 9, UNDA; *IFCO News*, February 14, 1974; "Reverend Lucius Walker Biographical Information," IFCO Records, box 3, folder 6, SCRBC.

61. Early, "Tough Assignment"; "IFCO: How Firm a Foundation?"; and IFCO 20th Anniversary Conference Program.

62. "Report of the Program Evaluation Committee to IFCO Board of Directors," December 18, 1973, IFCO Records, box 1, folder 4; and "Application to Division of Church and Society, National Council of Churches of Christ from IFCO," January 1, 1974, box 2, folder 18, both SCRBC. See also "IFCO: How Firm a Foundation?"; Douglas Brian and Philip Young to Synod/Presbytery Executives, February 14, 1978, CCUM, box 53, folder 40; and IFCO Executive Director's Report to the Board of Directors, June 7, 1974, FJEP, box 80, folder 9, both UNDA; and IFCO 20th Anniversary Conference Program.

63. IFCO Board of Directors, "An IFCO Position Paper on Opportunities to Promote Mission within the Church," February 13, 1976, IFCO Records, box 2, folder 18, SCRBC.

64. "Memorandum regarding Present Status of IFCO," October 1, 1976; and Ann Douglas and Lucius Walker to IFCO Executive Committee, October 1976, both IFCO Records, box 2, folder 18, SCRBC.

65. Brian and Young to Synod/Presbytery Executives.

66. "Reverend Lucius Walker Biographical Information"; and NCC Press Release, November 2, 1978, IFCO Records, box 37, folder 9, SCRBC.

67. IFCO Board of Directors, "A Two Year Projection for IFCO's Programmatic and Financial Development," February 18, 1988, box 164, folder 02B; and IFCO, "Background to Foreground," box 82, folder 1, both FJEP, UNDA; and IFCO 20th Anniversary Conference Program.

68. IFCO 20th Anniversary Conference Program.

69. IFCO Board of Directors, "A Two Year Projection."

70. IFCO 20th Anniversary Conference Program.

Conclusion

1. Folwell, "From Massive Resistance," 214–16 (quote, 216); Orleck, "Introduction," in Orleck and Hazirjian, *War on Poverty*; and Bok, *Civil Rights*, 74–75.

2. For more on Graciela Olivarez, see Bauman, "Opal Jones and Francisca Flores." On the Reagan administration and the end of the CSA, see Orleck, "Introduction" and "Conclusion," in Orleck and Hazirjian, *War on Poverty*; and Bok, *Civil Rights*, 75.

182 Notes to Conclusion

3. Wood, *"Fe y Acción Social,"* 152. See also the Catholic Campaign for Human Development website, http://www.usccb.org/cchd.

4. McKanan, *Prophetic Encounters*, 241. See also John D. McCarthy and Jim Castelli, "Working for Justice: The Campaign for Human Development and Poor Empowerment Groups," draft report, Catholic University of America, Life Cycle Institute, November 1994, American Catholic History Research Center and University Archives, Catholic University of America (ACUA).

5. Wood, *"Fe y Acción Social,"* 146.

6. Ibid., 146–48.

7. Wood, *"Fe y Acción Social,"* 150–51; Rios, "The Ladies Are Warriors," 197.

8. Medina, "Challenges and Consequences," 100. See also Medina, *Las Hermanas*.

9. García, *Católicos*, 151, 152. See also García, "Religion and the Chicano Movement"; Stevens-Arroyo, "Emergence of a Social Identity"; NCCIJ Press Release, March 31, 1964, NCCIJ Papers, ser. 8, box 2, Marquette University Archives; and McNamara, "Catholicism, Assimilation, and the Chicano Movement," 127–30.

10. García, "Religion and the Chicano Movement," 133; Cruz quoted in García, *Católicos*, 138; "Católicos por La Raza," *La Raza*, February 1970, reprinted in Valdez and Steiner, *Aztlán*, 391, 392.

11. del Grito, "Jesus Christ as a Revolutionist," 393–94.

12. Stevens-Arroyo, "Emergence of a Social Identity," 109; Espinosa, Elizondo, and Miranda, *Latino Religions and Civic Activism*, 309. See also Wood, *Faith in Action*, 6–7. On African American and Chicano/a War on Poverty organizations, see Bauman, *Race and the War on Poverty*.

13. Schäfer, "Cold War State," 32; *Catholic Standard*, February 17, 1966, quoted in Lowell, *Great Church-State Fraud*, 178. See also Schäfer, *Piety and Public Funding*; Greene, "Welfare of Faith"; Greene, *No Depression in Heaven*; Netting, "Secular and Religious Funding," 588–89; and Monsma, *When Sacred and Secular Mix*, 104–5.

14. Schäfer, "Cold War State," 42; Kruse, *One Nation under God*, 287–88; Wood, *Faith in Action*, 4. See also "President Creates Faith-Based Office," Associated Press, February 13, 2009; Pipes and Ebaugh, "Faith-Based Coalitions"; Wineburg, *Limited Partnership*; Wuthnow, *Saving America?*, 1, 14–15, 298; and Greene, "Welfare of Faith," 132–33, 144.

15. Jaweed Kaleem, "Melissa Rogers Appointed to Lead White House Office of Faith-Based and Neighborhood Partnerships," *Huffington Post*, March 13, 2013, https://www.huffingtonpost.com/2013/03/13/melissa-rogers-white-house-faith-based_n_2868413.html. See also "White House Picks Church-State Lawyer Melissa Rogers to Head Faith Office," *Washington Post*, March 13, 2013; Miller, "Between Hope and Despair," 209; Obama, *Dreams from My Father*; and "President Creates Faith-Based Office."

16. For a thoughtful and insightful analysis of the relationship between the federal government and faith-based organizations, see Greenberg, "Doing Whose Work?" See also Smith and Stone, "Unexpected Consequences of Privatization."

17. Baroni eulogy in Higgins Papers, box 4, folder 1, ACUA. See also Satter, *Family Properties*, 380–81.

Notes to Conclusion

18. Biondi, "Rise of the Reparations Movement"; and Franklin, "Introduction."

19. Biondi, "Rise of the Reparations Movement," 8–9.

20. Franklin, "Introduction"; Coates, "Case for Reparations," 70.

21. Coates, "My President Was Black," 62. For Klinkner's research results, see Klinkner, "Easiest Way to Guess."

BIBLIOGRAPHY

Adams, Betty Livingston. *Black Women's Christian Activism: Seeking Social Justice in a Northern Suburb*. New York: New York University Press, 2016.

Ahmann, Mathew, ed. *Race: Challenge to Religion*. Chicago, Ill.: Henry Regnery, 1963.

Ahmann, Mathew, and Margaret Roach, eds. *The Church and the Urban Racial Crisis*. Techny, Ill.: Divine Word, 1967.

Alvis, Joel L., Jr. *Religion and Race: Southern Presbyterians, 1946–1983*. Tuscaloosa: University of Alabama Press, 1994.

America, Richard F. *Paying the Social Debt: What White America Owes Black America*. Westport, Conn.: Praeger, 1993.

Anderson, R. Bentley. *Black, White, and Catholic: New Orleans Interracialism, 1947–1956*. Nashville, Tenn.: Vanderbilt University Press, 2005.

Andrews, Kenneth T. "Social Movements and Policy Implementation: The Mississippi Civil Rights Movement and the War on Poverty, 1965 to 1971." *American Sociological Review* 66, no. 1 (2001): 71–95.

Ashmore, Susan Youngblood. *Carry It On: The War on Poverty and the Civil Rights Movement in Alabama, 1964–1972*. Athens: University of Georgia Press, 2008.

———. "More than a Head Start: The War on Poverty, Catholic Charities, and Civil Rights in Mobile, Alabama, 1965–1970." In *The New Deal and Beyond: Social Welfare in the South since 1930*, ed. Elna C. Green, 196–238. Athens: University of Georgia Press, 2003.

Atkinson, Ernest E. *A Selected Bibliography of Hispanic Baptist History*. Nashville, Tenn.: Historical Commission, Southern Baptist Convention, 1981.

Atkins-Vasquez, Jane, ed. *Hispanic Presbyterians in Southern California: One Hundred Years of Ministry*. Los Angeles, Calif.: Hispanic Commission, Synod of Southern California and Hawaii, 1988.

Bailey, Fred Arthur. "That Which God Hath Put Asunder: White Baptists, Black Aliens, and the Southern Social Order, 1890–1920." In *Politics and Religion in the White South*, ed. Glenn Feldman, 11–33. Lexington: University of Kentucky Press, 2005.

Baroni, Geno. "The Church and the War on Poverty." *American Ecclesiastical Review* 153, no. 3 (1965): 184–93.

Bibliography

Bauman, Mark K., and Berkley Kalin, eds. *The Quiet Voices: Southern Rabbis and Black Civil Rights, 1880s to 1990s*. Tuscaloosa: University of Alabama Press, 1997.

Bauman, Robert. "The Black Power and Chicano Movements and the Poverty Wars in Los Angeles." *Journal of Urban History* 33, no. 2 (2007): 277–95.

———. "'Kind of a Secular Sacrament': Fathers Geno Baroni and John Egan and the Catholic War on Poverty." *Catholic Historical Review* 99, no. 2 (2013): 298–317.

———. "The Neighborhood Adult Participation Project: Black/Brown Strife in the War on Poverty in Los Angeles." In *The Struggle in Black and Brown: African American and Mexican American Relations during the Civil Rights Era*, ed. Brian Behnken, 104–24. Lincoln: University of Nebraska Press, 2012.

———. "Opal Jones and Francisca Flores: Gender and Civil Rights Activism in the War on Poverty in Los Angeles." In *The War on Poverty and Struggles for Racial and Economic Justice: Views from the Grassroots*, ed. Annelise Orleck and Lisa Hazirjian, 209–27. Athens: University of Georgia Press, 2011.

———. "Race, Class and Political Power: The Implementation of the War on Poverty in Los Angeles." PhD diss., University of California, Santa Barbara, 1998.

———. *Race and the War on Poverty: From Watts to East L.A.* Norman: University of Oklahoma Press, 2008.

Bedau, Hugo Adam. "Compensatory Justice and the Black Manifesto." In *Injustice and Rectification*, ed. Rodney C. Roberts, 131–46. New York: Peter Lang, 2002.

Bernstein, Shana. *Bridges of Reform: Interracial Civil Rights Activism in Twentieth-Century Los Angeles*. New York: Oxford University Press, 2011.

Berry, Mary Frances. *My Face Is Black Is True: Callie House and the Struggle for Ex-Slave Reparations*. New York: Knopf, 2005.

Betten, Neil, and Michael J. Austin, eds. *The Roots of Community Organizing, 1917–1939*. Philadelphia, Pa.: Temple University Press, 1990.

Betten, Neil, and William E. Hershey. "Religious Organizations as a Base for Community Organizing: The Catholic Worker Movement during the Great Depression." In *The Roots of Community Organizing, 1917–1939*, ed. Neil Betten and Michael J. Austin, 162–81. Philadelphia, Pa.: Temple University Press, 1990.

Billingsley, Scott. *It's a New Day: Race and Gender in the Modern Charismatic Movement*. Tuscaloosa: University of Alabama Press, 2008.

Biondi, Martha. "The Rise of the Reparations Movement." *Radical History Review* 87, no. 1 (2003): 5–15.

Bok, Marcia. *Civil Rights and the Social Programs of the 1960s: The Social Justice Functions of Social Policy*. Westport, Conn.: Praeger, 1992.

Brackenridge, R. Douglas, and Francisco O. García-Treto. *Iglesia Presbiteriana: A History of Presbyterians and Mexican Americans in the Southwest*. San Antonio, Tex.: Trinity University Press, 1974.

Brauer, Carl M. "Kennedy, Johnson and the War on Poverty." *Journal of American History* 69, no. 1 (1982): 98–119.

Braxton, Edward K. "The National Black Catholic Congress: An Event of the Century." *U.S. Catholic Historian* 7, nos. 2–3 (1988): 301–6.

Bibliography

Brilliant, Mark. *The Color of America Has Changed: How Racial Diversity Shaped Civil Rights Reform in California, 1941–1978*. New York: Oxford University Press, 2010.

Brown, Dorothy M., and Elizabeth McKeown. *The Poor Belong to Us: Catholic Charities and American Welfare*. Cambridge, Mass.: Harvard University Press, 1997.

Brown, Scot. *Fighting for US: Maulana Karenga, the US Organization, and Black Cultural Nationalism*. New York: New York University Press, 2003.

Butler, Jon. "Jack-in-the-Box Faith: The Religion Problem in Modern American History." *Journal of American History* 90 (March 2004): 1357–78.

Campbell, Ernest T. *The Christian Manifesto*. New York: Harper and Row, 1970.

Carroll, Tamar. *Mobilizing New York: AIDS, Antipoverty, and Feminist Activism*. Chapel Hill: University of North Carolina Press, 2015.

Chappell, David L. *A Stone of Hope: Prophetic Religion and the Death of Jim Crow*. Chapel Hill: University of North Carolina Press, 2004.

Chappell, Marisa. *The War on Welfare: Family, Poverty, and Politics in Modern America*. Philadelphia: University of Pennsylvania Press, 2010.

Clark, Henry. *The Christian Case against Poverty*. New York: Association Press, 1965.

Clayson, William S. *Freedom Is Not Enough: The War on Poverty and the Civil Rights Movement in Texas*. Austin: University of Texas Press, 2010.

Cleage, Albert B., Jr. *Black Christian Nationalism: New Directions for the Black Church*. New York: William Morrow, 1972.

Cline, David P. *From Reconciliation to Revolution: The Student Interracial Ministry, Liberal Christianity, and the Civil Rights Movement*. Chapel Hill: University of North Carolina Press, 2016.

Cloward, Richard A., and Lloyd Ohlin. *Delinquency and Opportunity*. New York: Free Press, 1960.

Coates, Ta-Nehisi. "The Case for Reparations." *Atlantic*, June 2014, 54–71.

———. "My President Was Black." *Atlantic*, January–February 2017, 46–66.

Cobb, Daniel M. *Native Activism in Cold War America: The Struggle for Sovereignty*. Lawrence: University Press of Kansas, 2008.

Cohen, Naomi W. *Not Free to Desist: The American Jewish Committee, 1906–1966*. Philadelphia, Pa.: Jewish Publication Society of America, 1972.

Colby, David C. "Black Power, White Resistance, and Public Policy: Political Power and Poverty Program Grants in Mississippi." *Journal of Politics* 47, no. 2 (1985): 579–95.

Collier-Thomas, Bettye. *Jesus, Jobs, and Justice: African American Women and Religion*. New York: Knopf, 2010.

Cone, James H. *A Black Theology of Liberation*. 20th anniversary ed. Maryknoll, N.Y.: Orbis, 1990.

———. *Speaking the Truth: Ecumenism, Liberation, and Black Theology*. Grand Rapids, Mich.: Eerdmans, 1986.

Corbett, J. Angelo. *Race, Racism and Reparations*. Ithaca, N.Y.: Cornell University Press, 2003.

Bibliography

Cronin, John F. "The Church, the Synagogue, and the World." In *Torah and Gospel: Jewish and Catholic Theology in Dialogue*, ed. Philip Scharper, 197–211. New York: Sheed and Ward, 1966.

Dahm, Charles W. *Power and Authority in the Catholic Church: Cardinal Cody in Chicago*. Notre Dame, IN: University of Notre Dame Press, 1981.

Davies, Gareth. *From Opportunity to Entitlement: The Transformation and Decline of Great Society Liberalism*. Lawrence: University Press of Kansas, 1996.

Davis, Cyprian. "God of Our Weary Years: Black Catholics in American Catholic History." In *Taking Down Our Harps: Black Catholics in the United States*, ed. Diana L. Hayes and Cyprian Davis, 17–46. Maryknoll, N.Y.: Orbis, 1998.

———. *The History of Black Catholics in the United States*. New York: Crossroad, 1990.

Davis, Joseph M., and Cyprian Lamar Rowe. "The Development of the National Office for Black Catholics." *U.S. Catholic Historian* 7, nos. 2–3 (1988): 265–89.

del Grito, Dolores. "Jesus Christ as a Revolutionist." *El Grito del Norte*, February 11, 1970. In *Aztlán: An Anthology of Mexican American Literature*, ed. Luis Valdez and Stan Steiner, 393–94. New York: Vintage, 1972.

Deslippe, Dennis. "'We Must Bring Together a New Coalition': The Challenge of Working-Class White Ethnics to Color-Blind Conservatism in the 1970s." *International Labor and Working-Class History* 74 (Fall 2008): 148–70.

Dillard, Angela D. *Faith in the City: Preaching Social Change in Detroit*. Ann Arbor: University of Michigan Press, 2007.

———. "Religion and Radicalism: The Reverend Albert B. Cleage, Jr., and the Rise of Black Christian Nationalism in Detroit." In *Freedom North: Black Freedom Struggles Outside the South, 1940–1980*, ed. Jeanne Theoharis and Komozi Woodard, 153–75. New York: Palgrave Macmillan, 2003.

Dochuk, Darren. *From Bible Belt to Sunbelt: Plain-Folk People, Grass-Roots Politics, and the Rise of Evangelical Religion*. New York: Norton, 2010.

Dolan, Jay P., and Allan Figueroa Deck, eds. *Hispanic Catholic Culture in the U.S.* Notre Dame, Ind.: University of Notre Dame Press, 1994.

Dolan, Jay P., and Gilberto M. Hinojosa, eds. *Mexican Americans and the Catholic Church, 1900–1965*. Vol. 1. Notre Dame, Ind.: University of Notre Dame Press, 1994.

Dupont, Carolyn Renée. *Mississippi Praying: Southern White Evangelicals and the Civil Rights Movement, 1945–1975*. New York: New York University Press, 2013.

Dye, Keith A. "Lessons in Hearing Human and Divine Discontent: The Black Manifesto and Episcopal Leaders and Congregations in the Detroit Area." *Journal of African American History* 97, nos. 1–2 (2012): 72–91.

Egan, John J. "The Responsibility of Church and Synagogue as Institutions in the Community." In *Race: Challenge to Religion*, ed. Mathew Ahmann, 91–100. Chicago, Ill.: Henry Regnery, 1963.

Egan, John J., Peggy Roach, and Philip J. Murnion. "Catholic Committee on Urban Ministry: Ministry to the Ministers." *Review of Religious Research* 20, no. 3 (1979): 279–90.

Engel, Lawrence J. "The Influence of Saul Alinsky on the Campaign for Human Development." *Theological Studies* 59 (1998): 636–61.

Bibliography 189

Espinosa, Gastón. "The Pentecostalization of Latin American and U.S. Latino Christianity." *Pneuma: The Journal of the Society for Pentecostal Studies* 26, no. 2 (2004): 262–92.

Espinosa, Gastón, Virgilio Elizondo, and Jesse Miranda, eds. *Latino Religions and Civic Activism in the United States*. New York: Oxford University Press, 2005.

Farber, David, and Beth Bailey. *The Columbia Guide to America in the 1960s*. New York: Columbia University Press, 2001.

Feldman, Glenn, ed. *Politics and Religion in the White South*. Lexington: University of Kentucky Press, 2005.

Ferguson, Karen. *Top Down: The Ford Foundation, Black Power, and the Reinvention of Racial Liberalism*. Philadelphia: University of Pennsylvania Press, 2013.

Findlay, James F., Jr. *Church People in the Struggle: The National Council of Churches and the Black Freedom Movement, 1940–1970*. New York: Oxford University Press, 1993.

———. "The Mainline Churches and Head Start in Mississippi: Religious Activism in the Sixties." *Church History* 64, no. 2 (1995): 237–50.

Folwell, Emma. "From Massive Resistance to New Conservatism: Opposition to Community Action Programs in Mississippi, 1965–1975." PhD thesis, University of Leicester, 2014.

Forman, James. *The Making of Black Revolutionaries*. Seattle: University of Washington Press, 1997.

———. *Self-Determination: An Examination of the Question and Its Application to the African-American People*. Rev. ed. Washington, D.C.: Open Hand, 1984.

Franklin, V. P. "Introduction—African Americans and Movements for Reparations: From Ex-Slave Pensions to the Reparations Superfund." *Journal of African American History* 97, nos. 1–2 (2012): 1–12.

Friedland, Michael B. *Lift Up Your Voice like a Trumpet: White Clergy and the Civil Rights and Antiwar Movements, 1954–1973*. Chapel Hill: University of North Carolina Press, 1998.

Frisbie, Margery. *An Alley in Chicago: The Ministry of a City Priest*. Kansas City, Mo.: Sheed and Ward, 1991.

Frye, Jerry K. "The 'Black Manifesto' and the Tactic of Objectification." *Journal of Black Studies* 5, no. 1 (1974): 65–76.

García, Mario T. *Católicos: Resistance and Affirmation in Chicano Catholic History*. Austin: University of Texas Press, 2008.

———. "Religion and the Chicano Movement: Católicos por La Raza." In *Mexican American Religions: Spirituality, Activism, and Culture*, ed. Gastón Espinosa and Mario T. García, 125–49. Durham, N.C.: Duke University Press, 2008.

Geary, Daniel. *Beyond Civil Rights: The Moynihan Report and Its Legacy*. Philadelphia: University of Pennsylvania Press, 2015.

George, Carol V. R. *One Mississippi, Two Mississippi: Methodists, Murder, and the Struggle for Racial Justice in Neshoba County*. New York: Oxford University Press, 2015.

Bibliography

Geschwender, James A. *Class, Race, and Worker Insurgency: The League of Revolutionary Black Workers.* Cambridge: Cambridge University Press, 1977.

Gill, Jill K. *Embattled Ecumenism: The National Council of Churches, the Vietnam War, and the Trials of the Protestant Left.* DeKalb: Northern Illinois University Press, 2011.

Goldstein, Brian D. "'The Search for New Forms': Black Power and the Making of the Postmodern City." *Journal of American History* 103, no. 2 (2016): 375–99.

Goudsouzian, Aram. *Down to the Crossroads: Civil Rights, Black Power, and the Meredith March against Fear.* New York: Farrar, Straus and Giroux, 2014.

Greenberg, Anna. "Doing Whose Work? Faith-Based Organizations and Government Partnerships." In *Who Will Provide? The Changing Role of Religion in American Social Welfare*, ed. Mary Jo Bane, Brent Coffin, and Ronald F. Thiemann, 178–97. Boulder, Colo.: Westview, 2000.

Greene, Alison Collis. *No Depression in Heaven: The Great Depression, the New Deal and the Transformation of Religion in the Delta.* New York: Oxford University Press, 2016.

———. "The Welfare of Faith." In *Faith in the New Millennium: The Future of Religion and American Politics*, ed. Matthew Avery Sutton and Darren Dochuk, 132–49. New York: Oxford University Press, 2016.

Greenwood, Elma L. *How Churches Fight Poverty.* New York: Friendship Press, 1967.

———. *One-Fifth of a Nation.* New York: Friendship Press, 1966.

Hall, Jacquelyn Dowd. "The Long Civil Rights Movement and the Political Uses of the Past." *Journal of American History* 91, no. 4 (2005): 1233–63.

Handy, Robert T. *A History of Union Theological Seminary in New York.* New York: Columbia University Press, 1987.

Hanhardt, Christina B. *Safe Space: Gay Neighborhood History and the Politics of Violence.* Durham, N.C.: Duke University Press, 2013.

Harrington, Michael. *The Other America.* Baltimore, Md.: Penguin, 1962.

Hayes, Diana L., and Cyprian Davis, eds. *Taking Down Our Harps: Black Catholics in the United States.* Maryknoll, N.Y.: Orbis, 1998.

Heineman, Kenneth. "Model City: The War on Poverty, Race Relations, and Catholic Social Activism in 1960s Pittsburgh." *Historian* 65, no. 4 (2003): 867–900.

Herberg, Will. *Protestant, Catholic, Jew.* New York: Doubleday, 1955.

Hill, Laura Warren, and Julia Rabig, eds. *The Business of Black Power: Community Development, Capitalism, and Corporate Responsibility in Postwar America.* Rochester, N.Y.: University of Rochester Press, 2012.

Hinojosa, Felipe. *Latino Mennonites: Civil Rights, Faith and Evangelical Culture.* Baltimore, Md.: Johns Hopkins University Press, 2014.

Hough, Joseph C., Jr. *Black Power and White Protestants: A Christian Response to the New Negro Pluralism.* New York: Oxford University Press, 1968.

Hoy, Suellen. "Lives on the Color Line: Catholic Sisters and African Americans in Chicago, 1890s–1960s." *U.S. Catholic Historian* 22, no. 1 (2004): 67–91.

Bibliography

Jackson, Thomas F. *From Civil Rights to Human Rights: Martin Luther King, Jr., and the Struggle for Economic Justice*. Philadelphia: University of Pennsylvania Press, 2007.

Johnson, Karl Ellis. "'Trouble Won't Last': Black Church Activism in Postwar Philadelphia." In *African American Urban History since World War II*, ed. Kenneth L. Kusmer and Joe W. Trotter, 245–62. Chicago, Ill.: University of Chicago Press, 2009.

Jones, Patrick D. "'Not a Color, but an Attitude': Father James Groppi and Black Power Politics in Milwaukee." In *Groundwork: Local Black Freedom Movements in America*, ed. Jeanne Theoharis and Komozi Woodard, 259–81. New York: New York University Press, 2005.

———. *The Selma of the North: Civil Rights Insurgency in Milwaukee*. Cambridge, Mass.: Harvard University Press, 2009.

Joseph, Peniel E., ed. *The Black Power Movement: Rethinking the Civil Rights–Black Power Era*. New York: Routledge, 2006.

———. "Community Organizing, Grassroots Politics, and Neighborhood Rebels: Local Struggles for Black Power in America." In *Neighborhood Rebels: Black Power at the Local Level*, ed. Peniel E. Joseph, 1–19. New York: Palgrave Macmillan, 2010.

———. "Rethinking the Black Power Era." *Journal of Southern History* 75, no. 3 (2009): 707–16.

———. *Waiting 'til the Midnight Hour: A Narrative History of Black Power in America*. New York: Owl Books, 2007.

Joseph, Robert T. "Sargent Shriver's Spiritual Weapons in the 'War on Poverty.'" *U.S. Catholic Historian* 34, no. 4 (2016): 55–78.

Kelley, Robin D. G. *Freedom Dreams: The Black Radical Imagination*. Boston: Beacon, 2002.

Kiffmeyer, Thomas. *Reformers to Radicals: The Appalachian Volunteers and the War on Poverty*. Lexington: University of Kentucky Press, 2008.

———. "'To Judge Harshly': The Troubled Legacy of America's Struggle with Poverty." *Reviews in American History* 43, no. 2 (2015): 369–77.

Klinkner, Philip. "The Easiest Way to Guess If Someone Supports Trump? Ask If Obama Is a Muslim." *Vox*, June 2, 2016.

K'Meyer, Tracy E. *Interracialism and Christian Community in the Postwar South*. Charlottesville: University of Virginia Press, 1997.

Koeth, Stephen M. "'The Mental Grandchildren of Monsignor John A. Ryan': George G. Higgins, John F. Cronin, S.S., and the Role of the National Catholic Welfare Conference in Post-War American Politics." *U.S. Catholic Historian* 33, no. 1 (2015): 99–135.

Korstad, Robert R., and James L. Leloudis. *To Right These Wrongs: The North Carolina Fund and the Battle to End Poverty and Inequality in 1960s America*. Chapel Hill: University of North Carolina Press, 2010.

Kruse, Kevin M. *One Nation under God: How Corporate America Invented Christian America*. New York: Basic, 2015.

Bibliography

Kurashige, Scott. *The Shifting Grounds of Race: Black and Japanese Americans in the Making of Multiethnic Los Angeles*. Princeton, N.J.: Princeton University Press, 2010.

LaFarge, John. *Interracial Justice: A Study of the Catholic Doctrine of Race Relations*. New York: America Press, 1937.

Lechtreck, Elaine Allen. "'We Are Demanding $500 Million for Reparations': The Black Manifesto, Mainline Religious Denominations, and Black Economic Development." *Journal of African American History* 97, nos. 1–2 (2012): 39–71.

Lecky, Robert S., and H. Elliott Wright, eds. *Black Manifesto: Religion, Racism and Reparations*. New York: Sheed and Ward, 1969.

Lee, Sonia Song-Ha. *Building a Latino Civil Rights Movement: Puerto Ricans, African Americans, and the Pursuit of Racial Justice in New York City*. Chapel Hill: University of North Carolina Press, 2014.

Lewis, Oscar. *The Children of Sanchez: Autobiography of a Mexican Family*. New York: Vintage, 1961.

———. *Five Families: Mexican Case Studies in the Culture of Poverty*. New York: New American Library, 1959.

Lowell, C. Stanley. *The Great Church-State Fraud*. Washington, D.C.: Robert B. Luce, 1973.

MacDonald, Dwight. "Our Invisible Poor." *New Yorker*, January 19, 1963, 82–132.

MacGregor, Morris J. *A Parish for the Federal City: St. Patrick's in Washington, 1794–1994*. Washington, D.C.: Catholic University Press, 1994.

———. *Steadfast in the Faith: The Life of Patrick Cardinal O'Boyle*. Washington, D.C.: Catholic University Press, 2006.

Maffly-Kipp, Laurie F. *Setting Down the Sacred Past: African-American Race Histories*. Cambridge, Mass.: Harvard University Press, 2010.

Manis, Andrew M. "'City Mothers': Dorothy Tilly, Georgia Methodist Women, and Black Civil Rights." In *Politics and Religion in the White South*, ed. Glenn Feldman, 125–56. Lexington: University of Kentucky Press, 2005.

Mann, Arthur. *The One and the Many: Reflections on the American Identity*. Chicago, Ill.: University of Chicago Press, 1979.

Mantler, Gordon K. *Power to the Poor: Black-Brown Coalition and the Fight for Economic Justice, 1960–1974*. Chapel Hill: University of North Carolina Press, 2013.

Marsh, Charles. *God's Long Summer: Stories of Faith and Civil Rights*. Princeton, N.J.: Princeton University Press, 1997.

Martensen, Katherine. "Region, Religion, and Social Action: The Catholic Committee of the South, 1939–1956." *Catholic Historical Review* 68, no. 2 (1982): 249–67.

Marx, Gary T. *Protest and Prejudice*. New York: Harper and Row, 1967.

———. "Religion: Opiate or Inspiration of Civil Rights Militancy among Negroes." *American Journal of Sociology* 32 (1967): 64–72.

Matusow, Allen J. *The Unraveling of America: A History of Liberalism in the 1960s*. New York: Harper and Row, 1984.

McGraw, James R. "Down by the Riverside." *Renewal* 9, no. 6 (1969): 3.

McGreevy, John T. *Catholicism and American Freedom: A History*. New York: Norton, 2003.

Bibliography

——. *Parish Boundaries: The Catholic Encounter with Race in the Twentieth-Century Urban North.* Chicago, Ill.: University of Chicago Press, 1996.

——. "Racial Justice and the People of God: The Second Vatican Council, the Civil Rights Movement, and American Catholics." *Religion and American Culture: A Journal of Interpretation* 4, no. 2 (1994): 221–54.

McKanan, Dan. *Prophetic Encounters: Religion and the American Radical Tradition.* Boston: Beacon, 2011.

McNamara, Patrick H. "Catholicism, Assimilation and the Chicano Movement: Los Angeles as a Case Study." In *Chicanos and Native Americans: The Territorial Minorities,* ed. Rodolfo O. de la Garza, Z. Anthony Kruszewski, and Tómas A. Arciniega, 124–30. Englewood Cliffs, N.J.: Prentice Hall, 1973.

Medina, Lara. "The Challenges and Consequences of Being Latina, Catholic, and Political." In *Latino Religions and Civic Activism in the United States,* ed. Gastón Espinosa, Virgilio Elizondo, and Jesse Miranda, 97–100. New York: Oxford University Press, 2005.

——. *Las Hermanas: Chicana/Latina Religious-Political Activism in the U.S. Catholic Church.* Philadelphia, Pa.: Temple University Press, 2004.

Meeker, Martin. "The Queerly Disadvantaged and the Making of San Francisco's War on Poverty, 1964–1967." *Pacific Historical Review* 81, no. 1 (2012): 21–59.

Miller, Steven P. "Between Hope and Despair: Obama and Evangelical Politics." In *Faith in the New Millennium: The Future of Religion and American Politics,* ed. Matthew Avery Sutton and Darren Dochuk, 199–216. New York: Oxford University Press, 2016.

——. "Billy Graham, Civil Rights, and the Changing Postwar South." In *Politics and Religion in the White South,* ed. Glenn Feldman, 157–86. Lexington: University of Kentucky Press, 2005.

——. *Billy Graham and the Rise of the Republican South.* Philadelphia: University of Pennsylvania Press, 2009.

Monsma, Stephen V. *When Sacred and Secular Mix: Religious Nonprofit Organizations and Public Money.* Lanham, Md.: Rowman and Littlefield, 1996.

Morgan, Lynda J. *Known for My Work: African American Ethics from Slavery to Freedom.* Gainesville: University of Florida Press, 2015.

Morgan, Richard E. *The Politics of Religious Conflict: Church and State in America.* New York: Pegasus, 1968.

Moynihan, Daniel P. *Maximum Feasible Misunderstanding: Community Action in the War on Poverty.* New York: Free Press, 1969.

Murray, Charles. *Losing Ground: American Social Policy, 1950–1980.* New York: Basic, 1984.

Murray, Paul T. "54 Miles to Freedom: Catholics Were Prominent in 1965 Selma March." *National Catholic Reporter,* March 7, 2015.

——. "From the Sidelines to the Front Lines: Mathew Ahmann Leads American Catholics into the Civil Rights Movement." *Journal of the Illinois State Historical Society* 107, no. 1 (2014): 77–115.

194 Bibliography

Murray, Peter C. *Methodism and the Crucible of Race, 1930–1975*. Columbia: University of Missouri Press, 2004.

Netting, F. Ellen. "Secular and Religious Funding of Church-Related Agencies." *Social Service Review* 56 (1982): 586–604.

Newman, Mark. *Getting Right with God: Southern Baptists and Desegregation, 1945–1995*. Tuscaloosa: University of Alabama Press, 2001.

Newman, Patty. *Pass the Poverty Please*. Whittier, Calif.: Constructive Action, 1966.

Nickels, Marilyn W. *Black Catholic Protest and the Federated Colored Catholics, 1917–1933: Three Perspectives on Racial Justice*. New York: Garland, 1988.

——. "Thomas Wyatt Turner and the Federated Colored Catholics." *U.S. Catholic Historian* 7, nos. 2–3 (1988): 215–32.

Nieto, Leo D. "The Chicano Movement and the Churches in the United States." *Perkins Journal* 29, no. 1 (1975): 32–41.

Noll, Mark A. *God and Race in American Politics: A Short History*. Princeton, N.J.: Princeton University Press, 2008.

Obama, Barack. *Dreams from My Father: A Story of Race and Inheritance*. New York: Crown, 2004.

Ochs, Stephen J. *Desegregating the Altar: The Josephites and the Struggle for Black Priests, 1871–1960*. Baton Rouge: Louisiana State University Press, 1990.

O'Connor, Alice. *Poverty Knowledge: Social Science, Social Policy, and the Poor in Twentieth-Century U.S. History*. Princeton, N.J.: Princeton University Press, 2001.

Oltman, Adele. *Sacred Mission, Worldly Ambition: Black Christian Nationalism in the Age of Jim Crow*. Athens: University of Georgia Press, 2008.

Orleck, Annelise. *Storming Caesars Palace: How Black Mothers Fought Their Own War on Poverty*. Boston: Beacon, 2005.

Orleck, Annelise, and Lisa Hazirjian, eds. *The War on Poverty and Struggles for Racial and Economic Justice: Views from the Grassroots*. Athens: University of Georgia Press, 2011.

O'Rourke, Lawrence M. *Geno: The Life and Mission of Geno Baroni*. New York: Paulist Press, 1991.

Pascoe, Peggy. *What Comes Naturally: Miscegenation Law and the Making of Race in America*. New York: Oxford University Press, 2009.

Pehl, Matthew. *The Making of Working-Class Religion*. Urbana: University of Illinois Press, 2016.

Phelps, Wesley G. *A People's War on Poverty: Urban Politics and Grassroots Activists in Houston*. Athens: University of Georgia Press, 2014.

Pipes, Paula F., and Helen Rose Ebaugh. "Faith-Based Coalitions, Social Services, and Government Funding." *Sociology of Religion* 63, no. 1 (2002): 49–68.

Pulido, Alberto L. "Are You an Emissary of Jesus Christ? Justice, the Catholic Church, and the Chicano Movement." *Explorations in Ethnic Studies* 14, no. 1 (1991): 17–34.

Quevedo, Eduardo, Jr. "The Catholic Church in America." *Con Safos* (Fall 1968): 11.

Rabig, Julia. "'A Fight and a Question': Community Development Corporations, Machine Politics, and Corporate Philanthropy in the Long Urban Crisis." In *The Business of Black Power: Community Development, Capitalism, and Corporate Responsibility in Postwar America*, ed. Laura Warren Hill and Julia Rabig, 245–73. Rochester, N.Y.: University of Rochester Press, 2012.

———. *The Fixers: Devolution, Development and Civil Society in Newark, 1960–1990.* Chicago, Ill.: University of Chicago Press, 2016.

Raboteau, Albert J. *American Prophets: Seven Religious Radicals and Their Struggle for Social and Political Justice.* Princeton, N.J.: Princeton University Press, 2016.

Rickford, Russell. *We Are an African People: Independent Education, Black Power, and the Radical Imagination.* New York: Oxford University Press, 2016.

———. "'We Can't Grow Food on All This Concrete': The Land Question, Agrarianism, and Black Nationalist Thought in the Late 1960s and 1970s." *Journal of American History* 103, no. 4 (2017): 956–82.

Rios, Elizabeth D. "'The Ladies Are Warriors': Latina Pentecostalism and Faith-Based Activism in New York City." In *Latino Religions and Civic Activism in the United States,* ed. Gastón Espinosa, Virgilio Elizondo, and Jesse Miranda, 197–217. New York: Oxford University Press, 2005.

Robertson, Nancy Marie. *Christian Sisterhood, Race Relations and the YWCA, 1906–46.* Urbana: University of Illinois Press, 2007.

Robinson, Randall. *The Debt: What America Owes to Blacks.* New York: Penguin, 2000.

Rodriguez, Marc Simon. *The Tejano Diaspora: Mexican Americanism and Ethnic Politics in Texas and Wisconsin.* Chapel Hill: University of North Carolina Press, 2011.

Rose, Stephen C. *The Grass Roots Church: A Manifesto for Protestant Renewal.* New York: Abingdon, 1966.

———. "Putting It to the Churches: Reparations for Blacks?" *New Republic,* June 21, 1969.

———. "Reparations Now!" *Renewal* 9, no. 6 (1969): 14.

Ruotsila, Markku. *Fighting Fundamentalist: Carl McIntire and the Politicization of American Fundamentalism.* New York: Oxford University Press, 2016.

Sánchez-Walsh, Arlene M. *Latino Pentecostal Identity: Evangelical Faith, Self, and Society.* New York: Columbia University Press, 2003.

Sanders, Crystal R. *A Chance for Change: Head Start and Mississippi's Black Freedom Struggle.* Chapel Hill: University of North Carolina Press, 2016.

Sanua, Marianne R. *Let Us Prove Strong: The American Jewish Committee, 1945–2006.* Waltham, Mass.: Brandeis University Press, 2007.

Satter, Beryl. *Family Properties: Race, Real Estate, and the Exploitation of Black Urban America.* New York: Henry Holt, 2009.

Schäfer, Axel R. "The Cold War State and the Resurgence of Evangelicalism: A Study of the Public Funding of Religion since 1945." *Radical History Review* 99 (Fall 2007): 19–50.

———. *Piety and Public Funding: Evangelicals and the State in Modern America.* Philadelphia: University of Pennsylvania Press, 2012.

Schaller, Lyle E. *The Churches' War on Poverty.* Nashville, Tenn.: Abingdon, 1967.

Schuchter, Arnold. *Reparations: The Black Manifesto and Its Challenge to White America.* Philadelphia, Pa.: Lippincott, 1970.

Bibliography

Schultz, Kevin M. *Tri-Faith America: How Catholics and Jews Held Postwar America to Its Protestant Promise*. New York: Oxford University Press, 2011.

Schultz, Kevin M., and Paul Harvey. "Everywhere and Nowhere: Recent Trends in American Religious History and Historiography." *Journal of the American Academy of Religion* 78, no. 1 (2010): 132–33.

Sharps, Ronald L. "Black Catholics in the United States: A Historical Chronology." *U.S. Catholic Historian* 12, no. 1 (1994): 119–41.

Shattuck, Gardiner H., Jr. *Episcopalians and Race: Civil War to Civil Rights*. Lexington: University of Kentucky Press, 2000.

Shearer, Tobin Miller. *Daily Demonstrators: The Civil Rights Movement in Mennonite Homes and Sanctuaries*. Baltimore, Md.: Johns Hopkins University Press, 2010.

Shriver, R. Sargent. "America, Race and the World." In *Race: Challenge to Religion*, ed. Mathew Ahmann, 143–44. Chicago, Ill.: Henry Regnery, 1963.

Smith, Steven Rathgeb, and Deborah A. Stone. "The Unexpected Consequences of Privatization." In *Remaking the Welfare State: Retrenchment and Social Policy in America and Europe*, ed. Michael K. Brown, 232–52. Philadelphia, Pa.: Temple University Press, 1988.

Southern, David W. *John LaFarge and the Limits of Catholic Interracialism, 1911–1963*. Baton Rouge: Louisiana State University Press, 1996.

Spencer, Robyn C. *The Revolution Has Come: Black Power, Gender, and the Black Panther Party in Oakland*. Durham, N.C.: Duke University Press, 2016.

Stevens-Arroyo, Anthony M. "The Emergence of a Social Identity among Latino Catholics: An Appraisal." In *Hispanic Catholic Culture in the United States: Issues and Concerns*, ed. Jay P. Dolan and Allan Figueroa Deck, 105–20. Notre Dame, Ind.: University of Notre Dame Press, 1994.

Stossel, Scott. *Sarge: The Life and Times of Sargent Shriver*. Washington, D.C.: Smithsonian Institution Books, 2004.

Sugrue, Thomas J. "The Catholic Encounter with the 1960s." In *Catholics in the American Century: Recasting Narratives of U.S. History*, ed. R. Scott Appleby and Kathleen Sprows Cummings, 61–79. Ithaca, N.Y.: Cornell University Press, 2012.

———. *Sweet Land of Liberty: The Forgotten Struggle for Civil Rights in the North*. New York: Random House, 2008.

Sullivan, Amy. *The Party Faithful: How and Why Democrats Are Closing the God Gap*. New York: Scribner, 2008.

Sutton, Matthew Avery. *American Apocalypse: A History of Modern Evangelicalism*. Cambridge, Mass.: Harvard University Press, 2014.

Swartz, David R. *Moral Minority: The Evangelical Left in an Age of Conservatism*. Philadelphia: University of Pennsylvania Press, 2012.

Tanenbaum, Marc H. "The Role of the Church and Synagogue in Social Action." In *Torah and Gospel: Jewish and Catholic Theology in Dialogue*, ed. Philip Scharper, 165–96. New York: Sheed and Ward, 1966.

Thompson, Francesca. "Black Power and the Catholic Church." *U.S. Catholic Historian* 7, nos. 2–3 (1988): 346–52.

Bibliography

Treviño, Roberto R. "Facing Jim Crow: Catholic Sisters and the 'Mexican Problem' in Texas." *Western Historical Quarterly* 34, no. 2 (2003): 139–64.

Unsworth, Tim. "Chicago's Jack Egan, Jack Egan's Chicago." *America*, March 19, 1994.

U.S. House of Representatives Budget Committee. *The War on Poverty: 50 Years Later*. Washington, D.C.: U.S. Government Printing Office, 2014.

Valdez, Luis, and Stan Steiner. *Aztlán: An Anthology of Mexican American Literature*. New York: Vintage, 1972.

Walters, Ronald W. *The Price of Racial Reconciliation*. Ann Arbor: University of Michigan Press, 2008.

Watt, Alan J. *Farm Workers and the Churches: The Movement in California and Texas*. College Station: Texas A&M Press, 2010.

Webb, Clive J. *Fight against Fear: Southern Jews and Black Civil Rights*. Athens: University of Georgia Press, 2001.

Weiner, Josephine. *The Story of WICS*. Washington, D.C.: Women in Community Service, 1979.

Weisenfeld, Judith. *African American Women and Christian Activism: New York's Black YWCA, 1905–1945*. Cambridge, Mass.: Harvard University Press, 1997.

Wells, Ronald A. "Cesar Chavez's Protestant Allies: The California Migrant Ministry and the Farm Workers." *Journal of Presbyterian History* 87 (Spring–Summer 2009): 5–16.

West, Michael O. "Whose Black Power? The Business of Black Power and Black Power's Business." In *The Business of Black Power: Community Development, Capitalism, and Corporate Responsibility in Postwar America*, ed. Laura Warren Hill and Julia Rabig, 274–303. Rochester, N.Y.: University of Rochester Press, 2012.

White House Council of Economic Advisers. *The War on Poverty 50 Years Later: A Progress Report*. Washington, D.C.: U.S. Government Printing Office, 2014.

Williams, Lawrence H. "Christianity and Reparations: Revisiting James Forman's 'Black Manifesto,' 1969." *Currents in Theology and Mission* 32, no. 1 (2005): 39–46.

Williams, Rhonda Y. *Concrete Demands: The Search for Black Power in the 20th Century*. New York: Routledge, 2015.

——. *The Politics of Public Housing: Black Women's Struggles against Urban Inequality*. New York: Oxford University Press, 2004.

Wilmore, Gayraud S., and James H. Cone, eds. *Black Theology: A Documentary History*. Maryknoll, N.Y.: Orbis, 1979.

Wilson, William Julius. *The Declining Significance of Race: Blacks and Changing American Institutions*. Chicago, Ill.: University of Chicago Press, 1980.

——. *The Truly Disadvantaged: The Inner City, the Underclass and Public Policy*. Chicago, Ill.: University of Chicago Press, 2012.

Winbush, Raymond A. *Should America Pay? Slavery and the Raging Debate on Reparations*. New York: HarperCollins, 2003.

Wineburg, Bob. *A Limited Partnership: The Politics of Religion, Welfare, and Social Service*. New York: Columbia University Press, 2001.

Wood, Richard L. *Faith in Action: Religion, Race, and Democratic Organizing in America*. Chicago, Ill.: University of Chicago Press, 2002.

———. *"Fe y Acción Social*: Hispanic Churches in Faith Based Community Organizing." In *Latino Religions and Civic Activism in the United States*, ed. Gastón Espinosa, Virgilio Elizondo, and Jesse Miranda, 145–58. New York: Oxford University Press, 2005.

Woodsworth, Michael. *Battle for Bed-Stuy: The Long War on Poverty in New York City*. Cambridge, Mass.: Harvard University Press, 2016.

Wuthnow, Robert. *Faith-Based Services and the Future of Civil Society*. Princeton, N.J.: Princeton University Press, 2009.

———. *The Restructuring of American Religion: Society and Faith since World War II*. Princeton, N.J.: Princeton University Press, 1988.

———. *Saving America? Faith-Based Services and the Future of Civil Society*. Princeton, N.J.: Princeton University Press, 2004.

Zielinski, Martin A. "Working for Interracial Justice: The Catholic Interracial Council of New York, 1934–1964." *U.S. Catholic Historian* 7, nos. 2–3 (1988): 233–62.

INDEX

Abernathy, Ralph, 136–37
activism: and black nationalism, 74–75; and charitable choice, 153; Chicano/a, 73, 150–51; clerical social, 18–24, 27–28, 31–35, 53, 65–66; and Forman, 88–89; and IFCO, 68, 71–73, 79, 84; Latino/a, 151; and NBEDC, 85–86; and NCC, 45–46; and participation of the poor, 45; scholarship on, 3–5; Shriver on, 14. *See also* civil rights movement
Ad Hoc Committee for Justice, 99, 112
Africa Information Service, 142
African Americans: and Baroni, 18–19; Black Manifesto, 135, 137; black nationalism, 74–75; and CDGM Head Start program, 51; and faith-based organizations, 149; and IFCO, 71, 141; and Jewish organizations, 69–70; and Mennonite Church, 133; and NBEDC, 83–85; and NCBC, 72; and NCC, 37, 137; scholarship on, 3–5. *See also* black economic development; reparations
Ahmann, Mathew, 15–17, 25–27, 29–32
AJC. *See* American Jewish Committee
Alinsky, Saul, 22–23, 77–78, 148–49
American Baptist Church, 122–23
American Baptist Convention, 102–3
American Church Union, 139
American Jewish Committee (AJC), 68–70, 117–19
Anabaptists, 133
Anti-Poverty Bulletin (periodical), 40–41
antipoverty efforts: Black Manifesto, 129–30; Board of Missions, United Methodists, 115; and Catholic social activism, 14–35; CDGM Head Start program, 51; Chicano/a activism, 85–86, 150–51; and church-state relationships, 55; CSA, 148; and economic development, 83–85, 88–92;

and economic justice, 16; ecumenism, 6, 146; evangelicals, 63; ICAP, 56, 58–61; interfaith organizations, 53–59; and juvenile delinquency, 6, 38–39; Latino/a communities, 149–51; NBEDC, 85–86; NCC, 39–51, 61–62; NCCIJ, 25–32; and opportunity theory, 6; participation of the poor, 7; and race, 25–26, 34, 37, 41–43, 98, 111; reparations, 158; scholarship on, 5–7; Shriver on, 65–66; and social activism, 3–5, 155; Unified Field Program, 45–48, 50; urban ministries, 31–33; WICS, 57. *See also* Catholic antipoverty efforts
antipoverty programs: and Black Manifesto, 121–24, 133–35, 137–38; and black power, 73–75; and charitable choice, 153; and Council of Economic Advisers, 2; and economic development, 83; and faith-based organizations, 149–55; federal support of, 157; funding of, 128–31; ICAP, 60; IFCO, 76, 122–24, 128, 139–46; NCBC, 96; NCC, 49–50, 54–55, 109–11; OEO, 62–63, 65–66, 147; participation of the poor, 105; privatization of, 154; and reparations, 156; and Riverside Church, 97
Anti-Poverty Task Force, NCC, 39–40, 45–55, 64
Archdiocese of New York, 96–97
Atlantic (magazine), 156–57

Back of the Yards neighborhood, 22
Barber, Hugh, 127
Baroni, Geno, 18–23, 25–27, 31, 33–35, 62, 155
Beazley, George, Jr., 131
Beck, Paul, 126
BEDC. *See* Black Economic Development Conference

BERC. *See* Black Economic Research Center
Bernardin, Joseph, 32, 34
Bernstein, Maurice, 69
Bernstein, Phillip, 53
A Better Way initiative (Ryan), 2, 5
Beyond These Hills (documentary), 62
Biondi, Martha, 156
black capitalism, 83–85, 89–91
black Catholics, 28–30
Black Christian Nationalism, 74–75
black clergy, 28–30, 72–74, 121, 135–37
black community antipoverty agencies,
    74–75, 77, 90–91, 98, 110, 119. *See also*
    Interreligious Foundation for Community
    Organization
Black Congress, 76–80
black economic development: BEDC, 98;
    BERC, 141; Black Manifesto, 87–92,
    105, 109–11; Board of Missions, United
    Methodists, 115; Committee of Sixteen,
    114; community organization(s), 83–86;
    funding efforts, 137–38; IFCO, 76, 142–46;
    Methodist Church, 128–30; National Black
    United Fund, 142; participation of the poor,
    84–85
Black Economic Development Conference
    (BEDC): Black Manifesto, 91–92, 94,
    97–100, 103–8, 110–16; Disciples of Christ,
    131; Episcopal Church, 121, 134; IFCO,
    138–40; Methodist Church, 128–30, 135;
    reparations, 97–99
Black Economic Research Center (BERC),
    140–41
black entrepreneurship, 89, 91
black evangelicals, 72
black freedom movement, 4–5, 88
Black Lives Matter movement, 157
Black Manifesto: and American Baptists,
    102, 122–23; analysis of, 129–30; and
    Baroni, 33; and BEDC, 91–92, 94, 97–100,
    103–8, 110–16; and BERC, 140–42; and
    black power, 88–92; black religious
    leaders' responses, 135–37; and Board of
    Missions, United Methodists, 102–8, 115,
    122–28, 130, 138; and Catholic Church,
    96–98; and Chicano/a activism, 150–51;
    and Christ Church Cranbrook, 134–35;
    and contemporary efforts, 156; criticism
    of, 137–38; demonstrations, 98–109, 113,
    118–19; and Disciples of Christ, 130–31;

Economic Liberation Committee, 102–8;
    and Episcopal Church, 101–2, 121; and
    IFCO, 81, 89–92, 115–19, 122–32, 138–42,
    146; and Jewish agencies, 117–19; and
    Lutheran Church, 95; and Mennonite
    Church, 133; and Methodist Church,
    122–32; and NBEDC, 87–92; and NCBC,
    95–96; and NCC, 88, 92–93, 109–15,
    130–32; and opposition to War on Poverty,
    120–21; overview, 6; and Presbyterian
    General Assembly, 99–101; responses to,
    121–27, 130, 131–32, 134–35; and Riverside
    Church, 92–97; scholarship on, 88; and
    United Church of Christ, 102; and Walker,
    95, 105; and white parishioners, 137. *See
    also* reparations
Black Methodists for Church Renewal
    (BMCR), 73, 104–5, 128, 130, 135
black nationalism, 28–29, 74–75, 78, 80–81,
    84–86
Black Panther Party, 76, 79–82, 88–89
black power: BERC, 141; Black Manifesto,
    88–92, 119, 133, 136, 139; black theology,
    74; BMCR, 73, 135; and Catholic Church,
    29–31; and CDGM Head Start program,
    51; and civil rights, 27–28, 72–73, 88, 119;
    and community control, 34; and Forman,
    88–89, 95; IFCO, 67–68, 73–74, 76–78,
    145; and Methodist Church, 109, 128–29;
    NCBC, 72; NEBDC, 83–86, 91–92
"Black Power and the White Church"
    (conference), 28
Black Presbyterian Leadership Conference, 73
black theology, 74–75, 86, 95, 110, 119
A Black Theology of Liberation (Cone), 75
black women religious, 28–30
Blake, Eugene Carson, 57
BMCR. *See* Black Methodists for Church
    Renewal
Board of Christian Social Concerns, United
    Methodist Church, 82
Board of Missions, Lutheran Church, 47
Board of Missions, United Methodist Church,
    65–66, 82, 102–8, 115, 122–28, 130, 138
Board of National Missions, United
    Presbyterian Church, 68, 82
Board of Social Ministry of the Lutheran
    Church, 46
Board of World Ministries of the United
    Church of Christ, 108

Index

Bookbinder, Hyman, 62
Bremond, Walter, 76, 78, 79
Browne, Robert S., 89–91
Burgess, Ernest, 6
Bush, George W., 153

Cabral Institute, 142–43
California Migrant Ministry, 79
Campaign for Human Development (CHD), 33–35, 148–49, 152
Campbell, Ernest T., 92–94, 96–97
Cannon, Corine, 100–101
Cardinal Stritch, Samuel, 22–23
Carothers, J. Edward, 48, 50–52, 82, 137
Carter, Jimmy, 148
"The Case for Reparations" sermon (Campbell), 97
Catholic antipoverty efforts: and black freedom movement, 4–5; and Black Manifesto, 96–98; and black power, 29–31; church-state relationships, 35; civil rights movement, 14–21, 23–35; community control, 28–29, 151–52; community organization(s), 31–35; federal programs, 12–14, 20–21, 26–27; funding, 33–34; and racism, 14–15, 28
Catholic Clergy Conference on the Interracial Apostolate, 28
Catholic Committee of Community Organization (CCCO), 31
Catholic Committee on Urban Ministry (CCUM), 31–35
Catholic Interracial Councils (CICs), 14–15, 28
"A Catholic Position on Reparations," 98
Catholic Standard (newspaper), 152
Catholic Worker movement, 22
Católicos por La Raza, 150–51
CBL. See Contract Buyers League
CCUM. See Catholic Committee on Urban Ministry
CDCs. See community development corporations
CDGM. See Child Development Group of Mississippi
Center for Democratic Renewal, 145
Center for Third World Organizing, 151
charitable choice, 153
CHD. See Campaign for Human Development
Chicago Declaration of Evangelical Social Concern, 63

Chicago Mandate, 69
Chicana Service Action Center (CSAC), 73
Chicano/a activism, 73, 85–86, 150–51
Child Development Group of Mississippi (CDGM), 51
Chisholm, Shirley, 141
Christ Church Cranbrook, 134–35
Christian Advocate (magazine), 126
Christian Century (magazine), 137–38
Christian Church. See Disciples of Christ
"Christian Manifesto" (McIntire), 126
"The Church and the Inner City" (Baroni), 20–21
"The Church and the Urban Racial Crisis" conference, 31
"The Church and the War on Poverty" (Baroni), 19–20
"The Church and the World" conference, 105
churches and synagogues: antipoverty programs, 13–14, 154; and Black Manifesto, 6, 120–21; charitable choice, 153; and demonstrations, 118–19; and federal money, 152; and ICAP, 53, 57, 61; and IFCO, 68–69, 75–76, 86, 146; King on, 15–16; and reparations, 87–92, 94–96, 102; Shriver on, 64
"The Church's Response to the Black Manifesto" (Wilmore), 136
church-state relationships: Catholic Church, 35; ecumenical participation, 62; and NCC, 45, 47, 54–56; and OEO, 8; and poverty during Trump presidency, 157; public-private antipoverty effort, 152–54; Shriver on, 65–66
CICs. See Catholic Interracial Councils
Citywide Citizens Action Committee, 80
Civil Rights Act of 1964, 19, 70
civil rights legislation, 15–19, 57, 132, 150
civil rights movement: AJC, 69–71; and Baroni, 18–21; Black Manifesto, 136–38; and black power, 27–28, 72–73, 88, 119; Catholic social activism, 14–21, 23–35; Chicano/a activism, 150–51; clergy support, 57; community organizing, 48; and ecumenical movement, 63, 71; and Egan, 23–25; IFCO, 67–69; NCC, 37–38, 43, 61; NCCIJ, 15–19, 25–27; and Riverside Church, 93; Shriver on, 65
Clark, Henry, 44
Cleage, Albert, Jr., 71, 74–75, 80

clerical social activism, 18–24, 27–28, 31–35, 53, 65–66
Clinton, Bill, 153
Cloward, Richard, 6, 38–39
Coates, Ta-Nehisi, 156–58
Cody, John Patrick, 23, 32
COINTELPRO (counterintelligence program), 80–82
Cold War subsidiarity, 152
Commandos (black power group), 28
Commission on Religion and Race, NCC, 39, 43
Committee of Sixteen, NCC, 111–15
Committee on Church and Race, Presbyterian General Assembly, 99–100
Committee on Civil Rights, Truman, 69
Committee on Racial Justice, Division of Christian Life and Mission, 113
Communities Organized for Public Service (COPS), 149, 153
community action: Anti-Poverty Committee, 46; Baroni, 19; black economic development, 109–10; CDGM Head Start program, 51; church-state relationships, 55; Conference of Mayors, 47; economic development, 83–85; EOA, 6–7; faith-based organizations, 154; ICAP, 58; IFCO, 27, 31, 68–69, 76, 79; NBEDC, 84–86; NCC, 42–45, 49–50; Neighborhood Centers, 20–21; participation of the poor, 7, 26, 29, 48–50; role of religious organizations, 12–15, 27; WICS, 57
community action agencies (CAAs), 7
community control: BERC, 141; black Catholic organizations, 28–29; black economic development, 83–86; and black power, 34, 135; Cleage on, 75; IFCO, 68; NCBC, 111; NCUEA, 155; and participation of the poor, 99
community development, 78–79, 84, 109, 142
community development corporations (CDCs), 83
community organization(s): and AJC, 70; and black economic development, 83–86; and Black Manifesto, 137; and Catholic Church, 31–35, 151–52; and CHD, 148–49; and COPS, 149; and Egan, 22–25; funding of, 76; and IFCO, 27, 68–69, 72–79, 143–46; and juvenile delinquency, 6; and Latino/a communities, 149–50; and NCUEA, 153;

and participation of the poor, 48; and reparations, 98
Community Services Administration (CSA), 147, 148
Cone, James, 74–75
Conferences on Religion and Race, 15–16, 18, 23–25, 30, 37, 70–71
conservatism, 5, 35, 59, 63, 153–55
Contract Buyers League (CBL), 23, 148
Contract Buyers of Lawndale (CBL). See Contract Buyers League
Cooke, Terence Cardinal, 96
COPS. See Communities Organized for Public Service
Council of Black Catholic Laymen, 28
Council of Catholic Negro Laymen, 28
Council of Christian Unity, 131
Council of Economic Advisers, 2
Council of Women, 41. See also Migrant Ministry programs
Craine, John, 121
Crusade against Poverty, 33–34
Cruz, Richard, 151, 158
CSA. See Community Services Administration
CSAC. See Chicana Service Action Center

Day, Dorothy, 22
"Decree on the Jews," 71
del Grito, Dolores, 151
Delta Ministry, 79
Department of Church and Economic Life, NCC, 39–41
Department of Racial and Cultural Relations, FCC, 36–37
Department of Urban Services, NCCIJ, 27
de Porres Grey, M. Martin, 28
Detroit News (newspaper), 134
Dillard, Angela, 88
Direct Action and Research Training Center, 149
Disciples of Christ, 115, 130–31
disruptions of churches, 92–102, 113, 116
Division of Christian Life and Mission, NCC, 46, 49
Division of Church and Society, NCC, 142–43
Division of Church Strategy and Development, United Presbyterian, 68
Division of Overseas Ministries, NCC, 113, 123
Division of Social Concern of the American Baptist Convention, 122–23

Index

Dodge Revolutionary Union Movement, 81
Dollger, Mary, 125–26
Douglas, Ann, 142, 144
DuBois, Joshua, 154
Dye, Keith, 134

The East Los Angeles Community Union (TELACU), 73, 86
Economic Development Council, Detroit, 83–84
Economic Liberation Committee, 102–9
Economic Opportunity Act (EOA), 6–7, 41–42, 48, 55, 83, 147
ecumenical activism, 63, 68
ecumenical antipoverty coalitions: and Black Manifesto, 119; creation of, 8; evolution of, 155; and faith-based organizations, 149; and ICAP, 56, 61; and IFCO, 79, 141–43, 146; Shriver on, 64–66
ecumenical religious organizations, 72–74, 153
ecumenism, 53, 70–71, 73, 141, 144
Egan, John J. (Jack), 22–25, 31, 32–35, 151, 155
Egan Payday Loan Reform Act, 155
Elementary and Secondary Education Act of 1965, 55
Emrich, Richard, 134
EOA. *See* Economic Opportunity Act
Episcopal Church, 72, 101–2, 121, 131–32, 134
Episcopal general convention, 121
Episcopal Society for Cultural and Racial Unity, 72
Espy, Edwin, 37, 50–52, 108, 112–15
evangelicals, 62–63, 72, 153–54
Evangelicals for Social Action, 63

faith-based antipoverty efforts, 148–49, 151–56. *See also specific religious groups and churches*
FBI investigation, IFCO, 80–82
FCC. *See* Federal Council of Churches
federal antipoverty efforts: agencies, 148–49; attacks on, 147; and Catholic antipoverty efforts, 12–14, 20–21, 26–27; and church-state relationships, 152–53; and Committee of Sixteen, 114; and evangelicals, 63; funding of, 54–55, 148; NCC, 37–42; Shriver on, 65
Federal Council of Churches (FCC), 36–38, 48. *See also* National Council of Churches (NCC)

Federated Colored Catholics, 14
Felder, Cain, 104–6
feminism, 3–4, 150–51
Fifield, Harry, 137
Fifteenth Street Presbyterian Church, Washington, D.C., 23
Findlay, James, 4, 37, 88
Flemming, Arthur, 112–14
Ford, Gerald, 59, 147
Forman, James: and black capitalism, 89–91; and Chicano/a activism, 150–51; and demonstrations, 107–8, 118–19; disruptions of churches, 92–102; and Economic Liberation Committee, 104–9; NBEDC address, 87–90; and NCC, 92–93, 109–15; on reparations, 92; responses to, 125–32, 135–37. *See also* Black Manifesto
Fosdick, Harry Emerson, 93
Fouke, Hugh, 126
fundamentalists, 126, 153
Fund for Reconciliation, United Methodist Church, 124, 127–29

Gallagher, Raymond, 53–54
Gallardo, Gloria, 150
Gamaliel Foundation, 149, 151–52
Garvey, Marcus, 74
General Assembly, NCC, 132
General Assembly of Presbyterians, 1, 36, 99–102
General Synod of the Reformed Church, 108
Gildea, Robert, 132
Gold, Bertram, 117–18
Gothard, Louis, 78
government antipoverty efforts. *See* federal antipoverty efforts
Graham, Billy, 62–63
Grass Roots Manifesto (Rose), 122
Greene, Shirley, 37–38, 40–41, 47–48, 50, 60
Greenwood, Elma, 44–45
Groppi, James, 27–28

Harrington, Michael, 6, 38–39
Harris, James T., 29, 71
Head Start, Economic Opportunity and Community Partnership Act, 147
Head Start programs, 40–42, 46, 51, 55, 59, 70
Heller, Walter, 6
Hesburgh, Theodore, 32
Heschel, Abraham, 15

204   Index

Hiatt, Philip, 15
Higgins, George, 155
Hillenbrand, Reynold, 15, 22
Hilliard, Raymond, 25
Hines, John, 101–2
Hinton, Thomas, 59–61
Hirsch, Richard G., 63, 70
Hoffman, Philip, 70
Hoover, Theressa, 107
Hoppe, Robert, 138–39
House Committee on Education and Labor, 41, 59
House of Representatives Budget Committee, 2
Howard, J. Gordon, 128
Hubbard, Walter, 97
Humphrey, Hubert, 57
Hunter, David R., 79, 82–83

IAF. *See* Industrial Areas Foundation
ICAP. *See* Interreligious Committee against Poverty
IFCO. *See* Interreligious Foundation for Community Organization
IFCO Program Committee, 143–44
Indianapolis News (newspaper), 121
indigenous communities, 77, 79, 84, 139, 143
Industrial Areas Foundation (IAF), 22, 149
Institute for Urban Affairs, 77
institutional action, 39
integration, 15–16, 72, 124, 127–29, 136
Interchurch (magazine), 131–32
Interchurch Center, 99–104, 107–9, 112–13
interfaith organizations, 53–59, 141
interracial civil rights organizations.
    See National Catholic Conference for Interracial Justice; Student Interracial Ministry
interracialism, 14–18, 25, 34, 122
interreligious activism, 73–74
Interreligious Committee against Poverty (ICAP), 53, 56–61, 69
interreligious efforts against poverty, 55–57, 61, 141
Interreligious Foundation for Community Organization (IFCO): and activism, 68, 71–73, 79, 84; and AJC, 117–19; and BEDC, 105–6, 108, 116, 138–40; and BERC, 141–42; and Black Manifesto, 89–92, 115–19, 122–32, 138–42, 146; and black

nationalism, 28–29; and black power, 67–68, 73–74, 76–78, 145; and black theology, 74–75; and BMCR, 135; and Board of Missions, United Methodists, 82, 138; and board representation, 71–72; and budget challenges, 75–76; caucuses of, 115–17; and community organization(s), 27, 68–69, 72–79, 143–46; as ecumenical antipoverty coalition, 141–43; FBI investigation of, 80–82; and grants, 144–45; LAPD inquiry, 79–82; and Latino and Native populations, 77–79; logo of, 73; and NBEDC, 83–86; and NCBC, 96; and NCC, 92, 114, 142–44; and NCCIJ, 27, 31; overview of, 6, 27, 67–69; and participation of the poor, 68, 78–80; Twentieth Anniversary Conference, 146; and Walker, 67–69, 71–73, 77–78, 82–84, 115–16, 138–45

"Jesus Christ as a Revolutionist" (del Grito), 151
Jewish organizations, 5, 9, 53–57, 68–71, 87–88, 117–19
Job Corps, 40, 42, 46, 57, 59–61, 65
Johnson, Lyndon B., 2, 6–7, 37, 58, 64–65, 120
Jones, Rufus, 63
Jones, Tracey K., 106–7, 115
"Judaism in Pursuit of Economic Justice" conference, 70
juvenile delinquency, 6, 38–39

Kahlenberg, Mareta, 102
Karenga, Maulana (Ron), 74, 76, 79
Kefauver, Estes, 38
Kelley, Dean, 55
Kennedy, John F., 6–7, 16–17, 25
Kennedy, Robert, 83
Kerner Commission, 155
Kilgore, Thomas, 43, 102
King, Martin Luther, Jr., 15–17, 70, 93
Klinkner, Philip, 157–58
Knight, Walker, 64
Kopp, Audrey, 30

LaFarge, John, 14–15
LAPD (Los Angeles Police Department), 79–82
La Raza (newspaper), 150–51
Las Hermanas, 150–51

Latin American Committee of the Woodlawn Organization, 22

Latino/a communities, 71, 77, 133, 142, 149–51

Lawson, James, 71

League of Revolutionary Black Workers, 81, 89, 91–92

Lechtreck, Elaine, 88, 156

Lee, Oscar, 15

liberation theology, 19–21, 150–51

local churches and congregations, 7, 39–43, 45–49, 78, 114, 138

"long war on poverty," use of term, 3

Lopez, Obed, 99

Los Angeles Black Congress, 76–80

Los Angeles City College, 150

Los Padres, 151

Loyola Marymount University, 150

Lutheran Church, 46–47, 95

Macdonald, Dwight, 6–7

Machle, Edward, 101

Madison Avenue protests, 12–13

Manning, John, 18

March on Washington, 17–19, 27–28, 37, 43, 69

Marmion, William, 121

Marshall, Calvin, 140

Marshall, Robert, 95

Marshall, Thurgood, 70

Matthai, Frederick C., 134

McDaniel, James, 52

McGreevy, John, 4

McIntire, Carl, 126

Mcintyre, Frances, 150

McPherson, N.C., 127–28

Mennonite Church, 133–35

Meredith March against Fear, 17–18

Methodist Church. *See* United Methodist Church

Mexican American communities, 99–100

Migrant Ministry programs, 41, 48, 79

Millions for Reparations rally, 156

Minority Ministries Council, 133

Mission Memo (newsletter), 138

Moore, James, 43

Moore, Paul, Jr., 63

Morrison, Robert, 134–35

Moyers, Bill, 13

Moynihan report, 2

Mueller, Reuben H., 41–42, 129

National Advisory Council on Economic Opportunity, 48–49

National Anti-Klan Network. *See* Center for Democratic Renewal

National Association of Evangelicals, 153

National Association of Laymen, 98

National Black Catholic Clergy Caucus (NBCCC), 28

National Black Economic Development Conference (NBEDC), 33, 81, 83–86, 87–92, 95

National Black Evangelical Association, 72

National Black Lay Catholic Caucus, 28

National Black Sisters Conference (NBSC), 28

National Black Training Institute, 77–78

National Black United Fund, 142

National Catholic Committee on Reparations, 98

National Catholic Conference for Interracial Justice (NCCIJ), 14–19, 25–32, 97–98

National Catholic Social Action Conference, 21

National Catholic Welfare Conference (NCWC), 57

National Center for Urban Ethnic Affairs (NCUEA), 32, 155

National Citizens Committee for the Child Development Group of Mississippi, 51

National Coalition of Blacks for Reparations in America, 156

National Committee of Black Churchmen (NCBC): and Black Manifesto, 95–96; and black theology, 74; and Committee of Sixteen, 111–15; and Economic Liberation Committee, 103, 108; financial support, 121, 130–32; formation of, 72

National Committee of Negro Churchmen. *See* National Committee of Black Churchmen (NCBC)

National Conference of Catholic Bishops (NCCB), 33–34, 98

National Council of Churches (NCC): and activism, 45–46; and African Americans, 137; antipoverty efforts, 39–51; Anti-Poverty Task Force, 45, 52–55, 64; and Black Manifesto, 88, 92–93, 109–15, 130–32; and CDGM Head Start program, 51; church-state relationships, 45, 47, 54–56; civil rights movement, 37–38, 43, 61; Commission on Religion and Race,

206 Index

National Council of Churches (*continued*)
39, 43; Committee of Sixteen, 111–15;
and community action, 42–45, 49–50;
and demonstrations, 95, 108; Division of
Christian Life and Mission, 46, 49; Division
of Church and Society, 142–43; Division of
Overseas Ministries, 113, 123; and federal
programs, 37–42; General Assembly,
132; history of, 36–38; and IFCO, 92, 114,
142–44; and juvenile delinquency, 38–39;
LAPD investigation of, 79–80; and moral
issue of poverty, 61–62; and OEO, 47–55;
and participation of the poor, 48–50; and
Shriver, 40–42, 64
National Jewish Community Relations
Advisory Council, 118–19
Native American communities, 26, 71, 77,
142–43
NBCCC. *See* National Black Catholic Clergy
Caucus
NBEDC. *See* National Black Economic
Development Conference
NBSC. *See* National Black Sisters Conference
NCBC. *See* National Committee of Black
Churchmen (NCBC)
NCC. *See* National Council of Churches (NCC)
NCCB. *See* National Conference of Catholic
Bishops
NCCIJ. *See* National Catholic Conference for
Interracial Justice
NCUEA. *See* National Center for Urban
Ethnic Affairs
NCWC. *See* National Catholic Welfare
Conference
The Negro Family (Moynihan), 2
Neighborhood Centers, 20–21
New Federalism, 147
New Yorker (magazine), 6–7
New York Times (newspaper), 51, 72
Nixon, Richard, 33–34, 120, 147
Noble, Jeanne, 57
Novins, Stuart, 62–63

Obama, Barack, 152–54
O'Boyle, Patrick, 19
OEO. *See* Office of Economic Opportunity
(OEO)
OFBCI. *See* Office of Faith-Based and
Community Initiatives
OFBNP. *See* Office of Faith-Based and
Neighborhood Partnerships

Office of Economic Opportunity (OEO):
abolishment of, 147; and BERC, 141;
and ICAP, 59–61; and Madison Avenue
protests, 12–13; and NCC, 41–42, 45, 47–55;
and NCCIJ, 26–28; overview, 7–8; political
challenges, 33–34, 120; and religious
groups' involvement in War on Poverty,
62–66, 152; and women, 57
Office of Faith-Based and Community
Initiatives (OFCBI), 152–53
Office of Faith-Based and Neighborhood
Partnerships (OFBNP), 152–54
Office of Urban Affairs, 19, 23, 31
O'Grady, Gerald, Jr., 134
Ohio Catholic Education Association
convention, 13–14
Ohlin, Lloyd, 6, 38–39
Olivarez, Graciela, 148
One-Fifth of a Nation (Greenwood), 44–45
open housing laws, 15
opportunity theory, 6, 22, 38
Ortega, Gregoria, 150
The Other America (Harrington), 6, 38–39

Pacific Institute for Community Organization,
149
parish, role of, 20, 23
Park, Robert, 6
participation of the poor: and activism, 45;
and antipoverty programs, 105; black
economic development, 84–85; Cleage on,
75; and community action, 7, 26, 29, 48–50;
and community control, 99; and COPS,
149; Greene on, 47–48; and ICAP, 58–59;
and IFCO, 68, 78–80; and NCC, 48–50
Patton, Frank, 81
payday loan industry, 155
Payton, Benjamin, 72
Pentecostal women, 149–50
Personal Responsibility and Work
Opportunity Reconciliation Act, 153
Poor People's Campaign, 129–30
"Poverty, Race and Religion: Challenge to a
Catholic Community" convention, 25
"Poverty's Challenge to Interracial Action"
convention, 25–26
Powell, John, 133
Presbyterian Church. *See* United Presbyterian
Church
Presbyterian General Assembly, 1, 36, 99–102
Presbyterian Standing Committee report, 1

Index

Presentation Parish, 23
President's Committee on Juvenile Delinquency, 6, 38
Project Head Start. *See* Head Start programs
public-private antipoverty efforts, 152–54

race relations, 24–26, 70, 107
racial justice, 24, 27, 43, 63, 113, 133
racism: Baroni on, 20–21; black clergy on, 135; and Catholic Church, 14–15, 28; and Christ Church Cranbrook, 134–35; and Disciples of Christ, 131; Forman on, 87, 110; institutional, 157; and Mennonite Church, 133; and Methodist Church, 130; Mueller on, 41–42; and NCCIJ, 18; and NCUEA, 155; and responses to Black Manifesto, 123–26; and Riverside Church, 94–97; and social action, 22; and Trump administration, 157–58
Rahn, Sheldon, 53
Raskob Foundation for Catholic Activities, 32
Reagan, Ronald, 5
Reddin, Tom, 79–81
Reformed Church in America, 108
Regier, Jon L., 50–52, 125–26
Relief for Africans in Need in the Sahel, 145
Religious Action Center of Reform Judaism, 70
Renewal (magazine), 122
reparations: and American Baptists, 123; and Black Manifesto, 6, 88–92, 94–98, 106–9, 156–58; and Christ Church Cranbrook, 134; contemporary efforts, 156–58; and Episcopal Church, 121; Kilgore on, 102; letter writers on, 125–27; and Mennonite Church, 133; and Methodist Church, 129–30; and Rose's Grass Roots Manifesto, 122; Wilmore on, 136
Response (magazine), 129–30
Reveille for Radicals (Alinsky), 22
Risco, Eliezer, 99–100
Riverside Church, 92–97, 126
Rockefeller, John D., 93–94
Rogers, Melissa, 154
Rollins, Metz, 96, 111–12
Roman Catholic Archdiocese of New York, 96–97
Rose, Stephen, 122
Rundle, Mrs. Paul, 124–25

Ryan, Paul, 2, 5

Saints Augustine and Paul Parishes, 19–21
Sanders, Beulah, 71
SATC. *See* Social Action Training Center
Schaller, Lyle, 52–53
Schultze, Charles, 47, 59
Second Vatican Council. *See* Vatican II
segregation, 14–15, 18, 37, 70, 127–28
self-determination: and Black Manifesto, 105; and Cabral Institute, 142–43; and CCUM, 32; Cleage on, 75; and Committee of Sixteen, 114; and IFCO, 71, 116; and indigenous groups, 79; versus integration, 136; and NCBC, 111; and NCUEA, 155; Tannenbaum on, 118
Selma to Montgomery march, 17, 28, 69, 88–89
Senate Sub-Committee on Employment, Manpower and Poverty, 58
Shearer, Tobin Miller, 133
Shelley, John, 47
Short, Roy, 128
Shriver, R. Sargent: and CDGM Head Start program, 51; and Chicago CIC, 15; and church-state relationships, 55–56; and ecumenical participation, 64–66; and moral issue of poverty, 36; and NCC, 40–42; and NCCIJ, 26; and OEO, 59, 62, 64–66; overview, 7–8, 13–14; public-private state, 152; speech to General Assembly of Presbyterians, 1; and WICS, 57
SNCC. *See* Student Nonviolent Coordinating Committee
Social Action Training Center (SATC), 79
Social Gospel, 36, 38, 41, 48, 88
Sonnabend, A. M., 70
South Africa, 115
Spivey, Charles S., Jr., 95, 137
Stennis, John, 51
Storey, Frank, 134
Student Interracial Ministry, 98–99, 122
Student Nonviolent Coordinating Committee (SNCC), 88–89
Suburban Action Centers, Philadelphia, 77
Sweazy, George, 101
Synagogue Council of America, 57, 118–19
synagogues. *See* churches and synagogues

Tanenbaum, Marc, 69–71, 116–18
Tate, Charles, 127

The Los Angeles Community Union (TELACU), 73, 86
Together (magazine), 129
Traxler, Margaret Ellen, 29–30
Truman, Harry, 69
Trump administration, 5, 157–58
twenty-first century antipoverty efforts, 151–58

Unified Field Program, 45–48, 50
Union of Black Clergy and Laymen, 72
Union Theological Seminary, 98, 102
United Auto Workers and Teamsters, 81
United Church of Christ, 101–2, 125
United Church Women, 65
United Methodist Board of Missions. *See* Board of Missions
United Methodist Church, 72–73, 82, 102–9, 123–30, 135, 139
United Methodist Church Western New York Annual Conference, 129
United Methodist Conference of New and Furloughed Missionaries, 107, 122
United Methodist Women, 129
United Presbyterian Church, 45, 52–53, 73, 98–102, 144–45
United Presbyterian Church Board of National Missions, 68, 82
United Presbyterian Church General Assembly, 36, 99–102
United States Catholic Conference (USCC), 31, 33–34
urban ministries, 31–35
Urban Racial Council, 133
urban renewal, 23
Urban Task Force, 33–34
U.S. Conference of Mayors, 25–26, 47
USCC. *See* United States Catholic Conference

Vatican II, 19–20, 35, 71, 150
VISTA. *See* Volunteers in Service to America
Volunteers in Service to America (VISTA), 42, 70, 147

Voting Rights Act, 37

Walker, Lucius: and AJC, 118; and BEDC, 138–40; and black clergy, 135; and Black Manifesto, 95, 105; on Egan's CCUM report, 32; and FBI surveillance, 80–82; and IFCO, 67–69, 71–73, 77–78, 82–84, 115–16, 138–45; and NBEDC, 84–85; and NCCIJ, 98; and Tanenbaum, 116–18
Ward, A. Dudley, 109
Ward, W. Ralph, 129
Washington Post (newspaper), 18
Watts Labor Community Action Committee (WLCAC), 73
Wayne State University, 85
West, Michael, 91–92
Western New York Annual Conference, United Methodist Church, 129
Westminster Neighborhood Association (WNA), 45
White, Woodie, 109
white nationalism and white supremacy, 147, 155, 158
Wicke, Lloyd C., 106–7
WICS. *See* Women in Community Service
Wiley, George, 71
Wilhelm, Carolyn, 129–30
Wilmore, Gayraud, 71, 136
WLCAC. *See* Watts Labor Community Action Committee
WNA. *See* Westminster Neighborhood Association
Women in Community Service (WICS), 57, 65
women organizers, 56–57, 129–30, 149–50
women religious, 30, 35, 41
Women's Division, United Methodist Church. *See* United Methodist Women
Womens Job Corp, 57
Wood, Rawson, 29

Yorty, Samuel, 47

Printed in the United States
By Bookmasters